Along the Enchanted Way

Along the Enchanted Way

A Romanian Story

WILLIAM BLACKER

JOHN MURRAY

First published in Great Britain in 2009 by John Murray (Publishers)
An Hachette UK Company

2

© William Blacker 2009

The right of William Blacker to be identified as the Author of the Work has been asserted by him in
accordance with the Copyright, Designs and Patents Act 1988.

A CIP catalogue record for this title is available from the British Library

ISBN 978-0-7195-9790-9

Typeset in 11.5pt Monotype Bembo by Servis Filmsetting Ltd, Stockport, Cheshire

Printed and bound by Clays Ltd, St Ives plc

John Murray policy is to use papers that are natural, renewable and recyclable products and made
from wood grown in sustainable forests. The logging and manufacturing processes are expected to
conform to the environmental regulations of the country of origin.

John Murray (Publishers)
338 Euston Road
London NW1 3BH

www.johnmurray.co.uk

To Constantin.

Contents

I saw the danger, yet I walked along the enchanted way,
And I said, let grief be a fallen leaf at the dawning of the day.
Patrick Kavanagh

Scampering about the dusty tracks of a village in the Transylvanian hills is a small Gypsy boy who seems, among the other darker-skinned children, to be a little out of place. He has blue eyes and light-coloured hair and people often refer to him as Neamţul, *the German boy. Amongst his greatest pleasures are watching the horses and carts clattering down the road and the cows making their way slowly back into the village in the twilight. During the day he tirelessly pursues, much to their consternation, the ducks and ducklings which waddle about on the banks of the stream, and in the evenings he lingers outside the* crîşma *dancing, after a fashion, moving his feet and clicking his fingers in time to the Gypsy music.*

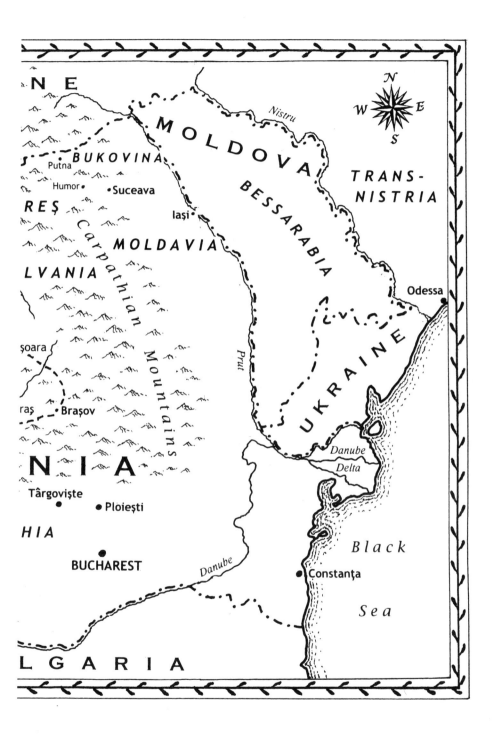

Prologue

10 January 2008

As the train wound its way along wooded valleys my mind was awash with memories. It was a slow train, with its blue but now rusting carriages still in service since Communist times. I had missed the flash new express and so had taken the old-fashioned option which stopped at every village station. Doors hung open and rattled, even a few windows were broken, and in places snow was settling on the floors. I pulled my coat around my body, and my hat down upon my head to preserve the last warmth left in me, and my neighbours, with a smile and a look of sympathy, offered me a swig of *țuică*, their home-made brandy. There was a companionship among us such as one rarely finds on the new express trains which flew by us through the night, a rush of air coming in through the broken windows as they passed, leaving the snow swirling in the corridors.

I was travelling to the very north of Romania, near the border with the Ukraine, in order to keep a promise I had made to an old friend. It was by no means an easy journey in midwinter. It would take another day to reach the isolated village in the northern Carpathian mountains, but I had promised.

The train hooted as we pulled up at a little station. An assortment of villagers, some Romanian, some Gypsy, clambered down on to the platform. The old man and woman who had given me the *țuică* climbed down too and waved me a merry wave as they headed off beside the train laden with their heavy bags.

Peering out of the window through the snow I could make out a dance going on in the hall in the village square. I remembered back to my first visit to Romania, also in the snow. In a village in northern Moldavia I had been taken to the Saturday evening dance. I remembered how the villagers had all paid a small entrance fee for the musicians, but from me the doorman resolutely refused to take any money. I tried to insist. 'No, no!' he said. 'You are a foreigner. You are our guest. We would not dream of asking you to pay.'

In the hall on one side of the room on benches along the wall sat the boys, and the village girls sat opposite them on the other side. I remembered it as though it had been the day before. When the moustachioed Gypsies took up their instruments to play, the boys walked across the room, took the girls by the hand and led them into the dances. They danced traditional dances, intermixed with waltzes and polkas, which they all knew perfectly. From the benches soft-faced mothers and grandmothers sat and watched, nodded and commented contentedly. Outside horses pulling sleighs rushed past snorting steam from their nostrils, the moon glittered on the snow and even then, right from the start, I knew there was no other place I wanted to be.

As the old blue train trundled on through the night, to forget the cold my mind drifted off to warmer occasions, and to musings about life in Romania. When eighteen years ago, in my mid-twenties, I had first headed towards this country I had had no idea what I would find. From reading Western newspapers I had expected to discover a drab Communist world of depressed workers whose spirits had been crushed by decades of conformity. But I had found something quite different. The villages and the countryside were awash with colour and brimming with cheerful, fresh-faced people. I had had no idea such a place was hidden away in this corner of Europe.

I remembered particularly a festival among the trees on the edge of the forest where fiddlers played in competition with the birds in the branches. The villagers dressed in white embroidered smocks – the girls in brightly coloured skirts and headscarves – joined arms, making a circle, stamping their feet rhythmically on the grass and singing the shepherds' songs at the tops of their voices. The dancing and singing went on all afternoon and evening in dappled shade, like some ancient bucolic festival. What, I thought to myself, could have been more colourful and full of life than this idyllic scene? Lying on the grassy bank of a stream, in the shade of flickering beech leaves, listening to the sound of trickling water and watching these smiling and laughing people, I scribbled in my notebook: How could we possibly have been persuaded that our modern way of living is any improvement on this? Was there something of a sham about the modern world? Were we, in Western Europe, for all our wealth and washing machines, any happier than these people? The answer was, to me at least, a clear and decisive 'No'.

I remembered how on my early journeys the people in Romania, almost everywhere I went, had welcomed me amongst them. Wherever I travelled, when night fell I was offered food and the best bed in the house; sometimes it might have had a straw mattress, sometimes it had a box of chicks or a lamb sleeping underneath it, but always it was warm and comfortable and I had a roof over my head. In the morning when I left, my hosts would be appalled if offered any form of payment, and instead would fill my bag with food. In those days there were few shops and food was almost impossible to buy along the way. I was overwhelmed by the generosity of the villagers and their old-fashioned courtesy. And now in the train I had once again been reminded of their simple kindness by the offer of *ţuică* to take my mind off the cold.

Among the many hospitable and courteous individuals I had been lucky to meet on my travels was the friend to whom I had made the promise. He was one of those old country people of Romania who, although not book-learned, was wiser and more knowledgeable than most of us, and most important of all, knew the great secret of being happy on little. I remembered the times we had spent together in the fields and forests, how with unswerving humour he had taught me all about country life in Romania, and had looked after me and protected me against the gossip and the occasional envy of others. It was now my turn to do something for him.

3

The train heaved and rattled its way over the hills. My mind returned to the present journey. Soon I would be crossing the snow-covered passes and descending slowly, always more slowly, down into the valleys of the old Maramureş.

I

East of the Wall

*They are not servile, even after centuries of serfdom, and are free in
manner and bearing yet without insolence . . . the poorer are our peasants the more noticeable is their serene goodness.*

Dostoevsky, *The Brothers Karamazov*

TOWARDS THE END of 1989, as everybody knows, the Berlin
Wall was tottering and the Communist regimes of Eastern
Europe were collapsing one by one. Most changes had been peaceful. Only Romania was in turmoil. There had been appalling mas-
sacres of innocent people, tanks rolling through the streets, and
soldiers and citizens fighting the President's elite troops, flushing
them out building by building. Then suddenly, on Christmas Day,
it was all over. President Ceauşescu and his wife were captured
and, after a hasty trial, were led out into the ice-covered backyard
of a militia garrison in the town of Târgovişte, put up against a
wall and machine-gunned down. 'But you are our children!' they
shouted as the soldiers raised their weapons. In Romania there had
indeed been a bloody revolution of the sort one rather expected of
Eastern Europe.

I set off to explore the newly 'liberated' countries of Central
Europe immediately after Christmas 1989 although I never thought
I would travel as far as Romania. 'The purity of a Revolution can
last for as much as two weeks,' Cocteau had once written, so it
seemed there was not a moment to lose. I drove out of London
through congested southern suburbs on a cold December morning,
crossed the Channel, and pointed the car eastwards. Eight hours

later I was driving down the long umbilical road to Berlin in a mist which seemed to divide one half of Europe from the other. In the skeletal branches of the trees by the side of the road perched numerous birds of prey, sitting and watching as if waiting for their moment to descend and pick at the bones of a dying ideology.

In the middle of the city hundreds of people with hammers and chisels were chipping away at the Wall. It was still the grey and forbidding barrier between East and West Germany, and a few weeks before people might have been shot if they had come too close; now no one was stopping them. In a few places the chisels had already made holes through which we could peer across the minefields towards East Berlin.

By the Brandenburg Gate East German police, the Vopos, stood on top of the wall with guns, but they merely looked on bemused as all around them hundreds of hammers were clinking on chisels, and did nothing as the structure upon which they were standing was slowly being demolished beneath their feet.

But the Wall was only being chipped at from the West. On the Eastern side there was an eerie silence. Many in East Berlin and beyond must have been listening to the chisels and wondering why the Wall was really there. Was it to keep those of the East in, or the evils of the West out? Perhaps like birds in a cage many of them might actually prefer the security that their prison afforded them. Perhaps the opening of the borders would be the opening of another Pandora's Box?

Whatever fears individuals might have had, the changes were unstoppable. On New Year's Eve a new taboo was broken. People dared to climb on to the top of the Wall. Girls kissed the border guards, posed with them for photographs, and stuck flowers in the barrels of their guns. The soldiers did nothing; they did not know what to do. They had no training for such an eventuality.

From there the crowds lowered themselves down into East Berlin, something the day before they would have been afraid to do. They then climbed on to the top of the Brandenburg Gate, pulled down the Communist flag and set it alight. Still the guards did nothing. I stood on the Wall and watched the anarchy and rejoicing all around me. It was the end of an era which had started long before I was born.

IN MOST OF Eastern Europe the controls and restrictions of the past forty years were suddenly lifted. Now anyone was free to travel wherever they wanted. So the next day I left the bright lights of West Berlin, passed through a newly opened door in the Wall, and drove east. By lunchtime I was in Dresden walking through streets among the burnt-out shells of buildings and piles of rubble left untouched since the bombing of 15 February 1945. In those days there were many places in Eastern Europe where little seemed to have changed since the Second World War, and the feeling strengthened the further east you went.

In Prague, whose spires, domes and baroque streets had been spared during the Hitler War, I saw evidence of more recent troubles. On buildings opposite the Romanian Embassy, halfway up the hill to the Hradcany castle, scrawled in red paint were protests against the killings which had taken place in the city of Timişoara on 17 December, and subsequently in towns all over Romania.

It was now 2 January. The Romanian Revolution was all but over. Should I continue eastwards, even as far as Romania, I wondered? It was still a long journey, and it was the middle of winter. In the end it was old architecture which persuaded me. I had heard of the famous painted monasteries of northern Moldavia. Looking at a map, it seemed as though I was nearly halfway there. They were situated beyond the Carpathian mountains in an area called the Bukovina, a land which until 1918 had been the farthest flung, easternmost province of the Austro-Hungarian Empire.

On 4 January it started to snow, but I had already determined to make my way to the monasteries. While flakes settled gently on the beards of the statues of Saints Cyril and Methodius on the Charles Bridge, I set off east again. I travelled through ice-bound Bohemia, Slovakia and Hungary, and after several days reached the Romanian frontier. Flags with the Communist symbols cut out of the middle fluttered above the huts of the border police. Romania, just a few days before, had ceased to be a Communist country.

Snow lay heavy on the ground, the trees beside the road were white with frost, and I entered a country frozen in time. Even the courtesy of the soldiers on the frontier seemed from another era. At every other border I had crossed in Eastern Europe I had faced interminable questions. Here they gave me advice on the roads, and where I might find a hotel, and waved me through with a smile. Half an hour later, I was approaching the town of Satu Mare.

Prague had been dark. There had been only a few simple street lamps. Like all places in those days east of the Wall, she was still commercially chaste, not caring to flaunt herself with neon lights and garish advertising. Satu Mare, however, was pitch black. There were no lights at all. Nor, it seemed, were there any people. All I could make out were tall, ghostly buildings looming on either side as I wove my way cautiously through the deserted streets.

I managed somehow to find the hotel. A candle flickered on the reception desk. There was no food or water, the maid told me, but there were beds and blankets. For supper I ate biscuits in the hall with the maid who brought vodkas from time to time to help us forget the cold. She was dressed in a black and white uniform over which she wore a heavy grey overcoat and a woollen hat, and sat smoking with her feet up on one of the armchairs. Occasionally soldiers in greatcoats and fur hats with rifles in their hands would come in, search the foyer with torches, looking for counter-revolutionaries, then put their guns flat on a table, and ask the maid to bring vodkas for them as well, which they drank down in one gulp before departing.

Then the candle sputtered and went out. It was time to go to bed. Fumbling up the stairs in the darkness all I could see as a point of reference was the tip of the maid's cigarette glowing.

I AWOKE TO the soft sound of horses' hooves on the snow outside and opening the window saw horses pulling carts trotting through the town's main square. With the hotel being out of food I searched the streets for a shop which might sell me something to eat. I found nothing, except a little street-side kiosk, heated by a wood-burning stove; inside sat an old crone, her head wrapped in woollen scarves. She was only able to provide me with stamps for letters. Taking a little brush and pot of glue, she stuck them carefully one by one on to my envelopes. There were seven stamps for each envelope. It was a tiring process.

Surviving still on dry biscuits I headed east again, along bumpy roads. After two hours, on entering a forest of tall beeches, their branches topped with snow like ermine on an empress's robes, the road began to climb. I drove upwards for half an hour and then over a mountain pass into an area marked on my rough map as 'Maramureş'. Slowly I descended through misty woods, not knowing what I would find, along a road which became rougher and rougher.

As the gradient levelled out, following a frozen stream whose waterfalls had turned into motionless cascades of ice, a few wooden houses began to appear. I proceeded cautiously along the snow- and ice-covered road, astonished at what I saw. East Germany, Czechoslovakia, Hungary, even the parts of Romania I had just travelled through: none of them were anything like this. Only here had I found the sort of Eastern Europe which I had imagined from reading *Old Peter's Russian Tales* when I was young; the Eastern Europe of wooden peasant cottages on the edge of forests inhabited by wolves and bears, of snow and sledges and sheepskin coats, and of country people in embroidered smocks and headscarves. I thought I had been born too late to see anything like the peasant life about which Tolstoy and Hardy had written, but I was wrong. Here there was a remnant of an old, almost medieval world, cut off by the mountains and forest I had just crossed, and I had stumbled upon it quite by accident.

When I stopped by the side of the road a peasant woman motioned me towards the snow-mantled porch of her house and showed me in. I was clearly a tired traveller in need of sustenance. Immediately a bowl of hot potato soup and a hunk of bread were placed on the table. She and her husband then sat on the bed and watched me with soft smiles of encouragement. As I ate, shafts of sunlight came through the small cottage windows and I was able to study the intricate designs on her and her husband's smocks. I had never seen anyone wearing a smock before, let alone smocks so beautifully stitched. I then looked down. Their legs and feet were wrapped in thick woollen cloth and on to their soles were strapped roughly sewn strips of leather, pointed at the toes, from which thongs wound up their legs as far as the knee. This was the ancient peasant footwear which, until the early twentieth century, had been common all over Europe, from the bast shoes of Russia made from birch bark, to the pampooties of the Aran Islands, or the rough sandals of Naples and the Ciocaria south of Rome. Now they are worn only in the Maramureş, the last place in Europe where they can still be seen.

For their hospitality my hosts refused anything in return, and when I left they waved until I was out of sight. They had provided me with my first meal in twenty-four hours.

ANOTHER DAY'S DRIVING and I reached the painted monasteries of the Bukovina, among the last masterpieces of Byzantine art, built after the fall of Constantinople and of the Byzantine Empire. They were tucked away in wooded valleys, deliberately remote so as to be well hidden from the Tartars.

Over the previous days I had become used to the dark greens and browns of the forest and the white of the snow, and it seemed as though I had left civilization entirely behind, but walking in through the first monastery gatehouse I was confronted by a sight which defied the remoteness of the spot. On the outside walls were frescoes painted in a dazzling array of colours. The lapis lazuli blue, the greens, reds and yellows were still vivid after four hundred years of sun, rain and snow, and were perfectly framed by the dark green forest on the surrounding hills. Many of the churches had depictions of the siege of Constantinople upon their walls. The fall of Constantinople to the Turks in 1453 had left the whole of Eastern Europe vulnerable. It was the founder of the first monasteries,

Stephen the Great of Moldavia, who had done so much to keep the Turks at bay after they had taken the imperial city. Such was his fame that the monks of Mount Athos sent him a piece of the 'True Cross' as a talisman of victory, and here in this faraway place it is still preserved. Few relics have a better provenance. The 'True Cross' was found in Jerusalem by Helena, the mother of the Emperor Constantine, at the beginning of the fourth century. This piece had been kept in the imperial treasury in Byzantium from where it had been given by the Emperor Romanus I in the ninth century to one of the monasteries on Mount Athos. From there it had been sent to Moldavia. As a talisman it seems to have worked; in 1502 Stephen told the Venetian envoy, 'I have fought thirty-six battles and of these I have won thirty-four.' Stephen's carved white marble tomb, which he had built for himself before he died, lies in the monastery at Putna. The date of his birth was inscribed and a space left for the date of his death. Stephen died in 1504 but the date was never added. For Romanians he never really passed away.

On 12 January that year there were church services all over Romania to remember the victims of the Revolution, which had started with the massacre in Timişoara. In the church at Humor, another of Stephen's painted churches, I knelt in front of the golden iconostasis among villagers dressed in traditional costume. The men wore sheepskin coats, white breeches and knee-length leather boots, the women brightly coloured headscarves and skirts. In the dim light, with the smell of incense in the air and smoke curling upwards from a thurible into the soot-blackened dome, a choir of peasants sang unaccompanied the beautiful hymns of the Romanian Orthodox Church. During the sermon tears poured down the cheeks of the congregation as the priest spoke of the men, women and children who had died.

Afterwards food and wine was distributed to be eaten and drunk in memory of the dead. The villagers insisted that, as a foreigner and thus honoured guest, I be the first to drink. They all crowded around, waiting, and watched me as I lifted my glass. Only after I had drunk did they begin.

★

FROM THE MONASTERIES, for the first time in many days I stopped going east. Instead I turned southwards, driving over hills and mountains, passing through thick pine forests which stretched for many miles in all directions, the branches of the trees weighed down and sagging with snow. In villages of wooden houses, outside the bars stood horse-drawn sledges, the horses stamping and snorting steam in the cold. Inside, in tall white fur hats and floor-length white coats lined with sheep's wool, with pockets and cuffs edged in black, their drivers drank strong liquor. But as always there was no food to be found. In the towns I kept my eyes open for queues which might indicate that there was bread for sale. At last I saw one. The people, noticing I was not Romanian, ushered me straight to the front. There I was presented with a loaf of bread for which the baker would accept no money, and from out of the queue, a dignified and aristocratic-looking old man came forward. He leant over and kissed my hand, and in faltering English, obviously not used for many years, said, 'Thank you for coming to our country. It means very much to us.'

As I passed through one village after another, driving slowly along snowy roads, there were beautiful old houses on all sides, both wooden and of stone and brick, with elegant plasterwork, decorated verandas, fretted eaves and shingled roofs. These villages were more intact than any I had seen elsewhere in Europe, and all the houses were still lived in by country people, whose cows, horses, pigs and chickens resided in stables, sties and coops in the courtyard. In many villages there was barely a modern building in sight. I had read in newspapers of President Ceauşescu's campaign to 'systematize' the villages of Romania. This process had apparently involved the bulldozing of the old villages and the forced relocation of the villagers into soulless apartment blocks. Now, as I looked around, I found it difficult to reconcile such reports with reality. In all the regions through which I had travelled there was, I was thankful to see, little evidence of such state-organized vandalism.

In Transylvania, on the road south, every ten miles I passed roadblocks with soldiers checking vehicles for counter-revolutionaries.

Then I entered the Saxon lands, and, before long, on rounding a corner on a hill above the Târnava river, I saw the spiky silhouette of the town of Sighişoara ahead of me.

I wandered through narrow medieval streets and up hundreds of wooden steps to the Gothic church at the top of the hill which looks down over the steep tiled roofs and finials of the town, then white and plump with snow. The keeper of the key lived in a tower by the church. The night before a wolf had climbed over the wall at the end of his garden and killed two of his sheep. He showed me the tracks. We were right in the centre of the town. To reach there the wolf must have loped through the cobbled streets and along the pavements. Walking back down those cobbled streets I passed a man with a squeeze box, drunk, playing and singing to himself as he staggered along. '*Libertate!*' he said, doffing his cap.

From Sighişoara I drove west to the town of Copşa Mica where antiquated factories blackened the countryside, coughing out thick smoke and choking the local population. Five miles before I reached it the snow turned grey. In the streets sooty-faced children, often dressed in rags, stood by the roadside and waved and made victory signs as I passed. There seemed to be no other cars. Then a steam train, thick white smoke billowing from its funnel, blew by on the railway track by the side of the road.

On a grey winter's evening I drove into Timişoara, the last big town before the border and scene of the massacre a month earlier. It was now 15 January. There were still tanks in the roads and troops of soldiers stood at street corners. From the rooftops I was watched through binoculars as I walked into the main square. In the square, shops were burnt out and their windows shattered or full of bullet holes; ornamental fountains and statues had been crushed by tanks whose tracks could be seen in the mud, now frozen, alongside foot-prints of protesters who had been there that night; young trees had gaping wounds in their trunks, ripped open by bullets, on one side small holes in the bark, on the other the white flesh of the wood torn apart.

A man came up and started talking. He wanted to tell me what had happened. The long narrow square had no streets leading off it; the only exits were at either end. He pointed to where the police and the Securitate had lined the rooftops while tanks cut off the escape routes below. The people were trapped. It was a massacre of unarmed men, women and children in a show of strength. Nobody knew how many died. 'They just shot them down,' he shouted, suddenly enraged as he remembered it all, 'the people could do nothing.' Tears were now flowing down his cheeks. He calmed down a little. 'And you know what happened next?' he said. 'Later the same evening, between two o'clock and four o'clock in the morning, God wept. It rained in torrents and washed away all the blood.'

It was this brutal repression which started the Revolution. The Romanians I had encountered all over the country were the kindest, gentlest and most civilized people I had ever met. They were appalled by such pitiless slaughter. It pushed them over the edge. After nearly twenty-five years of rule, Ceauşescu had miscalculated. Following the massacre everything happened quickly. Those unhappy with his regime seized their moment. The people supported them. Within a week Ceauşescu and his wife lay dead in a pool of blood in the backyard of the militia garrison in Târgovişte. The people's retribution had been swift.

2

Over the Hills to Halma

For he led us, he said, to a joyous land . . .
Where waters gushed and fruit trees grew,
And flowers put forth a fairer hue,
And everything was strange and new.
Robert Browning, *The Pied Piper of Hamelin*

IT WAS EARLY autumn, a year after my first visit, and I was walking from village to village over the hills of Transylvania. On reaching the margins of a wood I hesitated for a moment; here forests stretch for miles in all directions and I had no way of knowing how big this one was. Nonetheless, taking a deep breath, I walked in among the trees and was plunged from the burning hot sun outside into a cool green world of flickering light and shadow beneath a canopy of translucent leaves. There were no sounds except for the singing of distant birds. In places shafts of light plunged through the canopy like rays of sun through clouds, and lit up patches of the forest floor. In all directions trunks of beeches, oaks and horn-beams receded into darkness. I wondered what creatures might be lurking there watching me from the shadows, and felt the power these forests must wield over the imaginations of the local people. I had been walking for an hour, weaving my way between the silver tree trunks, and had still not emerged. Then at last I saw light ahead.

I came out of the dark forest along a woodcutter's path into a sunny meadow. Leaning on the stick I had cut for myself to fend off the ferocious dogs that guard the flocks of sheep against the wolves and bears which live in these forests, I blinked my eyes to accustom myself to the bright daylight. Down below me in a valley I could see the steeple of a church.

Tired and thirsty after a long walk in the heat of the Transylvanian summer I was relieved to have come across a village where I would find water. I walked with renewed energy along a path across recently scythed meadows, and dipped down in between the village houses and orchards, where the branches of the apple and pear trees were now heavy with fruit.

As I descended into the village I saw a girl in a courtyard lowering a bucket into a well. She was wearing a blue dirndl dress and had long blonde hair, tied behind in plaits like the country girls of Germany. On the train to Transylvania, and in the months before, I had been doing my best to learn Romanian and here was an opportunity to practise. I put my head over the fence and asked her, in halting phrases, if it might be possible to have a glass of water.

'*Können Sie vielleicht Deutsch?* – Can you speak German?' she replied.

'*Ja, ein wenig* – Yes, a little.'

'*Also, wenn Sie wollen können wir freilich Deutsch sprechen. Bitte, kommen Sie herein* – Then if you would like we could of course speak German. Please come inside,' she said.

Her father, who had been scything in the garden, appeared around the side of the house, and her mother on hearing voices came out on to the veranda. They too both had fair hair and blue eyes. They looked different from Romanians, and spoke fluent German. I was confused. We were so far from the German parts of Europe, almost in the Balkans; I assumed they must have come to live there recently, fed up with the bustle of modern life in Western Europe.

'No,' they told me, 'our family has been here for eight hundred years.'

THEY INSISTED I drink wine instead of water and invited me to sit down at a wooden table in the shade of a spreading vine. An older lady, the grandmother of the house, in aprons and wearing a wide-brimmed straw sunhat, laid a clean white tablecloth over the scrubbed pine, carefully smoothing it to the corners, and soon wine, glasses and a plate of freshly baked cakes were arranged in front of us.

'Our ancestors came here in the twelfth century from Northern Europe,' the father told me, filling my glass with wine. 'Just like you, we are Saxons. You are Anglo-Saxons and we are Transylvanian Saxons.'

He proceeded to tell their story. The Saxons had, it seemed, come there on the invitation of the Hungarian king to guard against marauding tribes of nomadic horsemen from the east who harried the southern marches of his kingdom, and they had been there ever since. He explained how, for all those eight hundred years, the Saxons had lived surrounded by Romanians and Hungarians, but had remained distinctly, stalwartly Saxon. They had married only among their own people and had kept their old Germanic names. They had built villages just like those they had left behind in Northern Europe, still spoke their archaic 'Saxon' language, still wore traditional Saxon clothes – which I later discovered bore an extraordinary resemblance to those depicted in Flemish Renaissance paintings – and still practised medieval customs passed down to them by their Saxon ancestors.

Through all the upheavals and toings and froings of eight hundred years in this distant and constantly fought-over frontier on the edge of Christendom, the Saxons had preserved their distinctive difference. Their massive church towered up above us on the hill behind the house. With its ring walls, bastions and pointed roofs, so foreign in style and so defensive in purpose, it told the story.

'This is how it was, and for the moment still is,' the man's wife said. 'But now we are all going. Everyone has decided to leave. The German government has offered all Saxons German citizenship, and because we can earn better money in Germany everyone has lost their heads and are packing their bags. You see the house over the road. The people who lived there left last week. They took just a few suitcases. They were not allowed to take anything more. The house is still full of their things but they have emigrated.' *Ausgewandert* was the word they used; it sounded as though they had just wandered away. 'They asked us to look after the house, and of course we will, but everyone else says they will be leaving too. Already over a hundred people have gone. If everyone goes we will go as well, what else can we do? And if we go then who will look after the houses?'

'But surely now is the time to stay here,' I said. 'Now that the Communists have been removed surely you can pick up the pieces and start a new life.'

'Yes we could,' they said, 'if others would stay. But as the Saxons say, "*Die Letzten werden die Hunde Beissen* – the dog bites those who are last." Others do not want to stay, and we do not want to be last and to get bitten. After eight hundred years the Saxons have had enough. They do not trust the new government and they are worried that the offer of German citizenship may not continue and that they might miss out. And if we are left alone what will happen to Gerhilde? She will have no Saxon friends. If she wants to marry a Saxon, as is customary, we will have to leave. We will have no choice.'

Gerhilde in her dirndl and blonde plaits sat and listened. She seemed like an apparition from another era. I did not see how she could survive married to a factory worker in a soulless modern suburb of Frankfurt or Karlsruhe. Around us the chickens pecked at the grass and on the bench next to Gerhilde sat her old grandmother with a soft smile on her face and a calm look in her eyes. Next to her the cat was curled up asleep in the cool shade of the vines leaves.

'But if you all go, who will look after your houses and your magnificent church?' I asked.

'Who indeed? Nobody. They will fall into ruin and the Gypsies will help themselves to what is left.'

'It is very sad,' I said.

'Yes, but what can we do?' said the sweet-faced grandmother shrugging her shoulders.

'*Alles ist vorbei* – Everything is over for us now,' sighed the father.

'You must try to stay,' I told them. 'You will not find in Germany anywhere as beautiful as here.'

'We know,' they said.

THEY HAD MENTIONED the Gypsies. I had heard much of them, and indeed had seen them often even during the short time I had been in Romania. They were a bright and exotic flash in the landscape. 'Roumania without its gypsies', wrote Konrad Bercovici, the Romanian émigré writer, 'is as inconceivable as the rainbow without its colours or a forest without birds.' Gypsies were indeed everywhere to be seen, but up until now we had rarely come in contact.

Often I had watched them from a distance as they travelled the country roads in their ragged wagons, or as they sat in the shade of a tree, resting during a journey, their horses tugging at the grass on a nearby verge. Certainly they were effortlessly picturesque; dark faced and barefooted, with ribbons and shells in their hair, and with swathes of multicoloured skirts splayed out over the grass, they seemed always to strike poses as though arranged for an artist to paint them. Around their necks they wore arrays of gold coins; just as Greek mountain shepherds used to keep their wealth in British gold sovereigns, so many of the Gypsies of Transylvania kept, and still keep, it in Austro-Hungarian thalers and florins, on which can be seen the portrait of a bewhiskered Franz Josef or even, occasionally, of a plump Maria Theresa.

Encountering such Gypsies on the road was like coming across a flock of tropical birds in an oak tree. But it was difficult ever to get close to them. Not that they would fly away: quite the contrary. As you approached there would be a rush of children towards you, followed quickly by their mothers, hands extended, faces and tongues imploring. If you gave a coin to one there came a chorus of '*Da şi mie! Da şi mie!* – Give to me as well!' from all the others. The chaos of such encounters would drive away all but the most patient or foolhardy. For Patrick Leigh Fermor in the 1930s things were little different. They 'entangled us in cries and supplication and a mesh of brown arms like tendrils,' he wrote in *Between the Woods and the Water*, 'which we could only unloose by flinging coins beyond their heads like confetti.'

'Are there a lot of Gypsies here?' I asked Gerhilde's parents.

'The place is full of them,' they said.

'And do you have a good relationship with them?'

'In a way, yes, in a way, no. Not all of them are so bad,' they said, 'but they are not the same as us. We work all day every day in the fields to have enough food for the winter. They do not work like that. They want to eat, of course, but they do not want to cultivate. Instead they work, paid by the day, because otherwise they would starve, and to be fair when they work they work very hard, either in the fields, or milking our cows, or doing metalwork, or building, or whatever it might be. But they spend what they receive immediately. So when winter comes along, lo and behold, they have no money and no food and they come to beg from us. They are hopelessly disorganized but they don't seem to care. Of course we give them what we can, and they sometimes do odd jobs for us in the winter like chopping wood. If we go I do not know what will happen to them. They will have no one left to work for and no one to beg from.'

As we chatted a group of dark-skinned girls walked past on the path by the house. These I assumed were some of the Gypsies, although they were not dressed quite as exotically as those I had seen by the sides of the road. They turned their heads to look into the courtyard, and giggled as they made their way down the track to the centre of the village.

We had been talking a long time and the sun was now low on the horizon.

'If you would like to stay the night we can make a bed up for you,' said the father. 'The next village is still several hours' walk from here and you have to go through the forest.'

I accepted their kind offer.

★

BEFORE NIGHTFALL I went for a walk in the village square. A stork was circling over the roofs, and came in to land on a nest high up on the top of one of the bastions of the great church. A woman nearby saw me watching it.

'The storks will soon be gone,' she said. 'They go every year on 22 September, flying south to warmer countries. But they will be back on 22 March.'

'The same day every year?' I asked.

'Yes,' she said. 'And we too will be going soon, but when we go we will not be coming back.'

'You are Saxon,' I said.

'*Ja.*'

I wandered in the direction of the *crîşma*, the village bar, from where I could hear music. I walked through the door. Everyone was in spirited conversation and I sat at a table in a corner with a glass of beer. At the far end of the room two Gypsies were playing, one a violin and the other an accordion. Their music flowed easily and effortlessly, between drinks, smiles and chat, each one improvising in harmony with the flourishes of the other. The instruments seemed to be a part of their body, so naturally did they play, and the music, although not sophisticated, had a strange Eastern rhythm which created an hypnotic effect. When I left the *crîşma* that evening to return to the Saxons' house I felt as though I was under a spell.

AFTER A HEARTY breakfast of eggs I said goodbye to the Saxons and headed for the next village. 'It will take a few hours to reach Floreni,' they said.

As I departed I asked them the name of their village.

'It is called Halma,' they told me, 'at least that is what the Romanians say, but we call it Helmsdorf. It is called Helmsdorf because the lid of the font is said to be made from a Turkish helmet.'

'Be careful of the Gypsies,' they warned me as they closed the gate behind me. 'At least you have a good stick — *ein anständiger Stock!*'

From the house I walked through the ancient Saxon settlement contemplating the decorative plasterwork and the colourful façades of the soon-to-be-abandoned houses. It was hard to understand how the Saxons could bring themselves to leave behind such an enchanting place and with it their eight hundred years of history.

In reflective mood I passed through the village square. Its margins were lined with pear trees and across it there curled a trickling stream. The Saxons had told me that the best drinking water was to be found in the middle of the village and seeing a group of Gypsies reclining on the banks of the stream I called to them to ask where the well might be.

'*Acolo* – Over there,' shouted one, pointing.

'Wait, we will help you with the bucket,' shouted another, and they all jumped up. There were a couple of girls and a boy.

I had always been warned to be wary of Gypsies, not just by the Saxons, but these looked harmless enough, although as they came over I could see there was something provocative and challenging in their eyes, and the smiles of the girls were brimming with secrets.

As the boy pulled on the bucket the girls asked me where I came from.

'I am from England,' I said. 'And you?'

'*Sîntem Ţigani* – We are Gypsies,' they replied, in a teasing tone as if to suggest they knew I would have been warned about them already.

'Do you live here? Or are you travelling?' I asked.

'We live here,' they replied.

'But I thought Gypsies travelled from place to place,' I said.

'Some do, but we don't,' they said. 'Our families are musicians. Musicians live in one place.'

'What instruments do you play?' I asked them.

They laughed. 'Girls don't play music, we just dance, or sing.'

One of them gave a quick demonstration, moving her arms and hips like a *houri*, and they all dissolved into laughter.

'And what do you do for the rest of the time?' I said.

'*Nimic* – Nothing,' they replied, shrugging cheerfully.

The sun sparkled on the water in the bucket as they poured it into my bottle. The warmth and the light breeze of a late summer's afternoon seemed the ideal conditions for lying by the stream and doing nothing.

'Have some apples,' said one of the girls, polishing them on her skirt. She had bright and audacious eyes. 'They are very sweet.'

I thanked her as she handed them to me, and asked which was the road to Floreni.

'You just follow this track and go up through the forest over there,' she said, pointing to the trees on the hill.

'But why are you going to Floreni?' they asked.

'I wanted to sleep there tonight,' I said.

'You should stay here. It is much more fun here,' they said, their eyes alive with innuendo.

'Perhaps another time,' I replied.

'Perhaps you are afraid of us?' said the girl who had given me the apples. 'You should not believe what people say about Gypsies.'

She had a point. Perhaps I was a little afraid of them – afraid of people about whom I knew almost nothing except from stories and from the occasional roadside sighting. But in a way it was their own fault. The Saxons had a solidity and homeliness about them which inspired confidence. The Gypsies were different. Their glances, movements and words seemed designed to unsettle you. There was something disquieting and unpredictable about them. It was difficult to know what was going on behind their flashing eyes.

'No one has said anything nasty about you,' I replied, worried that the Saxons might have trouble if I said otherwise. 'Thank you again for the apples,' I said as I walked off towards the fields.

'. . . and have fun doing nothing,' I shouted over my shoulder.

'We do!' they shouted back.

This was the first time that I met Marishka.

3

To the House of Mihai

Veşnicia s-a născut la sat – Eternity was born in the village.
Lucian Blaga, *Sufletul Satului* (The Soul of the Village)

WHEN I WAS young I lived in the south of England in a beautiful house tucked away at the end of a hidden valley. The house, surrounded by woods and hills on three sides, was blessedly cut off from the rest of the world, and there I passed a delightful and secluded childhood. My father and mother, both of whose families came from Ireland, ran the place in an Irish way. During the day the doors of the house were always open, and we children were allowed to roam at will over the hills. One of my greatest pleasures in those days was to go for long walks in the surrounding country with our faithful, shaggy brown-and-white springer spaniel who, when I stopped in the shade of a clump of beeches to sit and admire the view of the rolling Sussex Downs and beyond it the sea and the Isle of Wight, would leave off chasing rabbits and sit next to me, leaning up against my arm and resting his head on my shoulder.

The scene before us was idyllically beautiful but always, deep down, I sensed there was something wrong. The truth was that, however beautiful it might have been, it was also ghostlily empty. There were no people, or almost none. Sometimes an old back-woodsman, a relic from the past, whose very rarity would make me jump, might emerge from the bushes with a couple of rabbits or pigeons hanging over his shoulder. Otherwise there was nobody. I had read *Lark Rise to Candleford*, and Thomas Hardy, and kept half imagining that I might meet a shepherd tending a flock of sheep, or come across a Gypsy encampment in a dell, or schoolchildren walking home over the hills from the village school with satchels on their shoulders. But I never did. At the time I took this emptiness as being the norm. I resigned myself to the fact that the world had changed since Hardy's time.

Now, however, I had been to Romania. There I had seen that such emptiness was not the way the countryside had to be. In Romania the fields and woods were teeming with people. Wherever I had gone I had met men and women who would stop working, lean on their scythes or hoes, and talk to me as though they had all the time in the world. Then in the evening, having walked for miles across fields filled with swathes of wild flowers colouring and sweeping over hillsides, and through deep and sometimes frightening forests which reached for miles in all directions, I would come to a dirt track that led to a village. These villages might have been remote but they too were filled with people, young and old, all delighted to see strangers and always generous enough, however poor they might have been, to give me a meal or a bed for the night.

I was determined to return again to this beguiling country, but when I did not know.

THE 'WHEN' WAS sorted out in 1993. An insoluble financial crisis came upon us and my father was forced to sell the beautiful home which had, for all my life, been our refuge from the modern world. Now suddenly it was gone. I wandered around the garden for the last time, seeing all the places where I had spent the happiest days of my childhood, and then walked away and left that particular happy valley for ever.

One year passed and then another and my life in England drifted harmlessly by. I tried for a while to live in London, but it was hopeless. The more I trod the city streets the more I knew I had not been born to walk on pavements. My country childhood had left me unsuited to life in the big city. I longed for the sheltering peace of the valley again, a peace that the world in which I was now living seemed almost entirely devoid.

Two years after we sold the old house I knew I needed to find a new place to go. Fortunately, by then, there was an obvious first choice. In Romania there were any number of beautiful and tranquil valleys in which to escape once again from the more disagreeable realities of modern life.

Indeed I could not dislodge the idea of Romania from my mind. It had seemed like the wing of a mansion which had been closed up for a hundred years. I longed to go in and explore before people started to move things around. But I wanted to explore it properly, and was sure that I should go there for at least a year, to see the whole cycle of the seasons, and to observe every detail of the old way of life. The books and poetry I had read about English and Russian country life of the nineteenth century were not enough. They served only to whet my appetite. I wanted to hear the noises for myself, to smell the smells, learn how to scythe, to make ricks and to plough with horses, to go to their harvest fairs, dance their dances and to sing their songs. I wanted to breathe in to the full the last gasps of the fresh world which I had stumbled upon, before it changed and disappeared for ever.

BY EARLY 1996 I managed at last to free myself from the possessions and responsibilities which tied me to England, and on a spring morning, with a lightness in my step and whistling a merry tune, I set off from London. By the middle of May I found myself once again crossing the mountains of northern Romania, just as I had done six years before. Leaving the modern world behind with a sense of elation, I descended into the isolated valleys and villages of the Maramureş, returning to the lands where six years before I had seen the remarkable shoes.

For a week I walked over hills and through forests searching for a place to live, sleeping wherever I could find shelter. One day, towards evening, after many miles of walking, drinking water from hidden springs shown to me by shepherds, I found myself on a ridge looking down on a small village. I walked down from the hill and stopped at a wooden cottage in a dell surrounded by trees. It was accessible only by cart or on foot. Here lived, in one earth-floored room, an old lady and her grandson. I asked them if there was somewhere I could stay the night, and they pointed to a haystack which was protected from the rain by a shingled roof. 'The hay has just been cut,' they told me, 'it is the best room in the house.'

In the light of an oil lamp I ate a supper of bread and milk. A goat had wandered into the room and jumped up on to the bed next to the old lady. She grabbed it by the back leg and milked it into a bowl which, when she had finished, she placed in front of me on the table, with a broad smile on her face.

She then asked me some questions.

'Where is it you come from?'

'From England,' I replied.

'And where would that be?' she asked.

'Well, it's a long way away from here,' I said.

'Ah, in the outside world. I see. And in which direction is it?' she said.

'It is to the north-west, over there,' I said, pointing, 'but two thousand kilometres away on the other side of Europe.'

'And you came all the way from there to here?' she asked in apparent wonderment.

'Yes,' I said. For a moment she seemed lost in thought, and then added, 'But how on earth did you find the way?' She imagined the whole world to be made up of little paths like the ones which led from her village to the others nearby, and from there into the forest and over the mountains.

After a night in the fresh air, with my head resting on a cushion of flowers and grass, I came down the ladder to breakfast. A plate of eggs was placed in front of me, and some more goat's milk. 'Eat!' said the old lady.

The cat watched me from a ledge above the stove, chickens came in and out of the door, and the goat was nibbling in the courtyard. The old lady began to speak. Overnight she had prepared more questions.

'Do you have a cow in England?'

'No,' I replied, 'I don't.'

'Do you have a goat then or sheep?' she went on. I had to admit that I did not.

'A pig perhaps?'

'No.'

'Nothing?' she asked, amazed. 'Don't you have any grass where you live?'

'Oh yes, there is grass,' I said, thinking of the garden, and pleased to be able to lay claim to having something at last.

'Then why don't you have a cow?' she persisted.

'Well, I buy milk and meat in shops,' I explained.

'Then what on earth do you do with all the grass?' she said, walking away, shaking her head in bemusement, and scattering maize for the chickens.

She returned five minutes later.

'Perhaps you have a horse?' she said.

Thank goodness, I thought. 'Yes, I do have a horse, or rather my father does; and in fact many people in England have a horse rather than a pig or a cow.' But this news did not please her.

'Oh dear, oh dear. No. You cannot possibly have a horse and not a cow,' she said as if explaining matters to a child. 'You should always have a cow first. Cows are much more useful than horses.'

When I set off to continue my journey, she refused any payment for her hospitality. Instead she gave me bread and goat's cheese to put in my bag, and offered me some advice as well which I was left to ponder as I walked along paths smelling of spring up the hill and into the forest. 'Don't forget, when you return to England, go to the market, sell the horse and buy a cow.'

ON A GREEN sward, on hills high above the valleys and the villages, I stayed the next night at a sheepfold. The shepherd spread out a blanket on the ground in an open-fronted hut made of hazel wands. What little heat there was, was provided by a fire which burned just inside the opening. Into my hands he placed a warm cup of ewe's milk. As I drank he went out and sat on a rock. There he picked up a long metal horn, raised it to his lips and blew. The blasts echoed round the hills about us. It was the first time I had ever seen a true shepherd's horn being used by a shepherd. I watched him as he sat absorbed in blowing out the plangent notes. When they were by themselves, he told me, up on the hills by the forest it was good to blow on the horn and to hear from far away another shepherd replying and not to feel alone.

In front of us the mountains stretched into the distance and across the horizon. The shepherd looked at them.

'I have spent much of my life up here. We come up every year, we milk the ewes three times a day, every day, we make cheese, then we become old and we die,' he said, 'and I don't even know what is beyond those mountains.'

As the sun set behind the western hills he asked me whether the sun rose and set in the same way in England. I assured him it did. And do you have winter and summer? And wind and rain? And are there hills in England? And are all people as tall as you? The questions came thick and fast.

'It is interesting for us to know these things,' he said. 'I hope you do not think me impolite in asking.'

ON THE ROAD I was joined by a small group of travelling Gypsies weighed down with copper pans for sale in the next village. There was a mother, father and four children. They were friendly and for a while we walked together. The girls were all dressed in bright traditional Gypsy clothes, with red tassels and ribbons intended to ward off evil spirits plaited into the tresses of their hair. Sea shells also hung from their plaits and on strings around their necks. I wondered where the shells had come from.

'Have you been to the sea?' I asked.

'Yes! Yes, we have,' they replied beaming, jumping up and down and skipping.

'Really, how wonderful. And did you like it there?'

'Yes, it was beautiful!' they shrieked with joy.

At this point the father intervened.

'Don't lie to the gentleman!' he boomed. Then he turned to me and said: 'They were given to them by their grandmother. She had been to the Black Sea many years ago.'

A FEW EVENINGS later, on the day before Whitsun, I came down through orchards into a village called Breb. The villagers, weary from the day's work, were walking home from the fields in the twilight, hoes or scythes on their shoulders and round-bottomed wicker baskets on their backs. They greeted me, smiling, and asked where I was heading. 'To the house of Mihai, son of Gheorghe, son of Ştefan,' I replied. I had heard that he and his wife Maria, because they did not have children, might have room for me to stay.

I found Mihai in a smoke-filled rustic distillery, dressed in bell-sleeved smock and wearing *opinci* – the remarkable shoes cross-gartered with leather thongs up to the knee, which I had seen on my first visit to Romania in 1990. Outside stood a cart carrying a barrel filled with a seething mixture of plums, pears and apples which Mihai was shovelling into a bulbous copper still.

With a broad smile of welcome, Mihai wasted no time in passing me a battered aluminium mug of *horincă* – the plum brandy of the Maramureş – and signalled for me to drink.

'*Noroc! Şi să trăiţi la mulţi ani!* – Good fortune! And may you live for many years,' he said.

I swallowed, then choked, spluttered, and put my hand to my chest, unable to speak. Mihai laughed. His double distilled brew was evidently up to strength.

Back home Mihai gave me another mug of his freshly made *horincă* while his wife Maria, also dressed in embroidered smock and *opinci*, made up a bed for me, and prepared a supper of sausages and potato soup.

'You must be hungry after your long walk. Eat as much as you can,' they said. As I was about to go to my room, Mihai, son of Gheorghe, son of Ştefan, told me: 'I wanted to let you know, you can stay here as long as you like.' In the end I stayed for four years.

That night I slept deeply, soothed by the sound of the stream and drugged by the fresh mountain air. When I arose the next morning Mihai and Maria were in the kitchen. Outside the cock, with green tail feathers fit for an Emperor of Austria's hat, strutted about by the barn, and the pig, Grigor by name, was taking his morning potter about the yard.

A plate of scrambled eggs with fried pig fat (Grigor's predecessor, I fear) was placed in front of me, along with a glass of thick, creamy milk and another of *horincă*. I instinctively refused the *horincă* but changed my mind when I saw the look of disappointment on Mihai's face.

THE MARAMUREŞ IS a land cut off by mountains to the south and, since 1945, by the border with what was the Soviet Union to the north. Until 1920 eighty per cent of its surface was covered in forest. Still today there is something distinctly sylvan about the Maramureşeni, especially when one sees them huddled together in their wooden churches praying to God to help them eke out a living, with their mostly wooden tools, from their small patches of ground encircled by the echoing forest.

In valleys surrounded by forests and mountains, with no towns of any size nearby, remote and poorly connected to the outside world, the Maramureş remained one of the most unaltered regions of Europe. So well preserved had been their traditional way of life that, in more recent times, a selection of ethnologists and philologists from different parts of the world had travelled over the passes to study the lives, customs and language of these unique and isolated people. On my first days there I was asked by an old peasant, carrying a scythe and dressed in a linen smock, from which university I had come. It was not that there had been so many professors – very few, in fact, perhaps ten in twenty years – but that the only people who ever came there had been professors of one sort or another. Rather as John Synge had discovered when he went to the

Aran Islands in 1905, as they had never met anyone else, the peasants of the Maramureş appeared to believe the entire outside world to be made up of philologists.

I had gone there not as a scientist, however, but just to live and work together with them before their old way of life was changed for ever. Montaigne had looked out of the window of his tower in France, seen peasants working and ploughing in the fields and realized that they, with their simple daily round, were probably happier than he. Now was a last chance to put this to the test. The 1989 Revolution would soon be followed by the onset of the Western way of doing things. Time was clearly running out if one wanted to see and feel how country life had been several centuries ago. In Romania it had survived forty years of Communism, but the new order was likely to be altogether more destructive. It was only a matter of time before the modern world came marching over the mountains.

During the years I stayed there I was able to learn much about the lives of the Maramureşeni. They welcomed me among them, fed me, protected me, and talked freely about their ways. The village of Breb became like a home to me, and although from there I often travelled about the country, it was the place to which I always returned, to smiling and welcoming faces, and to the quiet wisdom and sanity of Mihai. It was a time before things began to change, before the advertising arrived, before young people began to become restless, influenced by what they heard of life beyond the mountains. The modern world had not yet begun its insidious work to undermine their happy and innocent way of life.

MIHAI WAS A delightful and gentle man with blue eyes and thick grey hair. He always wore a white smock, workaday ones during the week, and smart, clean ones of better, thicker material for Sundays and holy days. He had lived in the village and worked his family's land all his life. They possessed only a few hectares but it was enough to survive on. From working their few strips Mihai and Maria produced all their own food – they only had to buy salt and a little sugar when necessary – and there was always as much as you could eat on the table. Clothing too was all home made, with the exception of Mihai's trousers and the material for Maria's skirts which they bought at the market. When, after the 1989 Revolution, charities began bringing humanitarian aid to villages in Romania, some of the aid reached Breb. Mihai and Maria were very appreciative, but could not understand why on earth strangers should be sending them food and clothes when they had plenty of both. They did not eat the food or wear the clothes, but they were not wasted; the food was given to the pig, and the clothes were turned into cloths for drying dishes or mopping the floor.

Although Mihai had to work extremely hard to survive, at the same time he loved the country around him. He knew every tree, path and stream. He knew where to find crayfish, and where the bears slept in the forest. He knew the names of all the trees and flowers and the habits of every bird and animal. When describing a bird he had seen on the hill that day he would tell me where and how it nested, exactly when it arrived in Breb each year, what it fed on, its song and any other relevant detail. He pointed out the *Taptalaga* which began singing in the summer when the wheat was ready to harvest, and the *Storzi* which made their nests out of moss at the very end of the branches. His knowledge was the result of working for seventy years in the fields and the forests.

He loved his surroundings, and he knew his survival was intimately linked to them. Every tree and coppice on his land was treasured and nurtured. Some trees provided fruit or nuts, others provided the curved handles for scythes, the V-shapes necessary to make hay forks, the runners of sleighs, or the hard but yielding wood for making the yokes of oxen. If, when walking, he saw an ash branch with the right shape to make a two- or three-pronged hay fork he would cut it off with his axe, which he carried with him wherever he went, and bring it home. Sometimes whole trees had to be cut down for firewood or building, but there were always others growing to take their place planted by Mihai or his parents or grandparents.

Mihai also knew how to work leather and to make cart harnesses. On winter evenings he would sit on an old stool bench in the kitchen, put the leather in the jaws of the wooden vice, and cut and stitch until, after a month or two, a fine pair of harnesses were ready, as good as any in the area. Even the buckles he made himself, hammering to shape little pieces of metal on a tiny anvil; each buckle took him ten minutes to complete from start to finish. If need be he would also stitch you a pair of *opinci*. The tools lay in a box attached to the bench. There were knives, needles, awls, splicers, and, most beautiful of all, a special brass implement through which you pulled rough strips of leather to create belts and straps. It had been made in the early nineteenth century by Blanchard of Paris. Mihai pointed out the name engraved upon it. He was very proud of it. It had been given to him by an old leather-worker from a town on the other side of the mountains fifty years before.

In 1917 MIHAI's father had come back from fighting on the Italian and Serbian fronts in the Great War. In 1918 Mihai was born. At that time the Maramureş was a province of the Austro-Hungarian Empire – the part called Hungarian Ruthenia. Soon afterwards, in 1920 following the Paris Peace Conference, its southern part, south of the Tisa river, where Mihai lived, became a part of the Kingdom of Romania; then in 1940, as the result of an arrangement brokered by Hitler, it again became part of Hungary, and finally in 1945 a part of Romania again.

Sovereignty changed frequently: everything else stayed much the same. Their language remained Romanian, with a strong Slavic twist and a few peppery Hungarian words sprinkled in, as no doubt it had been for a thousand years. The style of their clothes too looked as though it had not altered much in a millennium. Advancing and retreating armies helped themselves to horses and carts, food, *horincă*, and probably the occasional woman, but otherwise left the Maramureşeni in peace. When the Russians came through in 1944, in their big fur hats, they cut down trees for the fruit, shot holes in the barrels of *horincă* to fill up their flasks and moved on. Mihai's brother-in-law told me, a year or two before he died, how in 1944 he, along with others from the village, had been taken by the retreating German army, through Austria and into Germany, to help dig trenches.

'The German trenches', he told me, 'were beautifully made by people from the Maramureş. We had known how to work with wood since we were children. We were the best and they took us everywhere with them. We drove posts into the ground and wove them together with hazel wands to stop the sides from falling in. The Russians, on the other hand, didn't use cover. It was very strange. They would come along in their thousands and the Germans, from their beautifully made trenches, mowed them down. The Russians lost many more men than the Germans for this reason, and the awful thing was that, whilst the Germans always buried their dead, the Russians left theirs where they fell. From the trenches we would watch the bodies swell up until, after a while, the worms made holes in them and they would burst, their bones disjointed, and they fell to pieces. It was unpleasant.' After this experience of the outside world, he came home and returned to village life as though nothing had happened.

Even the advent of Communism changed little. The villagers vehemently opposed being 'collectivized'. The Communists had come with tractors, with girls marching in front of them waving banners and singing patriotic songs, and ploughed over the divisions between the old strips. But at night the villagers dug up the fresh maize shoots from the newly enlarged fields and chopped down the state apple and plum orchards which had been planted on what they considered to be their land. In the end, the state left them alone, and they went contentedly back to the traditional way of doing things.

MIHAI WAS FAMOUS in the village for having fought and killed a wolf. When we had visitors and the talk turned to wolves, which it often did, he would fill all glasses with *horincă* and tell the story. He had been a shepherd before the Second World War and for the entire summer lived up on the high pastures beside the mountains which rose up to the south of the village. One day while he was watching the sheep a large wolf appeared out of the forest and loped towards him. This was not typical behaviour; usually wolves lurk in the darkness of the trees and choose their moment to pounce. This wolf was, however, rabid. It had already killed nine people in a neighbouring village. One of those attacked was left with his scalp and hair hanging off the side of his head, a wound from which he soon died.

It was an unusually big wolf and it bared its teeth as it came towards Mihai. Mihai's dog immediately went for it but was thrown aside. Mihai then swung his big shepherd's stick, but to little effect; the wolf jumped at him, grabbed him by the arm and threw him to the ground. The dog then saw its chance to attack, and while the wolf was distracted Mihai was able to scramble to his feet and hit it with his stick. The wolf turned towards him and again his dog attacked it from behind. And so it continued, the wolf turning first on one and then the other, Mihai and his dog moving gradually backwards as they fought. They walked backwards for a kilometre fighting the wolf until at last the blows of the stick and the attacks of the dog weakened it. When at last another shepherd, hearing the noise, came running to help, the wolf was easily beaten to death.

During the fight Mihai had been bitten on the arm. He came down from the hill and went to the doctor in the town. The doctor told him he must leave at once for the hospital in the city of Cluj in central Transylvania. It was a long way, but the only place where they could give injections against rabies. To reach Cluj he had to take the train, which in those days passed first through Czechoslovakia and then Hungary before turning back into Romania. It was a twenty-hour journey, avoiding the mountains, to go less than 120 kilometres as the crow flies. It might almost have been quicker to walk.

He sat in a compartment in his best peasant clothes, and chatted to the other passengers, mostly townspeople in suits and frocks. They asked him what his business was in Cluj. 'I was bitten by a wolf,' he said, 'and I am going to the hospital.' He then lifted the lid of the box sitting next to him on the seat. In it was the head of the wolf, its long fangs bared, its face in a twisted grin. The ladies started in surprise. Mihai laughed as he told the story. The doctor had told him to take the head with him to have it tested for rabies. He had not really meant to upset anyone. In the end, however, everyone in the train wanted to see the head. 'It was like at a fair,' he said, 'I could have made lots of money.'

The wolf did indeed have rabies, but remarkably Mihai survived. He had arrived much too late at the hospital for any injections to be effective, but the wolf's saliva had been wiped off its teeth by the thick sheep's wool of Mihai's coat, or so the doctors of Cluj surmised.

MIHAI BECAME A dear friend. He always took my part when others might laugh at my pretensions to living the peasant life, and when I would set off on my travels tears would roll down his cheeks. The people of the old Maramureş laugh and cry more easily than others. Nowadays, after thousands of years, life in the Maramureş is beginning to change. But as the world around them changed, Mihai and Maria remained the same.

MIHAI HAD TWO young cousins called Ion and Vasile. On Sundays they wore identical clothes and seemed to be twins even though there was in fact a year between them. This Whitsunday morning they stopped at the house to visit Mihai and Maria. On leaving they offered to accompany me to church. The forms and rituals of an Orthodox service were mostly a mystery to me and so I accepted gladly. Without their help I was sure to do something wrong.

We walked together down the track, following the stream in which white ducks swam, and passed through the wooden lych gate. As we entered the churchyard a hundred headscarved heads turned towards us.

The church in Breb was small. God liked small churches. He had after all allowed Constantinople to be destroyed because it had grown too big, or so it was said. Romanians therefore thought it best to build themselves modest churches. As a result, as here in Breb, there was not enough room inside for everyone. Since by tradition the men stood at the front, many of the women and girls had to stand outside on the grass, and when a man appeared they drew apart to make a path. At this time of year the path was perfumed by the scent of philadelphus blossom which the girls had picked from bushes on the way to the church and held as posies in their hands.

I walked self-consciously down this path, all eyes upon me, following Ion and Vasile, and entered through a low door into the semi-darkness of the narthex, which was also filled with women, dressed in headscarves, full pleated skirts and petticoats. They made way for us and again we ducked our heads to pass through another low door and walked into the naos, the main body of the church, where the men of the village stood huddled together, all in sheep's wool waistcoats and smocks, each standing in his appointed family place.

Ion, Vasile and I walked to the front, kissed the icon, and Ion led me to where I should stand. The boys' straw hats were passed from one man to another to be hung on wooden hooks on the wall in a line next to all the many others, their decorative ribbons dangling below them.

The service was in full flow. 'Doamne Miluieste', the Kyrie eleison of the Romanian Church, was intoned over and over again by the priest. Deacons chanted and swung frankincense-bearing censers whose smoke drifted upwards as though taking the prayers to heaven. The liturgy of St John Chrysostom, the Golden-Mouthed, seemed interminable in the heat of the crowded church, but the candles which flickered in front of the iconostasis, their glow reflecting faintly on the gilded carvings and smoke-stained icons, had a hypnotizing effect. The most pious remained there on their feet for over two hours, or, when a little bell was rung by the cantor, down on their knees. As they knelt to pray they placed neatly folded handkerchiefs on the wooden floor beneath them to keep their Sunday trousers clean.

At the frequent mention of the Father, Son and Holy Ghost everyone crossed themselves. I was not sure whether I should cross myself as well, nor, if I did, which way I should do it, from left to right or right to left, and most crucially, with how many fingers. In seventeenth-century Russia the question of whether to make the sign of the cross with two fingers or with three caused a schism which lasted for hundreds of years. St Avvakum, the famous Russian monk and confessor of Tsar Alexis, father of Peter the Great, refused to move with the times and make the sign with three fingers. He was exiled for ten years, imprisoned for twenty-two, twelve of those underground, and finally, aged sixty-two, was burnt at the stake. It was clearly not an issue to take lightly. The Old Believers, those who insisted on using two fingers, were driven to take refuge in remote parts of Russia. Some of them even reached Romania. These *Lipoveni*, as they are called, are still there, dwelling in wood and mud huts on small islands in the labyrinthine Danube delta, speaking Russian, dressing like Russian peasants, with long shirts and long beards, and resolutely making the sign of the cross with two fingers. These two fingers should be crossed in the same way as you see Jesus and the Saints holding up their fingers in old Russian icons. Carefully observing the villagers standing next to me I could see that in the Maramureş it was the custom to use three fingers, and so I did the same.

It was hot. The church was crammed with people and the windows were tiny. There barely seemed to be enough air for so many lungs, and when at last the service came to an end there was a discernible look of relief on faces as, leaving the subdued light of the church, we emerged blinking into the spring sunshine.

It being Whitsunday, a long procession was formed, headed by women carrying banners and singing hymns. It wound its way through the village and out on to the hill to a carved wooden wayside cross. There, under a blue sky, in the sweet-scented air, accompanied by the sound of singing birds, the service continued. The priest blessed the fields, saying prayers for a bountiful harvest to the north, south, east and west, and placed a wreath of corn and spring flowers over the cross.

'Does it please you, sir?' people asked me, proud of the spectacle of all the villagers dressed in their finest clothes, assembled on a hillside and worshipping God in the open air.

The procession wove back down the hill as the church bells rang and the wooden sounding board, the *toacă*, clattered. To the mesmerizing ferment of noise we processed three times around the church and then gathered outside the door as the priest called for quiet.

'Do not forget the importance of fasting. I should tell you that the next fast begins in eight days' time,' he said. 'And one last thing before you go, a white horse belonging to Gheorghe of the Valley has been lost — if anyone has seen it please could they let him know.'

With that all drew forward and one by one kissed the cross held by the priest who in turn tapped them on the head with an aspergill dipped in holy water, symbolic of the first Whitsunday (Pentecost) when St Peter had baptized three thousand men and women and started the Christian Church. Each was also given a piece of ritual bread. The congregation then walked away, holy water dripping down their faces or the backs of their headscarves. Sometimes the people do not eat the bread, but conceal it for later use in magical practices.

After the service a woman came up to me. She was, Ion informed me, a Gypsy even though dressed in Maramureş costume. She had a twinkle in her eye.

'Did you hear, sir, what the priest said in his sermon?'

'Yes, some of it,' I replied, impressed that she should be so interested in the sermon.

'He said that in order to be loved by God you have to give to the poor. And here I am, standing right in front of you,' she said beaming, 'a genuine poor person. You don't have to go through all the bother of going to look for one.'

I laughed, gave her a coin and she went happily off to buy a bottle of *horincă* in the village *crîşma*.

Ion and Vasile, before going on their way, accompanied me to the door of the house to make absolutely sure I arrived safely. Then

Maria, Mihai and I sat down to our Whitsunday lunch of lettuce soup, cabbage rolls with thick sour cream, pancakes, and brioche filled with crushed walnuts and plum jam. As it was Sunday there were many visits. Everyone entering said, '*Laudam pe Iesus* – We praise Jesus', and we replied, '*Lăudat să fie în veci, Amin* – May He be praised for ever, Amen.' The men who came shook hands with the other men but never with the women. Their handshakes were firm, and their hands as tough and solid as pieces of wood, but their demeanour and their manner were gentle.

The conversation moved around. Some talked of the price of piglets at the market, some of the bane of the dreaded Colorado beetle, others of the latest weaving patterns and new recipes for fancy cakes. One of the women was distressed. She was lamenting her daughter's marriage: 'We warned her not to marry into a poorer family, but she insisted. As a dowry we gave her everything a person could wish for: a pig, five hens and a pregnant cow. Before she was married she had sixteen different headscarves and any number of skirts from us. Since then her husband has not given her even one headscarf, nor any material to make a new skirt. I went over there the other day. The father was in bed covered by an old coat, the mother was sleeping on top of the stove, and there was wood all over the place, not even stacked up. It was like a barn. They smell of laziness, sitting around in their stuffy kitchen all day. Oh, in what a place has our daughter ended up!'

Like the shepherd on the hill, the visitors were full of questions. One of the old men, wearing a smock with white tasselled threads about the collar, was interested to know why I wore glasses. He asked in the politest possible way so as not to offend me, but as nobody in the Maramureş was short sighted he could not understand it.

'I don't see well without them,' I explained.

'Obviously not,' said Maria, 'as you haven't yet managed to find a wife.'

So in the afternoon Mihai set about trying to find one for me. He took me to the centre of the village where the Sunday promenade was in full flow. Rows of apple-cheeked maidens strolled along the rough village track, five or six abreast, arms coupled together, while their pear-shaped mothers sat on wooden benches, arms folded on their laps, chatting and smiling, but always keeping an eye.

'There you are,' said Mihai, 'take your pick.'

In front of me were girls of every shape and size parading up and down. Flora Thompson when describing an English village of the 1880s had written that 'a stranger coming to Lark Rise would have looked in vain for the sweet country girl of tradition, with her sunbonnet, hay rake, and air of rustic coquetry'. They had all gone into service in the great country houses of England. Here, however, there were still any number of them although, since it was a Sunday, they were not carrying hay rakes on their shoulders. They were dressed in immaculate white shirts and brightly coloured knee-length skirts, made more voluminous by pleats and stiff petticoats beneath them, and as they walked their flowery headscarves fluttered in the breeze. Their shirts were extraordinary works of virtuoso needlework, with stitching and smocking to astound the beholder. With puffed sleeves, embroidered star-shaped cuffs of hand-made lace, and similar ruffs at the neck and shoulders, they would not have looked out of place on a lady of the sixteenth century. All winter, girls even from the poorest households had been stitching away, counting the tiny threads in the best light by the window to make the patterns true and have their costumes ready for Easter. Now wearing smart Sunday shoes bought at the market, and taking care not to twist their ankles, these mannequins coyly picked their way along the rough stone track back and forth from the water mill to the Cooperative shop. The village lads in their white knitted jerseys and best home-made straw hats stood about in groups on the side of the road, doing their best to appear oblivious of the elaborate display put on for their benefit.

As I watched, a huge and hairy pig, covered in dried mud, trotted up the road with its ears flapping up and down in front of its eyes, grunting as it went. The line of delicate figurines was forced to break arms and step aside to let it pass.

4

With Hay in our Hair

This year ever since the early spring he had cherished a plan for mowing with the peasants for whole days together.

Leo Tolstoy, *Anna Karenina*

WHEN MIHAI SCYTHED the grass it was a joy to watch. He was able to make the blade so sharp it would cut a hair laid against it, and when he swung it he turned the grass in the orchard into a neatly cropped lawn. I very much wanted to learn how to do it. During my first days there, in the evenings, he would let me scythe in the garden to give grass to the cows, and took great care to show me how to hone the blade and to swing it properly. Then one day I asked to be allowed to help mow the fields as well. 'No!' was the resounding answer, in unison from Mihai and Maria. I was, as far as they were concerned, 'a gentleman', and they could not possibly countenance me sullying my soft city hands with real work.

'It would be too hard for you,' they said. In any case, it was simply not right to put a guest to work, however much he might beg you to let him. People would gossip, and trying to control gossip was like trying to catch a mouse in the long grass.

'But Tolstoy used to scythe in the fields,' I told them. 'He scythed because he enjoyed it.' They had not heard of Tolstoy, however, and with that my argument rather lost its momentum.

I decided, nonetheless, to buy myself a scythe – they could not object to that – and with it all the necessary equipment. In the small town of Ocna Şugatag there was a fair every Thursday. There I would find everything I needed.

43

So I hitched a lift on a neighbour's cart. Mihai, on other business, came as well. He was in jovial mood and had a bottle of *horincă* in the bag over his shoulder. As we trotted along the road we passed people on foot. Mihai shouted to them.

'*Hai cu noi!* Come with us to the market! Climb aboard!' If there was room they clambered up.

'May Jesus be praised,' they would say to the others on the cart.

'May He be praised for ever, Amen,' we would reply. Mihai then gave them an invigorating swig of *horincă*. The men shook my hand.

'Are you gong to buy a cow?' they joked.

'No,' Mihai replied on my behalf, 'he is going to see what the girls are like.'

'But cows are much more useful,' they rejoined, 'you can't survive here without a cow.'

'Actually I am going to buy a scythe,' I said, and, then, doing my best to join in the banter, 'since a cow can't survive without hay, can it?' They agreed, and I succeeded in making them laugh, but mostly, I think, because they found the idea of my scything too comic for words.

On reaching the ridge of the hill we saw in front of us a chain of tall snow-topped mountains stretching from the western to the eastern horizon. To the north were the Carpathian mountains of the Ukraine, and to the east the summits which separate the Maramureş from Moldavia. As it was such a clear day, perhaps the mountains we could see far off to the west were the most northerly peaks of the Carpathians, the Tatra mountains of Slovakia. Our destination, Ocna Şugatag and the fair, was just a mile or two in front of us, framed by the spectacular scenery.

Seen from above, Ocna Şugatag would be at the centre of a star-like arrangement of paths leading over the fields and through woods, from all the surrounding villages to the market. Along these paths, every Thursday, by foot or by cart, peasants in gathered skirts and headscarves, or best hats and pressed smocks, would travel. Over their shoulders they carried black and white checked bags filled with produce to sell. Some were followed by sheep with a couple of lambs trotting along beside them, others might be leading a reluctant cow or buffalo. Sometimes the cows would stop dead in their tracks and refuse to go a step further. Halfway along the road we passed a couple trying to coax their cow. The man was pushing from behind and his wife was pulling from in front. The cow remained rooted to the spot.

'Don't worry, Gheorghe,' shouted Mihai as we trotted by, 'there's another market next week.'

By the time we clattered into town most people had already arrived. Driving into the square we passed through a sea of swirling skirts and dazzling smocks and fresh, laughing country faces. The Thursday fair is both market and meeting place. In the mêlée were all kinds of people, from dignified old peasants, born when the Maramureş was still a part of the Empire, to 'the sweet country girls of tradition' promenading arm in arm down the main street. Those on our cart hailed friends in the crowd. Mihai pointed out how, from people's clothes, you could tell which village they had come from. If they wore a black and white waistcoat they were from Budeşti or Sîrbi, if one of brown fulled cloth with black edging they were from Breb, while brown with blue trimming was from the Sarasau near the Ukrainian border.

At the animal market we had to join queues of carts. '*Chea!*' shouted our driver to tell the horses to go to the right, '*Oho!*' for them to go to the left, and '*Zuruck!*' to go backwards – in Romania the horses understand German. After working our way through the crowd, which opened in front of us and then closed behind us like water, we found a space and parked amongst a hundred other carts in an open field on the edge of town, just five hundred yards from the centre. I marvelled to see so many horses and carts all gathered in one place. Until then I had not appreciated what it meant to be living in a land almost entirely innocent of the internal combustion engine. The horse and cart, or sleigh in the winter, were practically the only forms of transport, not just in my village but every-where.

It was a sight to be seen, and a colourful one. On the horses' backs were striped or checked blankets, blue, green, red, white and black, which had been woven by the women of the family on their creaking wooden handlooms during the winter. The horses – bays, chestnuts, roans, greys, and hafflingers with their long blond manes – stood there half asleep, occasionally reaching for the hay laid in front of them on the ground. Others neighed boastfully and nipped at people's bottoms in the crowd. Sleepy, saffron-coloured oxen lay ruminating, quietly resting their heads on their yokes, while black, scimitar-horned buffaloes stood with insolent looks upon their faces, outstaring passers-by.

Everywhere there were men and women in smocks busy buying, selling, bargaining, shrugging shoulders, licking their forefingers and slowly counting out money note by note. On the ground were lines of wooden boxes in which piles of contented piglets, noses twitching as they dreamt of delicious meals to come, lay snuggled up to their little pink siblings.

Down the road in the centre of the town, the rest of the market was in full flow. By the sides of the road itinerant salesmen had spread out their wares on the ground. There was everything a person might need. You could buy straw hats, wooden forks and rakes, enamel pots with wooden handles for carrying soup to the fields, round-bottomed baskets, sacks of flour, bran or oats, and of course scythes. There was also a miracle-working herbal elixir several bottles of which, with homemade labels, were placed on a little wooden table. A few teaspoonsful would be guaranteed, according to the handwritten notice placed next to them, 'to cure all known illnesses both interior and exterior'. A Gypsy woman, dressed in an exotic array of colours, squatted on the grass with pots, pans and cauldrons laid out in front of her. She rattled a metal spoon in the pots, bashed the cauldrons and invited passers-by to admire the clear sound they made. Further on a Gypsy with large moustaches lay snoozing among a pile of baskets, and beyond him sat a peasant cobbler offering for sale a variety of leather and rubber *opinci* of all different sizes, and thongs of all different lengths to go with them – leather *opinci* are considered more elegant, but the rubber ones are waterproof.

At the entrance to the food market a line of old ladies carrying chickens in their arms stood patiently. The chickens, equally patient, let out only an occasional squawk at the proddings of the barber's wife or the spouses of municipal dignitaries. Inside, plump, rosy-cheeked villagers sold cream and cheese made from either cow, buffalo or sheep's milk. Buffalo milk is the richest and most luxurious. According to a lady traveller of the nineteenth century, the Hungarian nobility drank only buffalo's milk, considering cow's milk unfit for aristocratic consumption.

Villagers who did not have animals were trying to make a little money selling the few simple things they did have; half a dozen eggs saved up over the week and brought to market wrapped in a hand-kerchief, a handful of carrots or an apple or two from last year, some walnuts, a pot of honey, or seeds which they measured out for sale in walnut shells. They had walked many kilometres to reach the market, and would have to walk many back.

A woman from the town was buying eggs from one of these good people. There were ten eggs, but one was cracked.

'I'll take the nine good ones,' the woman said.

'Wouldn't you buy all ten perhaps?' said the villager. 'What am I to do with just one egg?'

'But it is cracked,' the woman pointed out.

'That'll save you having to crack it when you get home,' suggested the villager smiling, and the woman bought all ten.

I found a stall which sold scythe blades. With the help of a friendly face from Breb who had appeared in the crowd, we hit them one by one on a stone to test for the right ring. In the end I selected a fine Russian model. Although Austrian scythes are universally recognized as being the very best, Russian scythes are the best you can find in the Maramureş, brought over by itinerant ped-lars from the Ukraine. To mow a field in Romania you need, they will tell you with their usual self-deprecating humour, 'a Russian scythe, a Hungarian whetstone and Romanian sweat'. Having, therefore, found myself a Hungarian stone and a suitable sheath to keep it in, I sought out Mihai and we both clambered aboard a cart heading back to the village. We sat on top of a wooden box containing slumbering piglets. Mihai caught sight of my new scythe and smiled.

The cart rumbled along the road. I drank swigs of *horincă* as bottles were passed around, and watched the spring landscape pass slowly by. I was blissfully happy to be in this exotic world among these trusting and cheerful people, all of whom, in their beautiful clothes, seemed like characters from another era. Sometimes I felt as though I was dreaming. I had run away from the modern world to a faraway land where no one could find me, and I could stay here as long as I liked.

BACK IN THE village I found a man who would make a handle for my new scythe. He had all the right wood laid aside, including the curved pieces of plum wood needed for the hafts which he had specially selected and cut from the tree the year before. A scythe handle is a bespoke item, and so he measured me up, noting especially the distance between the ground and the tip of my chin. A week later I took delivery, a neighbour showed me how to attach the blade at the appropriate angle, and I now had a scythe all ready to go.

Armed with Russian scythe and Hungarian whetstone with its water-carrying sheath attached to the belt, I presented myself in the courtyard. Mihai and Maria had been preparing for this difficult moment, and Mihai in particular did not want to disappoint me. They realized they had no choice but to let me play with my new toy, and Mihai patiently set about teaching me first how to hammer out the blade and then how to sharpen it.

THERE WAS STILL a week or two before the grass in the hay meadows would be ready to mow. So to keep myself busy I made efforts to improve my Romanian, and each day I would read a new chapter of the Teach Yourself book which I had brought with me.

Conventional Romanian is a mixture of Latin and Slavic with traces of Daco-Thracian, Greek and Celtic, and latterly of Turkish,

French and German. In its syllables, so they say, you can hear its history. The Romanian words *plug*, *uger* and *ax* all have Celtic origins like their English equivalents 'plough', 'udder' and 'axle', and archaeological evidence also suggests that a Celtic people passed through the lands which make up present-day Romania. Romania's greatest hero, Stephen the Great, the founder of the painted monasteries, appears to have had red hair and blue eyes; at least this is the way he is depicted in the frescoes of the monastery at Putna. There are linguistic traces of every people that has passed through this part of the world over the last few thousand years, and Romanian is a mixture of those traces, with a distinctly Slavic tilt, all hanging together on a lattice of Latin grammar.

I would sit in the kitchen, while Maria cooked and cleaned, and struggle with my grammar lessons, while at the same time searching the dictionary for words which I had heard people using. But often I would search in vain. They were not words which could be found in any dictionary. The Maramureş dialect contains many Slavic words, and a variety of metamorphosed Hungarian words, which are not used elsewhere in the country. Indeed, Romanians from over the mountains find the Maramureş brogue hard to understand. Professors, intrigued both by the anomalies of the dialect and its curious pronunciation, journeyed north from the capital. They sat the long-suffering peasants down and asked them to repeat words over and again while peering into their mouths with torches.

'It seems they had come all the way from Bucharest just to see how our tongues moved when we spoke,' said Mihai. 'We were surprised they didn't have anything better to do. How we laughed after they left!'

To further complicate my efforts to learn the language, the villagers, in their considerate way, thought it impolite to correct me. However much I begged them to tell me my mistakes, they never did. I simply had to listen to them and copy their way of speaking as best I could, and to ask the meanings of words I had not heard before. Later, when I moved south, I discovered an easy way to make people laugh. I had only to open my mouth. To everyone's delight they heard a foreigner speaking in a broad and often incomprehensible Romanian dialect.

While working, Maria cooking and I book-learning, we would receive periodic visits from the cat, or the chickens, and even from Grigor the pig. Grigor was allowed to potter about the yard, snuffling along the ground, eating whatever scraps he could find or scratching himself against the corner of the barn, and sometimes he would wander along the veranda to see how we were getting on. His great bulk would appear blocking the kitchen door. Raising his head to have a better view from behind his flapping ears, he would glance about, giving the occasional grunt and then start eating the sack doormat which, after fancy cakes, was one of his favourite snacks. Maria, who did not want to have to replace the doormat yet again, would grab the broom from behind the door and bash him on the head and then on the bottom as he turned, noisily complaining, and fled.

From the kitchen window I could watch people coming and going along the track. From about eleven o'clock until lunchtime it became busy with women striding, briskly and purposefully, to or from the fields, with baskets on their backs, to fetch lunch and to feed the animals. They walked upright, the basket keeping their shoulders back, taking long and graceful strides.

At twelve o'clock the children were released from school and rushed up the path past the house. The boys wore the traditional straw hat with ribbons fluttering like bunting down the back, and the girls were dressed in headscarves and skirts. Their books and pens were carried in black- and white-checked Maramureş bags slung over their shoulders.

After lunch most villagers were to be found in the fields. There was, however, still the ring of the hammer of the Gypsy blacksmith working on horseshoes or beating out a ploughshare in a neighbouring courtyard, and the occasional creak of carts and the calls of their drivers. There were also the cries of the Gypsies hawking pots, pans, wooden sieves, brooms or even spare parts for handlooms. Sometimes a line of covered wagons pulled by horses and full of outlandish-looking Gypsies would trundle into the village along the rutted tracks and stop outside the house. Dark faced, jingling with jewellery, and dressed in brightly coloured skirts which swept the ground, the Gypsy women seemed as though they had just arrived from India. Abandoning my study of irregular verbs I would stare out, intrigued, at these exotically dressed women and their men, wearing hats and improbable moustaches, who climbed out of the wagons and set off around the village with goods to swap for walnuts, old bottles, lamb pelts or woollen cloth. Their children would remain by the carts, the girls looking after the young babies or going through the steps of the Gypsy dances, barefooted, swirling their skirts and the ribbons tied into their long plaited hair.

Sometimes the children would come to the kitchen, point at their stomachs and look at us imploringly with their big dark eyes. Maria gave them a bowl of soup and a piece of bread. As they ate, I asked them if it tasted good, trying out my slowly improving Romanian. They looked back at me blankly.

'They don't understand Romanian,' Mihai explained, 'they speak only their own Gypsy language.'

At night the Gypsies would camp on the hill outside the village and their silhouettes could be seen moving about in front of the glow of the fire. The following morning they would disappear as mysteriously as they had come and you would never see them again.

BY THE END of June the grass had filled out with flowers. Purple clover, wild lavender, bright red campions, harebells, cornflowers and wild carnations decorated the fields, and Mihai declared the meadows were ready to mow. From then on, each day when the sun shone, with Mihai and his neighbours and relations, and with my scythe on my shoulder, I walked out of the village to make hay. While friends in England were mastering the latest computer technology, I was learning how to mow. 'This', as I wrote to a friend, 'is what *I* call progress.'

Together we swung our shining-sharp scythes and turned the meadows into lawns, while the girls with wooden pitchforks spread the grass out to dry. I was still learning, and although the swathes fell well enough in front of my scythe, it was hard work, and I looked with envy at the ease with which the others swished and cut, cleared around molehills, threw sticks away with the points of the blade, and left neat lines of grass to their left as though cut by a machine. They had been brought up to it since childhood, knowing how to scythe as others know how to swim or ride bicycles, and could mow all day without tiring. I had never met any people tougher or with greater stamina. I struggled to keep up with them and sweat poured off the end of my nose. But like Levin in *Anna Karenina*, 'I had not enjoyed anything more in my life'.

When mowing, sharpening is crucial. As I was not experienced my scythe was rarely as sharp as it should be, which caused me to tire more quickly than others. To have a razor-sharp scythe it is necessary to beat out the blade with a hammer on a little portable anvil. This takes about twenty minutes, but it was not easy to make the blade a smooth arc from one end to the other. Hitting the metal too hard resulted in a wavy edge of wafer-thin metal. Hitting it too softly meant the job would take an hour. You had to get it just right. During summer days, all over the hills you could hear the reassuring rhythm of the *chink, chink, chink* of hammers on scythes. And if you looked carefully you could see men dressed in white smocks bent over their anvils, one on the other side of a small valley, another under a tree by a stream, 'setting' their scythes ready for the afternoon's work.

Once the blade was hammered out you needed to hone its edge with the sharpening stone which was kept in a water-filled wooden scabbard attached to the belt. The blade honed, it was now possible to scythe for fifteen to twenty swipes until, once again, it needed to be wiped clean with a handful of grass and honed again. This process went on all day sometimes from before dawn, when the dew was still on the grass, until dusk.

Around midday Maria appeared with lunch. There was, at this time, a flow of women striding out with neat wicker baskets on their backs filled with food for those working in the fields. On almost every sunny day in the spring, summer and autumn, dozens of picnics could be seen taking place in picturesque spots all over the Breb *hotar*. One day it would be buffalo cream with bread, onions and *horincă* under the branches of a spreading beech with views looking out to the blue mountains of the Ukraine to the north, on another potato soup, maize bread and apple cake in the shade of an orchard beside a quietly running stream.

We sat on the ground, tired with work, and drank water from an enamel jug filled from a nearby spring. As we lifted the jug to our lips, the cool water spilled out and trickled down our cheeks. Maria then ladled soup into bowls. Salt, if needed, was sprinkled from a hollowed-out cow's horn carved by Mihai. Then with a knife the large round loaf of bread was blessed with the sign of the cross on its underside, and hunks were cut off and handed around. We ate with the appetite of those who work in the fresh air.

Mihai then brought out the *horincă* bottle from his bag. Along with the *horincă* conversation flowed. We swigged straight from the bottle and passed it from one to another with the benediction '*Să trăiţi la mulţi ani! –* May you live for many years!' Mihai would then begin to reminisce. There were no end of stories. He told us of the Cossack travelling show in 1939 where they threw their swords in front of them and plucked them out of the ground as they galloped past; of the Gypsy blacksmith of Breb who was an accomplished violinist until some fool hit his hand by mistake while he was working in the forge; of the fugitive from Communism who lived in the hills above the village for many years but was captured when the village priest hit him on the head with a hammer during confession and handed him over to police who had been hiding in the graveyard; or of the son of an Italian prisoner of war who had been brought up in Breb: the prisoner had been brought in to help the peasants with their farm work in 1916, and while there had had an affair with a Jewish girl. The man had returned to Italy in 1918 at the end of the war and months later a son was born to the Jewish girl. The Italian probably never knew he had a child. This boy, who was the same age as Mihai, was taken to Auschwitz with all the other Jews of the Maramureş in 1944.

'I felt sorry for the Jews when the Hungarian police came to take them away, even though we did not know why they were being taken,' said Mihai. 'There was a long line of carts on the track winding all the way up to the Ocna Şugatag road.'

I knew Mihai had had good relations with the Jews who had lived in Breb. One day a stranger had arrived at the gate, entered the courtyard and embraced Mihai with tears and smiles. She was a Jewess who, with her parents, had been taken from Breb in 1944. She had survived Auschwitz and, after the war, had emigrated to America. Now, on a nostalgic visit, she had gone straight to Mihai's house. She knew he was a friend.

From the field where we were working Mihai pointed to woods on the other side of the hill. 'That is the Jewish graveyard,' he said.

I looked but could see nothing.

'It is overgrown now, but if you go there you will see the stones, though most of them have fallen over. There are no Jews left to look after it.' For Breb the 'Solution' had indeed been 'Final'.

Young people would talk about other things. Ion, Mihai's cousin, would ask about 'the outside world'. I told him what he wanted to know but assured him that, in my opinion, people were as happy in these valleys as anywhere in the world.

'It is pleasant in Breb,' he agreed, 'but we have to work hard. Most of the young people would like to leave and find a job in the town if they could. If only we had machines here we could at least do the work faster,' he said.

'But if you had machines there would not be enough work for everyone, so some would have to leave the village. Everything would change. You would have to work alone. It wouldn't be like this,' I said.

He accepted it might be a problem.

'In any case, why do it faster?' I said. 'You have enough to eat, you have a comfortable home, with friends and family all around you. What do you lack?'

'I don't know,' he replied, 'perhaps nothing.'

★

AFTER LUNCH AND chatter we would lie in the shade of a conveni-
ent tree and doze for twenty minutes. Then it was back to work,
scything the strips from side to side all afternoon in the hot sun.
One evening, after a hard day's mowing, I was exhausted and still
faced with half an hour's walk back to the village. Seeing me flag-
ging, Ion offered to carry my scythe home for me.

'Now you see', said Mihai, 'how hard we have to work. But
when we go to the market to sell cream the townspeople complain
it is too expensive.'

But although the work was hard, there were many days of rest.
We never worked on Sundays, nor on any of the many saints' days
of which there were about thirty-five every year. Together with
Sundays there were nearly ninety days of rest in a year. If the sun
was shining on a saint's day, a day perfect for making hay, they
would sigh, 'Trust it to be sunny on a holiday.' Very occasionally
people risked working on a Sunday. Everyone was secretly pleased
when they received their comeuppance, which they always did in
one way or another. When a haystack was struck by lightning, as
they were from time to time, and burnt to nothing, everyone has-
tened to tell me that it had been made on a Sunday. It seemed, in
fact, that only haystacks made on Sundays were ever struck by
lightning.

There is one week in July, between the 20th and 27th, in which
five of the days were called the 'Dangerous Holidays'. Most villagers kept working as they were not the holiest of holidays, and the
weather was usually warm and suitable for haymaking; but you had
to be careful. It was the month of storms, and people, animals and
especially haystacks were often hit by bolts of fire from the sky.
Mihai and Maria listed ten people they knew who had been killed
by lightning strikes, and then in turn what each one had done
wrong. While I was living in Breb at least four people were killed
by lightning. I never discovered if they had been working on a
Sunday, or whether there had been some other misdemeanour – for
everyone was quite clear: lightning strikes did not just happen for
nothing.

★

ONCE THE FIELDS were scythed the grass had to dry. Mihai would keep his eyes skinned for clouds on the southern horizon. If a particular sort of cloud appeared in a particular place we would rush to make haycocks, which, once the rain had stopped, were undone and again spread about. Weather permitting, the grass was dry in a day or two, and we set about constructing one of the pear-shaped ricks which are such a feature of the Maramureş landscape. A tall pole, twenty foot long, was sharpened to a point, stuck into the ground, thin end upwards, and wedged steady with rocks. Then, on a bed of sticks raised up on stones, to allow air to flow underneath, we arranged the hay, layer upon layer, around the pole. As the rick grew gradually higher, a girl climbed on top to settle the forkfuls of hay as they were thrown up.

'Did you remember to put on your underwear this morning?' said Mihai before she clambered up. Soon the girl was high above us, and the hay was thrown up to her with long-handled wooden forks, made from specially sought-out stems of sycamore. As she teetered at the top, clinging on to the pole with one arm, I once asked Mihai whether anyone ever fell off. 'Yes, sometimes. Dumitru did. He was a bit drunk. He broke his neck. That's why he walks with a stoop. He shouldn't have been working on a Sunday.'

The top of the rick complete, the girl slid to the ground down a polished wooden pole made from a small pine tree. As she descended, unless she was very careful, her skirts would ride up and we would discover the answer to Mihai's earlier question.

In the evening, once every last scrap of hay had been raked up and all was neat and tidy, we gathered up the tools, and Mihai lashed them together with a tie of twisted grass. Then turning towards the setting sun he would take off his hat, make the sign of the cross and ask God to bless their labours.

'Well, goodnight, Ion,' he would say to his cousin. 'We will see what God will give us in the morning.' We walked home in the golden light and the warm still air of a summer's evening, strands of hay in our hair, tired but content. As we passed other meadows we called to people still at work – 'Come home with us. Leave something to do for tomorrow!'

At that time of the evening, as the sun's last rays gently stroked the slopes, on the paths leading into the village there were usually others returning from work, with baskets on their backs and tools on their shoulders, all as tired as we were but still happy to chat until we reached the different tracks which branched off to our separate houses. I made many friends in this way. One of these was Charlie. Some of Charlie's fields were near ours and once when I passed I shouted to him to leave something for the next day.

'There's always more work to do tomorrow,' he shouted back, 'except when you are in your grave.' He was in his eighties, had a wrinkled leathery face and blue eyes. He seemed every inch a Maramureşean, but in fact Charlie was American.

Charlie was born in Ohio and had an American passport which he proudly showed me one day, although it was, on inspection, long since out of date.

'I remember the celebrations at the end of the Great War in New York, the dancing in the streets, the ringing of church bells and people honking their car horns. They have', he told me authoritatively, 'lots of cars in America, you know.'

Whenever I saw him he would say 'Goodday!', the only English word he could remember, and pronounced, as a result, with all the more enthusiasm. He always had a beaming smile on his face when we met. Perhaps he felt that he and I were somehow special, having both come there from distant lands. On walks back from the fields, scythes on our shoulders, he would tell me his story.

'My parents', he told me, 'had emigrated from here to America before the first of the two big wars. In those days the Maramureş was under Hungarian rule and they did not treat Romanians well. My parents had had enough.'

I recalled photographs I had seen of emigrants from Eastern Europe dressed in elaborate peasant costumes arriving at Ellis Island. There had been a huge movement of people from the Ukraine, Ruthenia, Hungary and Romania in the early years of the century and Charlie's parents had been among them.

'My parents went to live in Ohio and it was there that I was born and brought up,' he went on. 'But when I was twelve, my mother was shot. A man tried to force his way into our house to rob us, she slammed the door in his face and he shot her. She didn't die, but after that my parents decided that America was not for them, and we packed our bags to return to the Maramureş. We tied all our dollars around our bodies under our clothes and came back on a steamship across the ocean. For many days and nights we saw nothing but sea and sky, until at last we spotted land, and a few days later we were steaming past Istanbul and up towards the Romanian port of Constanţa.'

'And what did you think when you arrived in the village?' I asked. 'It must have been very different from what you were used to in America.'

'It was,' he said. 'I didn't like it at all. I cried a lot. It was so different. There were no cars here and people were travelling about in carts pulled by oxen and buffalo. They wore homespun clothes and walked around barefoot or in *opinci* which looked so strange to me. And then when someone died it was awful. The women keened, wailing, clasping their heads with their hands in a terrible way which frightened me.'

'So little has really changed,' I said.

'No, indeed it hasn't,' he replied.

'And in which year did you arrive here?' I asked him.

'In 1924 . . . yes . . . 1924,' he repeated slowly, his blue eyes looking out at the green hills around us, and all the peasants in *opinci* walking back from the fields, 'and I've been here ever since.'

Charlie died in 2001. At last there was no more work for him to do the next day. He was buried wearing his best Maramureş peasant clothes and with his American passport in his hands. Respecting his wishes the women of Breb refrained from keening at his funeral. The Maramureş had been an alarming and bewildering place for a young boy fresh from America, but in the end he had had a happy life there. It was evident from the smile on his face and in his eyes as he walked with his scythe on his shoulders to and from the fields, or as he stood and watched the wedding processions pass his house as young people from the village were married and life in Breb went on. Nonetheless, in life as in death,

Charlie had clung to his American passport, a faded symbol of his difference from others.

In Romania there were many who did not quite belong, who knew themselves to be different. There were the Old Believers in the Danube delta who had fled persecution in Russia, still resolutely making the sign of the cross with two fingers; there were the Saxons, away over the mountains to the south in Transylvania. And then, of course, there were the Gypsies.

5

'A wild and dangerous people'

My mother said I never should
Play with the Gypsies in the wood.
Victorian nursery rhyme

I HAD BEEN in the north for almost three months and the first cut of hay was nearly finished. The wheat harvest would not start for a few weeks. It seemed a good moment for a brief excursion. I had often thought about the Saxons and the Gypsies of Transylvania and decided to pay a return visit to Halma. It was now four or five years since I had last been there.

In July all over Romania the meadows were being mown. As I travelled south I passed horses pulling heavily laden hay carts, and in the fields people were busily scything and raking. Seeing the wide sprays of wild flowers over the hillsides and all the many people working together in the fields made the English countryside of today seem a colourless and lonely place.

I arrived in Halma in the last light of evening and walked up to the house of Gerhilde and her parents. There were no chickens, no cat, no movement or life from inside the courtyard. I could see holes in the roof of the house, the wooden fence was in tatters, weeds grew up among the cobbles, and the barn was leaning precariously, ready to collapse. I then noticed light coming from one of the back rooms. A dog barked and an old Gypsy with fine moustaches came on to the steps, smiled and waved.

'*Să trăiţi!* – Long may you live!' he shouted.

'Where have the Saxons gone?' I shouted back.

'They left a long time ago,' he replied. 'It's a pity. As you see, now everything is falling down.' It was indeed falling down, but he was certainly not doing anything about it.

'Why don't you mend the holes in the roof then?' I asked.

'It's not my house. I just rent it off the town hall,' said the Gypsy.

There were, it seemed, a few Saxons still living in Halma, and I knocked at the gate of a house belonging to an old couple called Herr and Frau Knall. An old man emerged wearing a straw hat and a blue apron which, I later discovered, only came off on Sundays. He invited me in. At a table peeling carrots was his wife, Frau Knall, a plump Saxon lady of many aprons and smiles. A rounder and rosier-faced Hausfrau it would be hard to find, nor one with such a welcoming demeanour. They were kind enough to offer me a bed for the night and gave me a simple supper of bread and bean soup. 'On Wednesday and Friday Saxons eat beans,' they told me.

Before we ate, Herr and Frau Knall lowered their heads and put their hands together to say grace.

'*Komm Herr Jesu sei unser Gast, / Und segne was du uns bescheret hast.*'

'Amen,' we said together.

As we slurped our soup I asked them when the family of Gerhilde had left.

'They went about four years ago,' said Frau Knall. 'And they have not been back since. Gerhilde's grandmother went with them to Germany. She used to send us letters. She said she had nothing to do there. They had no land and no animals and there were only so many times she could clean their small flat. She told us that she cried every night thinking of Halma, and then within a year she had died. "*Ein alter Baum soll nicht verpflanzt werden* – You should not try to replant an old tree." That is what we say.'

EARLY THE NEXT morning as the sun came up I looked out of the white painted windows to see a wide street lined with solid, lime-washed Saxon houses, and beyond, and rising above them, the wooded hills and pastures. It was still the beautiful place I remembered. Swallows were skimming the stream which ran down the middle of the green, and from a huge nest, three or four feet wide, perched precariously on the tip of one of the church towers, a mother stork was leading her five progeny in early flying lessons over the ridges of the steep, terracotta-tiled roofs. Certain things remained constant.

By the time I came downstairs, Frau Knall had laid out a breakfast of boiled eggs, coffee, warm milk, toast and plum jam on a fresh white tablecloth.

'Would you like to see the church?' they asked me. I said I would, and so after breakfast Herr Knall picked up a bunch of jangling keys, put on his wide-brimmed straw hat, and we walked up the hill to the church. On the way Herr Knall pointed out the rectory, the village hall, the schoolmaster's house and the school, all now abandoned. Up ahead and above us rose the steeple which had been my guide when, on my first visit, I had emerged from the forest and descended into the village.

We entered a defensive ring-wall through a small and ancient wooden door, barred and strapped with iron, and came face to face, after just a few yards, with another tall wall and another iron-barred gate. Herr Knall turned the key in its lock and, creaking and groaning on its hinges, it swung open.

In front of us stood the church. Around it were neatly trimmed rose bushes and pruned fruit trees, and the grass that fringed the building had recently been scythed. But these domestic touches could not disguise the fact that this was more than a simple country church. We had passed through two ring-walls, strengthened with massive bastions, all with gun-slits, and on the church itself there were more gun-slits and other defensive mechanisms and chutes for hurling rocks on attackers trying to undermine the walls.

The fortifications bore witness to the dangers of living in this part of the world in the Middle Ages. The Saxons had come to settle here in the twelfth century under protection of the Hungarian king. But he was a distant figure. From day to day they had had to look after themselves. At any moment marauding raiding parties of

Tartars from the Black Sea coast, unpaid Turkish soldiers encouraged to live off the land, jealous Hungarian neighbours, or just bands of robbers, might appear on the horizon and sweep through the village. Warned by the tolling of bells or the beating of a huge drum, the villagers would rush to take sanctuary behind the massive walls of their castle-churches where water and provisions were always stored, and remain there for as many days as the raiders were inclined to waste. In the sixteenth century the Saxons became Lutherans. Luther's famous words, *'Ein' feste Burg ist unser Gott* – A strong fortress is our God', was, for the Saxons, more than metaphorical. Written in big letters above the gates of the fortress-churches or painted on medieval sacristy doors, it reminded the Saxons of the earthly as well as spiritual protection offered to them by their church.

For hundreds of years generations of Saxon masons, tilers, joiners and smiths had maintained their fortress-churches in original condition. But now, with most of the Saxons gone, the structures were crumbling. There were holes in the roofs, plaster was falling off, and joists were beginning to rot. The rickety ladders and walkways around the battlements still remained, as did the wooden swivelled flaps over the gun-slits, and many a happy hour could be spent clambering along battlements and learning the detailed mechanics of medieval fortifications. But there were now only a handful of Saxons left to carry out repairs and their numbers were dwindling. Herr Knall pointed out the holes in the roof.

'What can we do? It is too much for us now,' he said.

The doors of the church itself were left open for airing and we walked in. The interiors of the Saxon churches are often quite at odds with their warlike surroundings. They are delicately painted with pictures of flowers, birds, woods and primitive depictions of churches and villages. This church was no exception.

Although tiles might have been slipping from the roof, inside the church was neat and tidy. The parson who had occupied the rectory by the church had gone to Germany like all the other Saxons, but another from the nearby town came there once a month to hold a service for the few Saxons who remained. Herr Knall explained where all the different members of the community would sit; the men, women, old, young, married and unmarried all had their allotted places on numbered pews and benches.

'In the Saxon community there was a strict *Ordnung*, that is how we survived for so long.'

Now Herr Knall, with great pride, pointed to the altarpiece. It had been painted, carved and gilded at the beginning of the sixteenth century by the Master of Schässburg (Sighișoara) who had been a pupil of Johann Stoss, son of Veit, the famous craftsman of Cracow. Transylvania and Poland had been, in those days, ruled by the same king. It was framed in red and gold and had twelve painted panels describing the life of Christ. In the middle was a beautifully carved Renaissance figure of St John. It had been especially made for the church and had been there for five hundred years.

'It is a wonderful thing to have in your church,' I told him.

'Yes,' he said. 'It is like the heart of our village. We do what we can to keep a roof above it, but when we are gone, who knows what will happen.'

Little did I know then how this altarpiece would figure in my life.

I took a few pounds' worth of Romanian currency out of my pocket to put in the collection box as a contribution to the maintenance of the church. As we walked out I noticed that there were tears in Herr Knall's eyes. It was not so much the money, but the thought that anyone should have cared.

'We are old,' he said. 'We have lost all our people, they have gone to Germany, and there is little we can do to help our church now. But our last wish is that somehow our church will survive, and in some small way the Saxons will be remembered.'

'I will do what I can to help you,' I told him.

We descended the hill and returned to the house where Frau Knall was by now preparing lunch. We sat down and said grace. As we ate Frau Knall talked of her life. Any words or phrases I did not understand in German she explained to me in Romanian, or even in Saxon, which, knowing me to be Anglo-Saxon, she thought I might understand.

She told me how in 1945 she had been deported to Russia to work repairing damage caused by the German army during the war. All the deportees had been put into cattle trucks and carted off to the north-east in the middle of the freezing winter.

'I was there for four years, ten months and eighteen days,' she said, 'and I worked all that time without one single day of rest.'

In Russia she moved rubble, mended roads, and shovelled coal in the mines.

'In those days I wasn't as fat as I am now,' she said laughing, realizing I was having difficulty imagining her fitting down a mine. Of those in Frau Knall's group only half survived. The others died in Russia from disease, cold, shortage of food and lack of medicine. At last, in 1949, Frau Knall was allowed to return home to Transylvania, but it was to a different sort of life from the one she had known.

Since the Hitler War everything had changed for the Saxons, and while Frau Knall had been away a new Communist regime had taken over in Romania. The Saxons' houses, land and furniture had been confiscated or stolen, and Frau Knall and the rest of her family had had to live as lodgers wherever they could find a Romanian or Gypsy who would take them in. In 1952, however, she married Herr Knall, and in 1954 their house was given back to them. Through hard work and good husbandry, together they slowly managed to build up what they had lost.

Owing to the hardships experienced both during and after the war, many Saxons had lost the will to continue living in Transylvania. So when in the 1960s and 70s President Ceauşescu had begun selling exit permits to Saxons for a few thousand Deutschmarks many people took up the offer, and the idea of emigration as an option was lodged in Saxon minds. Following the 1989 Revolution, when the borders became easier to cross, and, as I had first heard from Gerhilde's family, Germany was willing to give citizenship to all Saxons, the floodgates were opened and within a couple of years the Saxon population had dwindled. Only a few thousand now remained and a unique 850-year-old culture was on the point of extinction.

Older Saxons did not want to leave, but their children insisted; afraid to stay on alone, reluctantly they agreed to go. In the following years many like Gerhilde's grandmother died of *Heimweh*, sitting in small flats in the suburbs of Hamburg or Frankfurt, dreaming of their beautiful homeland so far away. In Germany they had no fields to cultivate, no animals to tend, no vines to tie, no chickens to feed, and no deep and echoing forest on the hill. In the villages the great old bells in the towers of the Saxon churches would toll as yet another Saxon, who had died of homesickness, was buried in some municipal cemetery in distant Germany.

The Knalls had no children. But friends and neighbours, about to leave for Germany, tried to persuade them to come too: 'You'll be all alone if you stay here,' they said.

'It is not we who will be alone, but you,' Frau Knall replied, pointing to the Saxon graveyard on the hill. 'Here we have all our forefathers.'

Everything in the Saxon villages spoke of permanence. There were the solid stone and brick houses, whose beamed ceilings were carved with dates from the eighteenth century. There were the huge oak barns pinned at the joints with wooden nails a foot and a half long, and there were the great clumps and circles of ancient oak trees on the village lands. Above all, there were the vast castle-churches with their Gothic portals, walls ten feet thick, and mighty fortifications built by men who intended to preserve not only themselves, but also their children, and their children's children. Everything had always been done with future generations in mind. But now it was almost all over: these future generations had moved out. Now just a few old people, like Herr and Frau Knall, remained sitting on benches beside the road watching, bemused, as a new way of life took over.

The new way of life was one which the old Saxons struggled to understand. Having been in the majority they were now a tiny minority. As the Saxons had left, Gypsies moved in to fill the gaps. The Knalls did not like it. There had always been Gypsies, but they had lived in the *Ţigănie* on the edge of the village. Now they had moved to the centre to fill the houses left empty by the departed Saxons.

Herr and Frau Knall found it difficult to watch as their village became ever more dominated by Gypsies, and ever more neglected and dilapidated. The Saxon village hall was falling into disrepair. The Knalls blamed the Gypsies for stealing its tiles and bricks and tearing out the floorboards for firewood. Now with the doors open and wind blowing through it, it was no longer used, either for plays or village dances, and the remnants of the set of the last play remained, torn and broken, as a reminder of how things had changed. The Gypsies, it seemed, had no need of a hall or a stage; they were just as happy to dance in the streets.

IN THE AFTERNOONS I would leave the Knalls' house to go for walks in the village. Whenever I went out both of them were always full of warnings. The Knalls seemed obsessed with the Gypsies and their apparent indolence and alleged wickedness. But each time I left the house a Gypsy boy would appear as if from nowhere, as though he had been waiting for me. His name was Nicu, a *Băiaş* Gypsy, originally of the tribe of gold panners. He came with me like my shadow wherever I went, and every evening, having accompanied me about the village, he would ask if I might buy a loaf of bread for his brothers and sisters. By way of apology he told me, shrugging his shoulders, 'I am a poor Gypsy, what can I do? That is what God made me. I have to make the best of it.'

One evening I was standing with Nicu on a track up near the Saxon church watching the cows returning home from the fields. The cows went out every morning at first light. The villagers opened the doors of their stables and the cows and horses wandered out of the courtyard into the road, from where, guided by a cow-herd wielding a long whip which sounded like a gun-shot when cracked, they sauntered out to the slopes beneath the forest and grazed there contentedly all day long. Then as the sun began to go down they would make their way slowly back into the village where, without guidance, each cow would find its way to its own stable and wait there patiently to be milked.

It was while watching this picturesque scene in the last evening light that I noticed a dark-limbed Gypsy girl squatting barefoot beside a pear tree on the other side of the track. Nicu saw her too and called out.

'*Ce faci, Natalia?* – What are you up to?'

'*Nimic* – Nothing,' she said, turning her head lazily towards us. 'And you?'

'Just going for a walk,' replied Nicu.

As they talked one of the cows peeled off the group, scratched its head on the pear tree, and strolled into the courtyard of the house behind Natalia.

'Marishka!' shouted Natalia, turning her head, 'the cow is back.'

Next a horse came trotting into view.

'Nicu!' shouted Natalia. 'Make her go into the courtyard. It is Nicolae's.'

Nicu tried to stop the mare but she tossed her head, side-stepped and cantered off towards the middle of the village.

'Shall I go after her?' said Nicu.

'No, it doesn't matter,' said Natalia. 'She'll come back later.'

Natalia stayed where she was, watching us, and then, as if on a whim, she jumped up and ran to a nearby fruit tree, where on tip-toe she picked some blue plums, put them into the gathered lap of her skirt and came over to where Nicu and I were standing.

'I am Natalia,' she said. 'Would you like some plums?' With a smile of encouragement she offered them to me and poured them into my cupped hands. As she chatted merrily to Nicu I watched her as she talked. She was striking to look at with her chestnut hair, almost blonde at the ends, brown face and dark hazel eyes, their whites luminously bright. We settled down on the grass together – the Gypsies squatting on their heels as Indians do – eating plums and talking as the evening shadows lengthened.

Soon the sun was going down, glowing red up behind the trees of the forest on the hill. I knew the Knalls would be waiting for me and peering anxiously out through the slats of the shutters. It was not safe, they had told me, to be out after dark, even in the village; the Gypsies were wild and dangerous people. I stood up to leave. As I did so Natalia looked up, turning her 'dangerous' eyes towards me.

'You will come back tomorrow, won't you?' she said.

As usual, the next day after lunch I went out to walk about the village and was joined by Nicu. We went up through the orchards underneath the towering defensive walls of the Saxon church.

There reclining in the grass underneath an apple tree lay a swarthy and moustachioed man cleaning his fingernails with a long and ugly knife. As we passed him he slowly lifted his head and gave us a withering stare.

'That is Natalia's boyfriend,' said Nicu, once we were out of hearing, 'they call him "The Lad".'

As it happened, on the way back from our stroll we passed Natalia's house. The Lad was sitting menacingly on a bench on the other side of the road and we walked on by. But the windows of the house were thrown open and Natalia's head appeared.

'Where are you going?' she shouted sunnily, leaning on the sill. 'Come inside!'

As we entered through the gate I felt the glare of the scowling Lad warming the back of my neck.

In the house Natalia was stretched out languorously on a bed, her head propped up on her hand, a beautiful arrangement of skirts and brown limbs. And in the far corner of the room there was someone else. It was another of Romania's brown-skinned and dark-glancing daughters, lying in a similarly graceful pose across an armchair, her eyes calmly surveying me. This girl was Marishka.

'I've seen you somewhere before?' she said.

'Where?' I replied.

'I'm not sure. I thought I recognized you.'

'I was in this village a few years ago,' I said. 'I had walked over the hills. Some people filled my water bottle, gave me a few apples and pointed me the way to Floreni.'

'Were you carrying a stick?' she asked.

'Yes,' I said.

'It was me who gave you the apples,' she said smiling. 'I remember your glasses. We laughed that a foreigner was carrying a big stick like a shepherd.'

'Sit down,' said Natalia.

Nicu sat on the bed. I found a rickety chair. For a while they watched us. Their eyes were bewitching. They shot them in our direction hypnotizing us like flames, darting away occasionally, flickering about the room and then back, fixing us in their glare.

'*Ce mai faci?* – How are you?' I asked at last, addressing Natalia, as it was with her I had been talking the evening before.

'I'm well,' she said.

'And what have you been up to?' I asked.

'*Nimic* – Nothing,' she said. 'Nothing' was something which apparently happened all the time. I assumed it was the standard reply given to anyone they did not entirely trust.

'But surely you do something sometimes?' I said.

'No, not really. Only in the evenings. Then we dance and have parties, especially now when our parents are away working in Hungary. Almost every night.'

'So why did you say you did nothing?'

'Why not?' she said shrugging her shoulders. 'Anyway why do you ask so many questions? You sound like a policeman.'

'I'm sorry,' I said. 'You can ask me questions if you want.'

'All right. What are you doing here in Halma?' she asked.

'I want to learn German, and to see what life is like in a Saxon village.'

'If you stay here, you will see a lot,' said Marishka. 'You can be sure of that.'

Natalia then had an idea. Her face lit up.

'Why don't we go for a picnic tomorrow?' she said.

On the wall above the girls' heads I noticed some old embroidered cloths. These cloths had been left behind by the Saxons and still remained hanging on the walls of the houses which were now occupied by Gypsies. Upon one of them, in beautifully stitched and decorated letters, was written '*Gebet und Arbeit* – Prayer and Work'.

70

The two peoples, Saxons and Gypsies, who had come to Transylvania many centuries before, one from the cold north-west, the others from the exotic east, could barely be more different. And yet they had found themselves living side by side in a place where the paths from their separate homelands had met. Now the Saxons had gone and the Gypsies had inherited their houses, complete with the Saxons' mottos still hanging on the walls.

Natalia lay on the bed in a pose of extreme relaxation. The atmosphere of *dolce far niente* was overwhelming. 'Prayer and Work' was clearly not a maxim by which Natalia, Marishka or any of their friends lived, nor had any intention of living by.

Before I left to return to the Knalls I rashly agreed to come over in the morning to go for a picnic in the forest the next day. By the time Nicu and I walked out into the street the Lad had disappeared.

WHEN I HAD finished my boiled eggs and coffee the next morning I packed my bags and told Herr and Frau Knall I would be leaving. But instead of leaving I headed for Natalia's house, and with Natalia, Marishka, Marishka's boyfriend and Nicu we went for a picnic. They had brought food, wine and rugs and we walked up to the edge of the forest.

By the evening, with the hills blue and misty in the distance and the embers of the fire glowing, my intention of leaving evaporated. What with Natalia's charms, a glass or two of wine, much laughter and their invitations for me to stay the night, I changed my mind. As we walked down the hill into the village Natalia and Marishka sang songs all the way.

It was almost dark when we crossed the dusty village square and walked up to the Gypsies' house, the girls looking anxiously about, their eyes darting and alert, to see if there was anyone hiding in the shadows. As we approached the house there was a mounting sense of urgency. They hurried me quickly inside, although not before Eugen, Natalia's little brother, had led me to a corner of the courtyard to show me his collection of rabbits in their hutches.

Things seemed to be quiet. So Eugen, Nicu, Marishka and her boyfriend decided to return to the village square, leaving Natalia and me alone.

'Lock yourselves into the bedroom and turn off the light,' they told us. 'We'll lock the front door from the outside when we leave.'

It does not happen every day to be locked into a bedroom with a beautiful Gypsy girl. And I was locked in from both the inside *and* the outside. It seemed almost too good to be true. I did wonder for a moment why such strict security measures were necessary, but the thought passed quickly: I was only too happy to be imprisoned. There is a much-quoted Romanian saying, 'You cannot know how to make fire until you have kissed a Gypsy'. Now at last I might be able to find out what this meant.

As it turned out there was no opportunity for kissing. On the departure of the others, the situation rapidly deteriorated. Hardly had Natalia and I sat down together in the dark on the bed, than there came a violent bashing on the window which almost shook the frame off its hinges. The glass was smashed and the head of the enraged Lad appeared through the shattered fragments shouting and swearing. He had been waiting outside in the shadows until the others had left. With his knife he hacked at the broken glass around the frame.

'May my mother be struck down dead if I do not kill you both at this moment!' he screamed. The disadvantages of being locked in from the outside as well as the inside now dawned upon me. There was no escape route.

Natalia took swift action. In the swish of a skirt she was by the window and with a broomstick had pushed the Lad backwards off the sill. He fell to the ground six feet below. He was easily dislodged as the windows were just high enough to make it difficult to keep hold, a useful aspect of Saxon architecture which I had not previously appreciated. From below he issued blood-curdling threats and Natalia screamed back. It was a glorious Gypsy occasion. She attempted to reason with him but then the fury rose up and again he tried to climb in. I stood in the background, out of sight, trying to pretend I was not there, and wondering why on earth I had not just stayed at home in Breb. I remembered the Gypsies telling me that life was much more fun in Halma. This was not quite what I had envisaged, although it was certainly different. Bravely Natalia kept him at bay until at last we heard voices. It was the others coming back up the track. The Lad slipped quietly into the shadows.

We all slept on the same bed that night, Natalia with her head on my shoulder. One thing was sure, when the Knalls discovered I had stayed with the Gypsies they would not be amused.

We awoke the next morning to find all of Eugen's rabbits dead, strewn about the courtyard, one of them being chewed by the dog. The Lad had crept into the courtyard in the middle of the night and cut their throats, partly in revenge and partly, no doubt, as some sinister warning of what might shortly happen to me.

My presence was causing too much trouble for everyone. It was time for me to leave. But before I had gathered my things together a sinister-looking policeman arrived at the house.

'I would like a word with the foreigner in private,' he announced.

In a back room he asked me not to tell the others what he was about to say.

'My name is Barbu. You must be careful,' he warned. 'These are dangerous and violent people. They are the most dangerous Gypsies in the village. I advise you to leave, and if you ever come here again do not carry money or anything valuable with you, do you understand? It is not safe.'

I looked concerned and told him I would indeed leave and be careful. But somehow, even though I hardly knew them yet, I could not believe the Gypsies were quite as bad as he made out.

6

A Lost Letter

The contrast between silence and sound, darkness and light, like that between summer and winter, was more strongly marked than it is in our lives. The modern town hardly knows silence and darkness in their purity, nor the effect of a solitary light or a single distant cry.
Johan Huizinga, *The Waning of the Middle Ages*

IN MY POCKET was a scrap of paper upon which Natalia had scribbled her address. As I left she had pushed it into my hand and assured me that if I wrote to her she would write back. I travelled north past the smoking lime kilns of the Baba gorge and the charcoal burners in the Baiuṭi valley, then in the evening up and over the forested pass and down into the green and shaded valleys of the Maramureş, the cool air smelling sweetly of newly cut grass. An old peasant told me how he had once been away from the Maramureş. Reaching the pass and coming down the track through the forest towards Breb was, he said, like returning to paradise. This was the first time I had been away and as I descended through the freshly mown meadows and the coppices I knew what he meant. It was an enchanted landscape.

In Breb I went straight back to work in the fields. The first cut of hay had almost been finished and while I had been away they had started to reap the wheat. The last strips still had to be harvested, and so, sickle in hand, I joined them, pulling the weeds carefully out and laying the stalks on the ground in a neat pile, then gathering them into my arms, knotting them round with a tie of stalks and standing them up in stooks together with the other sheaves. As with the hay, twenty-foot-long poles were sharpened and planted into the ground in a line. Then the sheaves were hoisted up, impaled on the spiked ends and threaded down the shaft of the pole. There they were to remain for a month to dry in the wind and the sun.

Then in September, in the still autumn air, an unfamiliar sound could be heard. It was the whirring and chugging of the village threshing machines. Free-standing single-cylinder diesel engines sputtered and hissed into motion, and long flapping belts were thrown over slowly rotating drive wheels which began to turn wheels on the side of the threshing machines themselves. Gradually the great beasts – made in Budapest before the Great War but still going strong – came shuddering to life, one cog turning another as the belts took hold, until all the machines were alive, coughing and wheezing dust out of every orifice, clattering and clanking, shaking and wobbling on their old legs. Lines of horses and carts came in from the fields all day piled high with the sheaves of wheat, and in the evening left the dust-filled courtyards laden with bulging sacks of grain. Dogs and cats assembled too, to catch the field mice who had made the mistake of taking up residence in the sheaves, or even in the threshing machine itself. The mice jumped for their lives seconds before the sheaves were fed into the whirring machinery, and then gradually made their way down the juddering contraption to a ledge near the ground where they gathered and waited. The dogs and cats waited too, looking fixedly up at the little snacks sitting on the ledge. Panic-stricken by the noise, the vibrations and the dust, sometimes a mouse would jump. Then there was a great commotion. The dogs and cats all pounced at the same time and the field mice rarely escaped.

COMMUNICATIONS BETWEEN THE village of Breb and the outside world were usually effected through the good offices of Petrovici, 'the panting postman' of Ocna Şugatag, who had to trudge, summer and winter, the seven kilometres from the town to reach us. During the autumn work my thoughts often turned to

Natalia, and it was not long before I had written her a letter. Just as I had been fascinated by the Gypsy music, now it seemed I had been won over by Natalia and her hazel eyes.

A few days after my writing the letter, Petrovici arrived at our house to bring the post to Mihai and Maria. Tired and puffing after his long walk, a bowl of hot potato soup was placed on the table and he was told to sit down and eat. I took the opportunity to give him the letter and money for a stamp. He assured me he would hand it to the postmistress in town, and, slipping it into his polished leather postbag, doffed his hat and went on his way.

I WORKED EVERY day, and every day wondered whether a letter might have come for me while I was out in the fields. But nothing ever came. So when Petrovici passed by our house again I asked if he had posted the letter. Looking a trifle offended, and wiping the sweat off his brow, he assured me he had. So I asked his advice. Perhaps it had not arrived at its destination? As he sat down to eat the soup, which Maria always placed in front of him whenever he came, and to drink the glass of *horincă* which Mihai always poured for him, he explained that I would need to go myself to the post office in Ocna Şugatag and to send a registered letter. So on the next market day this is what I did.

Then the following week, I again joined the lines of villagers walking along the paths through the fields and orchards to the fair. I wanted to buy myself a new whetstone for the scythe; like all bad workmen I was constantly blaming one piece of equipment or another for my inability to keep the scythe razor sharp. At the same time I took the opportunity to visit the post office to ask the postmistress if the registered letter had been delivered. It had indeed, she told me with a smile. I returned happily to the village and waited for a reply, which I assumed would not be long in coming.

When walking home through the orchards I heard the sound of fruit dropping on to the grass all around me. And sure enough over the next days we harvested all the apples and pears in the garden, climbing high up, and balancing precariously on branches with bags slung over our shoulders to collect the fruit without bruising it. Then in the fields we gathered marrows, huge orange pumpkins, cabbages and maize stalks and returned in the cart to the village sitting on top of our multicoloured cargo. Every morning, with the neighbours' children to help, we collected the walnuts which had fallen during the night. When we shook the branches nuts came raining down upon our heads, bouncing off our hats.

It was now beginning to turn cold. Gradually the woods and trees which had been so fresh and alive in the spring began to settle down for the winter. The sheep had slowly been descending from their mountain pastures with their shepherds, and on 9 November, the same date every year, they were returned for the winter to their different owners. Christmas was not so far away, but still I had received no reply to the registered letter. I waited patiently, kept an eye out for Petrovici's smiling face, and each time I saw him I asked him. But no reply came.

I made up my mind to send the registered letter again.

THE FIRST DUSTING of snow fell at the beginning of December, and at last the panting Petrovici, stamping the snow from his boots, came into the kitchen triumphantly holding a letter addressed to me with a Romanian stamp on it. I opened it and perused the spidery writing. I read in amazement.

> William. We are telling you not to write any more to the Gypsies, they are dangerous people. You do not know what you are doing. We insist that you stop.

It was not signed.

So my letters had been intercepted.

'This is not the letter I was expecting,' I told the kindly Petrovici, and asked him for his advice as to what might have happened to the registered letter.

'I suppose you'd better try "Registered with Confirmation of Delivery",' he suggested, as he swallowed another spoonful of his favourite soup, 'although it is a bit more expensive.' A registered letter, he explained, is signed for only by the postman in the village where the letter is sent. 'Perhaps the postman left it on the gate, felt he had delivered it, and it was blown away.'

'A local postman therefore could,' I put it to him, 'if he wanted to, sign for it but not actually deliver it.'

'Yes,' he said, 'I suppose he could in theory, but I can't think why he would.' Petrovici was too good a man to suspect such subterfuge. In the case of my letters it seemed that someone had not only refrained from delivering them but had also taken the liberty of reading them. I was not amused, but having great hopes in the grand-sounding 'Registered with Confirmation of Delivery' let it pass.

The addressee, as the postmistress in Ocna Şugatag explained to me as I handed her the letter, has to sign and confirm receipt in person. It seemed foolproof. At least in this way I would be sure whether it had been delivered or not, and might make some progress in solving the mystery of what on earth was going on.

I went home to an afternoon's work helping Mihai, with horse and cart, to collect a haystack from the fields. As we descended the hill, Mihai told me how, forty years before, he had looked up while driving a hay cart, and had seen little balloons sailing by in the overcast late autumn sky. A couple of them floated down on the Breb lands and were retrieved. They had letters attached to them, which turned out to be desperate pleas for help from Hungarians whose country was being invaded by the Russians. It was 1956.

'We were not the right people to send messages to though, were we?' said Mihai. 'Just peasants working in the fields, what could we do?' It was touching that he thought the letters had been meant for them.

'At least the letters made it through to you,' I said.

'YES,' SAID THE Ocna Şugatag postmistress when I asked her about my letter on the next market day, 'it has been delivered.' But again days and then weeks went by and still I received no reply.

The next time I was at the market I again popped into the post office and joined a queue of peasant women in their pleated skirts and headscarves applying for their child allowance. Even the telephonist working at her bakelite switchboard was dressed in village clothes, and was wearing the headphones over the top of her headscarf.

On reaching the front of the queue I enquired again. 'Are you sure the letter was delivered?'

'It has been signed for,' they told me. 'There is nothing more we can do.'

'But how do you know it was actually signed for by the person to whom it was sent?' I asked.

'How can we possibly know that?' they replied.

'Well, how does this system of registered letters work then?' I asked.

'If you would like to make a complaint we can forward it for you,' they told me, although it was clear they thought I was making an absurd fuss. Nonetheless, I did make a complaint, which the postmistress, now looking a little thin-lipped, filled out.

A week later, I walked again to Ocna Şugatag, this time in the snow. Now people, all wrapped up against the cold, were travelling there by sleigh, sliding silently over the fields. At the market a lady selling *horincă* from a bottle standing on a stool in front of her on the snow, and poured into the same glass for each customer, was doing good trade. So was the fur-hat seller who carried his finest astra khans piled precariously one on top of the other upon his head. All around were people wearing the hairy woollen coats of the Maramureş which made them resemble the animals they were selling. The horses, with icicles hanging from their whiskers, all had layers of thick blankets on their backs, and the pink little piglets for sale, snuggled in hay, were now being kept in boxes well wrapped round with rugs.

Again I dropped into the post office. There was now an answer to the complaint. The letter, I was officially informed, had been delivered and signed for. I felt sure Natalia would have sent me a reply by now, and, having received the anonymous letter, I was not convinced. I told the postmistress. She, however, was beginning to tire of this story.

'I'm afraid there is nothing more we can do,' she replied. 'If you want to make another complaint you will have to write to the inspector of post offices in the city of Baia Mare.' The simple act of sending a letter to a friend was becoming truly Kafkaesque. It had now been over three months and I had achieved nothing. No doubt the Baia Mare office would refer me to someone else, and then after months of going from one office to another I would be referred back to Ocna Şugatag.

I struggled back towards the village in the snow. It was now deep winter. I had to lift my feet high at each step to make progress. The wind bit at my cheeks as I walked past frozen streams and snow-capped haystacks. Snow muffles sound, and all was quiet. Only occasionally was there the caw of a crow, or the creaking and tapping of trees as they swayed and touched each other in the wind. Even the horse-drawn sleighs going by made almost no noise as they passed, except for the clink of their harness and the soft tinkling of bells.

As I trudged along my mind turned again to the curious business of the disappearing letters and the mysterious warning note I had received. It would, I realized, have to remain a mystery for some time; had I wanted to go anywhere it was barely possible in these conditions. The winters here were long and hard. Temperatures dropped to below minus 30 degrees Centigrade. My old car was already frozen solid, and even if I had managed to get it started it would not have been able to climb the steep hill out of the village without being pulled by horses. I had, for the moment, been defeated by the Romanian postal system.

Halfway along the road back from the market I heard the faint sound of bells. A sleigh was approaching, going in my direction. I hopped on, covered my knees with a proffered rug and off we went at a startling speed, careering downhill into the village along the ice-covered road, bells jingling and red tassels flying. At the corners the sledge slid towards the ditch, and I thought we would overturn, but always we were dragged around by the horses with their sharp,

studded hooves. As we whooshed along the driver pulled out a
bottle of *horincă*, and all worries we might have had were soon
forgotten.

7

Every Element of Strangeness

*The Gypsies are . . . the Bedouins of our commons and woodlands . . .
they are not the outcasts of society; they voluntarily hold aloof from its
crushing organization, and refuse to wear the bonds it imposes. The
sameness and restraint of civil life, the routine of business and labour
. . . the dim skies, confined air . . . the want of freshness and natural
beauty – these conditions of existence are for them intolerable.*
Henry T. Crofton, *The Dialect of the English Gypsies*

I N DECEMBER THE weather and the daylight closed in. Mists hung
over a white village. The sun skimmed along the top of the mountain Gutin and by four o'clock had already sunk behind the western
hills in the direction of Hungary. The days were short and the evenings were long. Sometimes, because of the cold, I would not even try
to go outside but instead tucked myself in bed, under thick warm
blankets made by Maria, and read for many hours. *Anna Karenina,
The Brothers Karamazov* and all the books I had about nineteenth-
century country life were rapidly consumed and I was running out
of reading matter.

In my small collection were several books about the Gypsies.
Amongst them was one by a man named Angus Fraser, who intriguingly, according to the blurb, had been a civil servant in London, and
an adviser to Mrs Thatcher. His book I now read with fascination.

According to Fraser the nomadic people who later became
known as the Gypsies left north-west India in disparate groups
about a thousand years ago and, dallying along the way, headed
slowly towards Europe. Their language gives a clue to the route

they took. As John Sampson, the great scholar of the Welsh Gypsy dialect, put it, their language is 'a sort of diary of their wanderings' with 'here treasures carried from India, here scented and perfumed words from Persia, here Armenian antiquities'. Their word *bacht*, for example, meaning 'luck' is from Persian, while their word *grast* meaning 'horse' is said to derive from Armenian.

The dark-skinned nomads appeared in the Balkans in the four-teenth century, and from there spread up through Europe, reaching even its coldest and most distant parts. In 1529, according to the medieval accounts book from Holyrood House, a group of Gypsies danced for the pleasure of King James V of Scotland. Indeed, according to Fraser, James V had 'remarkably cordial relations with the Gypsies for most of his reign'. But it all ended badly. James, who had fathered at least nine illegitimate children, was said to have been hit over the head with a bottle while taking liberties with a Gypsy lady. Being in disguise he was then, as Fraser puts it, 'subjected to further indignities'. This put an abrupt stop to the special relation-ship. Gypsies were banned from Scotland upon pain of death. James died soon after, however, aged thirty. His only surviving legitimate child, who was born just a week before his death, was the ill-fated Mary, Queen of Scots. Might there, I wondered, have been a Gypsy curse?

In other parts of Europe too, thanks to their ingenuity as musi-cians and metalworkers, they had been welcomed by the very high-est in the land. In the royal account books of Hungary for 1489 there was an entry listing a payment 'to Gypsies who play the lute on the island of the princess' – the island was Csepel Island in the Danube near Budapest, the princess was Beatrice of Aragon, daughter of the King of Naples. Then in 1543 'the most excellent Egyptian musicians . . . descendants of the pharaohs' (there was a common belief at the time that Gypsies had come from Egypt) were playing at the court of Queen Isabella of Hungary, while others later still were dancing for Henry IV of France.

As metalworkers Gypsies were in the service of the Bishop of Pécs making cannon balls, and of Vladislas II of Hungary who gave an 'Egyptian' named Tamas Polgar the right to settle wherever he pleased with his twenty-five tents of Gypsy smiths. Sigismund, King of Poland, had a Gypsy blacksmith in his service, who rejoiced in the name of Mixidarius Wanko de Oppavia.

In the end, however, the unconventional troupes of Gypsies travelling over Europe unsettled the local populations. The authorities took action. In the seventeenth and eighteenth centuries Gypsies were banished *en masse* upon pain of death from most of the countries of Europe. 'Gypsy hunts' were organized and the Gypsies had to hide themselves in the forests and mountains, moving from one place to another, and disguising their tracks by nailing their horses' shoes on backwards. If caught they were executed, or condemned to a life as galley-slaves. Others were dispatched to the colonies. Families were ruthlessly split up and children were taken away and given to peasant families to bring up, regardless of whether they had committed any crime. It was a terrible catalogue of injustice. As Angus Fraser points out, in England nomads and vagrants were blamed for much of rural petty crime, but a careful look at the criminal records shows that violence and theft were usually the work of residents rather than Gypsies.

For a hundred years or more a shadowy and fugitive existence was the lot of the few Gypsies who remained free. Only in the nineteenth century, with the Romantic movement, there appeared those more sympathetic to the spirit of the Gypsies, and their spontaneous music and dancing. Goethe was the first idealize the Gypsies as noble savages, living close to nature and fighting for freedom and justice; then Liszt, Pushkin and Borrow took up their cause, and even the Habsburg Archduke Karl Josef Ludwig wrote a book on the Gypsy language. Gradually education, rather than banishment, torture or execution, became the method the 'civilized' world thought it might use to better the Gypsies. Fraser describes a venture by a certain John Baird in Kirk Yedholm in 1830 to 'improve' the Gypsies in Scotland. He hoped to convince them to give up their wandering ways. But the Gypsies were not to be so easily persuaded. In 1842 Baird reported of his experiment that 'the success hitherto has been next to an entire failure'.

★

IN THE ROMANIAN provinces, the Gypsies' expertise as metal-workers worked against them. Rather than gaining them favour, it brought them slavery. So skilled were they, and yet so elusive, that the Romanian princes, afraid of losing them, enslaved them *en masse* to ensure they were always available. This mass servitude lasted for hundreds of years. In 1837 the great Romanian reformer Kogălniceanu wrote of what he had seen in Iaşi, the capital of Moldavia:

> . . . people with chains on their arms and legs, iron clamps around their foreheads, and metal collars around their necks . . . floggings, and punishments such as starving, hanging over smoking fires, solitary confinement, and being thrown into snow or frozen rivers, this was how the wretched Gypsies were treated.

Only in 1856, fifty years after the slave trade was abolished in the British Empire, were they eventually freed and the selling of slaves was banned in Moldavia and Wallachia. On gaining their freedom many Gypsies returned to nomadic ways. Some travelled surprisingly far and wide. Indeed in the 1890s Dr Sampson, the philologist, encountered a group of them on Blackpool beach, and later others at Birkenhead. Admiring their necklaces of golden coins, he addressed them in Welsh Romany. Although they spoke a different dialect, they were able to understand him. To his astonishment, Sampson discovered that they had come all the way from Romania, having somehow managed to cross the Channel even with their horses, carts and voluminous tents. Wherever they went they must have caused a sensation. They spoke, wrote Sampson, their own beautiful version of Romany, 'more beautiful falling as it does from the lips of proud and splendid men and womankind who have indeed every element of strangeness added to their beauty'. He saw among them 'the most beautiful "*chais*" [girls] I have ever seen – gay, fearless, friendly, brilliant in every shade of red and yellow . . . they gleam and glitter in the sun, I have never seen anything like it. No such piece of pageantry was ever put on the stage.'

Another Englishman, Sacheverell Sitwell, on his travels near the monastery of Horezu in the foothills of the Carpathian mountains in the late 1930s, came across a family of *Căldărari* Gypsies, makers of stills and copper cauldrons. He too was impressed.

> The *Căldărari* are remarkably Indian in type; their skins are of a darkness that is utterly alien to Europe. The Gitanas of Triana or the Albaicin are fair in comparison with the Gypsies of Roumania. One of the women of this family who was nursing her child, made the perfect type of Gypsy Madonna, and had features which were most beautiful in their softness of expression.

Sitwell did not know, however, that he was witnessing the last carefree years of the Gypsies' roaming life. Without warning, in 1942, all the nomadic and many thousands of the settled Gypsies were rounded up and deported to camps in Transnistria by order of Marshal Ion Antonescu, the fascist dictator of Romania, and ally and stooge of Hitler. The Gypsy Madonna and her family would almost certainly have been among them. So too, I later discovered, was Natalia and Marishka's grandfather and most of his family. In Transnistria, over 20,000 Romanian Gypsies died of disease, starvation and cold.

WHEN AFTER THE war a Russian-backed Communist government took over in Romania it was deemed time to settle the Gypsies once and for all. They endeavoured to persuade them to take jobs in factories and 'to learn about and to respect the laws'. Then, in the 1970s, travelling by cart was made illegal and a systematic programme of 'civilizing' the Gypsies was set in motion. Many were given houses far more salubrious than the shacks in which they had previously lived. But when they moved into them they did not always use them for the purpose for which they were intended. In the typically upside-down way of the Gypsies, many families preferred to live in tents pitched outside and use the houses as stables for the horses.

Following the 1989 Revolution many of those who had been 'settled' took to the roads again. There was a new freedom, the word '*Libertate*' was on every lip, and the political disorder created conditions favourable to Gypsy life. The roads were empty, potholed and unsuitable for motor vehicles. Everywhere you went there were Gypsy carts. The *Corturari* – the tent-dwellers – were on the move again. And among the *Corturari* were any number of sub-groups. The most commonly seen were the *Căldărari*, the makers of the bulbous copper pot-stills, whom Sacheverell Sitwell had encountered. But there were also the *Lingurari*, the sculptors of wooden spoons and bowls, the *Cărămidari* – the brickmakers, and along with them the silversmiths, broom makers, and those who travelled the villages collecting cloth or old bottles and glass for recycling. They all jumped at the chance to live once more on the open road. It was perhaps the last great gasp of true, old-fashioned Gypsy life in Europe.

I saw them often. On one memorable day, an old Gypsy silver-smith passed through the village. Silversmiths were few and far between, and I stopped to watch him. He wore a brown felt hat, had flowing moustaches and carried a canvas bag on his shoulder. He walked slowly into the village square, found a comfortable patch of grass near the stream and sat down cross-legged on the ground. He then spread out a cloth in front of him, which contained his various tools. He had a miniature anvil, files of all shapes and sizes, tiny hammers, pliers, moulds, a set of conical forms upon which rings were beaten out, and little corked bottles of chemicals and powders for burnishing. Next to him on one side was a pile of old silver Austro-Hungarian coins, and on the other, as he worked, an ever-growing pile of cigarette butts. A crowd gathered round him and he took commissions. One girl brought a silver necklace which she asked him to turn into a ring; others ordered jewellery to be made from the coins. He worked with ease melting down, pouring into moulds, soldering and polishing. All watched transfixed. He worked so fast and so fluidly. To melt the metals down he had a simple blowtorch which consisted of a bottle of petrol and a thin metal pipe. He blew through the reed-like pipe and lit the end of it. If he kept blowing there appeared a pointed flame hot enough to melt any of the metals with which he was working. Travelling silversmiths in India use the same tools and the same methods.

When the petrol in the bottle was running low the Gypsy,

dragging on a cigarette he had been given by one of the spectators, looked around at the crowd of Romanians.

'Where can we steal a bit more petrol?' he asked, with a wink, smiling wickedly. In the watery glint of his eye at that moment was distilled a wry understanding of all the centuries of *gajo* stereotyping of the Gypsies.

8

Grigor's Demise and Other Events

The impulses of all such outlandish hamlets are pagan still: in these spots homage to nature . . . frantic gaieties . . . rites to divinities whose names are forgotten seem in some way or other to have survived medieval doctrine.

Thomas Hardy, *The Return of the Native*

I WAS INSIDE in the warm, while outside in the cold and the darkness, the streets rang with the clamour of bells and horns. The winter holy days were approaching, and every evening until late the streets were filled with such noise of cowbells and blowing of horns as could wake the wolves. The mummers were running down the streets, off to practise their Christmas play. The devils with lines of bells slung on their backs ran in a way intended to make as much horrifying clonking and clanging as possible; it could be heard long after they had passed, reverberating across the village and into the night. As they went they cracked their bullwhips and blew their horns, and the village dogs, driven into a frenzy, barked and howled at them all the way along their route.

ON CHRISTMAS EVE at nine o'clock I set off through the village with a group of unmarried boys and the girls they had invited to go with them. One of the lads had a violin, one a *zongorǎ*, the two-stringed Maramureş guitar, and one a home-made dogskin drum. All were dressed in fur hats and the thick and hairy sheep's wool coats of the Maramureş. We made our way in the moonlight in single file along the narrow paths trodden out in the three-foot-deep snow. As we walked the violin and *zongora* played, the drum beat out the rhythms, and the boys sang with all their might. They sang as loud as they could, wanting everyone to hear them, and, so they say, to scare away any evil spirits that might be lurking. Snow quietly fell and covered the tops of our hats and shoulders as we walked.

On arrival at the first house we sang carols outside and then, shaking the snow off our hats, coats and boots, hurried in to the warmth. Once inside, after a customary gulp of *horincă* and a mouthful of cabbage roll or cake, the musicians struck up, and each boy took a girl by the hand and danced the whirling dances of the Maramureş, which, as the evening went on, became ever faster and wilder. The older wooden houses shook and cupboards wobbled dangerously as the lads stamped on the floorboards and swung the girls around, their skirts flying and almost sweeping bottles and fancy cakes off the tables. I had to put out an arm to steady a swaying kitchen cabinet. After forty-five minutes we trooped out, singing as we went, on to the next house, leaving our hosts to straighten the icons and push the cupboards safely back against the wall, as though a whirlwind or an earthquake had passed. From house to house we went all night. Other groups of carollers were about and we could hear them singing and their violins playing in the distance as they too tramped along the deep beaten paths through the snow. At last, a rim of light was visible on the eastern horizon turning the snow-covered landscape a freezing, luminous blue, and daylight followed quickly. I reached my bed, exhausted, at eight o'clock that morning and missed church.

LEANING OUT OF the window when I awoke, I caught a glimpse of the mummers coming down the road on their way to take part in the Christmas play. Devils, clanging at every step, rushed by the families who were walking to the priest's house where the show would take place. The devils were covered right down to the ground in ragged skins – fox, rabbit, sheep, even wild boar. On their heads they wore hideous and fantastic helmet-like creations of rabbit skin, with dried white beans as teeth, chickens' skulls as noses, and curling rams' horns on the crown with stuffed rats rearing up in between them. When they appeared in their thick animal furs growling and cracking their whips, the children ran screaming to their mothers' sides and hid themselves in the folds of their skirts.

Then came the priest in robes and mitre, with a tangled beard and a large pair of dark glasses on his nose. Walking drunkenly down the track, he carried a long thick bullwhip in his hands which he cracked under the feet of a group of passing girls. 'Confessions! I'm taking confessions,' he said, laughing lewdly, 'but only girls' confessions!'

He then went up to them and, to shrieks and laughter, folded them into his outstretched arms. In doing so he dropped his Bible. The pages spilled out on the ground and he went down on all fours to pick them up. While on his hands and knees he took the opportunity to feel up the girls' legs. I thought I must still be dreaming. The girls escaped from the priest's clutches and ran away giggling. He then stood up tired and drunk, swaying in the middle of the track, and took off his dark glasses. It was one of the lads from the night before, still drunk and with a keen sense of satire, on his way to play the part of the priest in the Christmas play.

I WENT OVER, on the evening of Christmas Day, to visit a poor family who lived in an old wooden house nearby. They had five young children, who had, with a few sweets, and the odd apple and pear, decorated a Christmas tree in their house, and were insistent that I should see it. It was also, I knew, the birthday of one of the girls. She was now eight. I gave her a little envelope with two notes of 10,000 lei in it, the equivalent of three English pounds, and wished her a happy birthday. She opened the envelope and, saying nothing, went back to sit in the corner.

'Aren't you going to say thank you?' her mother asked her. The little girl came up to me and gave me one of the notes back.

'*E prea mult domnul* – It is too much, sir,' she said quietly. I gave the note back to her with a reassuring smile. This was the amount I had meant to give her, I told her. She went back and sat in the corner on her little wooden chair in her headscarf and pleated skirts, while the others talked, laughed and drank. After a few minutes I looked over to her and saw that she was crying.

ON 28 DECEMBER it was minus 30 degrees Centigrade and if you touched the icicles your hands stuck fast to them. I rarely went out, though was occasionally obliged to do so in order to visit the earth closet at the end of the garden. Nonetheless, I enjoyed the beautiful winter weather. The Brebians were more circumspect. The snow had fallen before the ground had properly frozen and it now acted as insulation. As a result there was still mud beneath the snow, despite the plummeting temperatures, and it was difficult to use the sleighs.

During the freezing weather Mihai had been sitting in the kitchen making a pair of *opinci* on his stool-workbench. As he worked he pointed out that the smoke from the chimney was blowing towards the old church. The weather would soon become milder, he told me. And he was right; the next day the icicles started dripping.

On New Year's Eve I discovered that the *opinci* Mihai had been making were a present for me. From then on I wore them with pride, much to the amusement of the village girls who could not contain their hilarity when I walked past them. The main thing, however, was that at last my feet were blissfully warm and comfortable. Wearing *opinci*, I discovered, was like being in bed all day.

IT WAS NOW the ninth day of Christmas. The night before, walking near the pigsty on my way to bed, I had heard the heavy breathing of Grigor sleeping soundly. Little did he know, as he dreamt of maize mush, yoghurt, potato peelings and fancy cakes left over from Christmas, and whatever else goes into his delicious swill, that the supper he had just eaten would be his last.

At six o'clock the next morning I heard outside the steps of those preparing the execution. Before long Mihai came to wake me up. I stumbled, barely awake, out into the yard. It was still dark. Four men were trying to push Grigor out of his sty. Grigor, however, was strongly objecting to being woken up at this unearthly hour before dawn. Something was clearly wrong. Never before had he been taken for a walk at six in the morning. During the commotion the burly men managed to tie a rope to one of his back legs. Eventually he was forced out and led behind the barn, the men calling, 'ne, ne, ne . . .' which usually signified food. When he was in position the rope attached to the back leg was pulled sharply and Grigor tripped and fell sideways with a thump on to the snow. He was now furious and struggled and roared with all his might. But three of the men jumped on top of him, one with a knee on his neck. The fourth, a medieval-looking character with a down-curving nose and pointed chin, scrabbled across the snow to where he had left the knife, rushed back and plunged it deep into Grigor's neck. I stood by and watched helpless as our companion of the courtyard was being done to death, feeling suddenly guilty that I had not raised even the slightest objection to what was happening. Blood began to sputter slowly out on to the snow and Grigor roared. It seemed to me it was perhaps a roar of furious outrage that we, his friends, could so betray him. The executioner then sliced about in the wound to make absolutely sure he had cut the appropriate artery in the darkness. The blood dribbled and then began to spurt out. Grigor kicked and struggled, but the men held him down. He continued to roar and scream in protest, but gradually the strength went out of him and the roars became weaker and weaker. After a minute or two it seemed all was over, but then in a final effort he let out a tremendous roar, tried to raise himself up, but fell limp and was dead.

Straw was immediately piled over him and set alight. It flared up high into the air, lighting up all the faces looking down at Grigor and giving a welcome warmth at this most chilly and depressing hour of the morning. Grigor's hairs were being burnt off. Soon the flames died down. The men scraped the blackened and wobbly body with a knife, and then, propping his legs open with a log, bundled on more straw to make sure they burnt the bristles on his undercarriage as well. As the men worked, dogs gathered and began to lick at and eat the blood-stained snow.

With one flank now smooth they heaved him over on to the other side to repeat the process. Remaining in the snow was the perfect shape of a pig in black and white. Once all the burning and scraping was finished it was time for scrubbing and washing. They put Grigor on a large wooden board and poured water over him. Steam rose up from his half-burnt body, as blood continued to trickle from the wound in his throat. All the carbon and dirt was now scrubbed off him with a scrubbing brush.

'You see how much he likes having his back scratched,' quipped one of the executioners. They scrubbed neatly behind his ears and even inside them with a corn cob, and then up his nose. Next they pulled off his hooves.

'Would you like an ear?' somebody asked me.

'What for?' I replied, thinking it was being offered to me as some sort of primitive trophy of my first pig slaughtering which I could then hang on my wall.

'To eat of course, what else?' was the reply amidst much laughter.

With a knife one of them sliced off half a singed but essentially raw ear and tore a chunk off with his teeth.

'Mmm, that's good,' he said as he chewed. The others did the same and offered me a slice.

'No thanks. It's a bit early in the morning,' I said. I really did not fancy eating a raw piece of my friend Grigor at six o'clock in the morning, a few minutes after he had been killed.

'But it's the best bit. It's a delicacy,' they told me. I was persuaded to take a piece, which I held between the tips of my thumb and forefinger.

'Well, go on, eat it!' they said. All eyes were on me.

I put the piece of skin and cartilage between my front teeth and took a tiny bite. I chewed and chewed but could not bring myself to swallow. It tasted of smoke and was half chewy and half crunchy, the skin and the cartilage respectively.

'Well, what was it like?' they asked

'Hmmm,' I said, moving my head from side to side to signify a degree of uncertainty on the subject. The last thing I wanted was to be given any more.

Finally, having chewed for five minutes, I managed to swallow. Then, as the others proceeded with the butchering, occasionally slicing off a piece of ear to chew, I moved off discreetly to give the remains of my piece of Grigor's ear to one of the dogs.

Grigor was now lying on his back, nose puckered up and face in a hideous grin. First his legs were cut off, one by one, then his head was severed. The eyes were gouged out and flung to the dogs. The head was then split in two with the axe from the woodshed, his tiny brain scooped out, and, along with his tongue, plopped into a saucepan.

At this point I retired from the cold and carnage outside into the kitchen to eat some breakfast, although certain things did not help my appetite. On the floor in front of me, soaking in a basin of red-stained water, was Grigor's head split in half. His snout, shredded ears and forehead were out of the water, teeth showing at the front, looking a bit like a lurking crocodile. On a plate beside me was another piece of Grigor's ear which someone had thoughtfully given me noticing I had finished the last piece.

So I went outside again. Two great slabs of fat were now being cut off from either side of the body, and then heaved on to a helper's shoulder and dropped in a great wooden barrel of salt water, to lie there with the legs to cure for several days. The rest of the corpse was rapidly cut up. The saddle was sliced from the spine, the lungs, liver, heart, kidneys were pulled out and put into basins. The ballooning intestines were tied at each end to stop Grigor's last supper from spilling out (he was not supposed to eat on his last night but Maria felt sorry for him), and the bladder was emptied on the midden. Before long Grigor was merely bits in basins on the kitchen floor, no longer the funny grunting fellow we used to know.

Maria then went down to the river with the intestines. She broke a hole in the ice and washed them. It was a cold and smelly business although she had a bucket of hot water to dip her hands into from time to time. The long strings of intestine had to be turned inside out, using a stick, and thoroughly cleaned in the freezing water. This would become the skin of the sausages, and as I saw the thick yellow liquid pouring out and staining the snow, and smelt its stench, I realized that eating them would never be quite the same again.

The rest of the day was spent making different sorts of sausage, jellied puddings and other preparations of obscure parts of pig, such parts with which we in England never knowingly come into contact. As usual nothing was wasted. The kitchen was full of foulsmelling steam arising from bubbling cauldrons on the range, and the floor was slippery with grease. I tried to stay there, but in the end the heat and reek drove me outside. There in the freezing, but at least fresh air, away from the smell of slaughter, crows pecked away at the deep red, blood-soaked snow. Grigor had been sacrificed so that we could live. The only trouble was, I did not feel I would ever be able to stomach anything made of pig again, let alone of Grigor.

DURING THE FREEZING months that followed Christmas we retreated into the warmth of the kitchen. The smell of Grigor's slaughter was now gone, and it was the only room in the house where a fire was kept going all day. Through the icicles hanging in front of the windows, we watched the snow quietly falling, melting a little during the day, then falling again, and so on for week after week after week. Sometimes the snow piled up so high on the roofs of houses or barns it seemed they might collapse under the weight. Mihai sat at his stool bench making *opinci* or cart harnesses. At other times he carefully carved and shaped light and streamlined rakes ready for the spring. He took extra trouble to cut and notch the heads with symmetric designs. I assumed this was to make them more beautiful, and complimented him on the trouble he was taking to decorate them. 'It is to make them lighter,' he told me. Maria set up her old creaking wooden loom, which took up nearly half the room, and wove blankets. All over the village women and girls were setting up their looms. They wove all day and in the evening complained of stiff necks.

AFTER DARK, IN the houses where there were unmarried girls, the weaving would often be interrupted by visits from groups of courting lads. Courting, or 'Going to the Girls', as it was called, was a formal activity with rules, none of which I was familiar with. Mihai, in the hope that I might find a nice sensible Maramureş girl with whom to settle down and so stay in the Maramureş, arranged for me to join a couple of neighbours, Vasile and Petru, on one of their expeditions.

So one freezing evening we set off into the dark and snowy night. Both Vasile and Petru burst into song the instant we started walking up the road. I followed them down twisting back lanes, across bridges over frozen streams, past the huge, carved gates so famous in the Maramureş, silhouetted by the moon, and steep-roofed houses, their eaves fringed with icicles and light glowing from their windows. Sleighs occasionally swept by, dogs barked and all around was the smell of manure. We arrived at one of the tall looming gates, ducked our heads through a low door, as the main gates were only opened for horses and sleighs, and entered a court-yard.

Clumping up wooden steps, along a veranda, and beating the snow off our boots on the fir branches laid on the threshold, we entered the receiving room. We were, it seemed, not the first visitors. There were already eight other lads a-courting, sitting around the edge of the room on polished pine benches wearing woollen waistcoats and fur hats. All of us had, apparently, come to court the same girl, who sat in pleated skirts and headscarf between two of the lads. On entering we shook hands with the lads, though not with the girl or her mother, and having completed the circuit took our places on the benches.

The girl had a sweet, rosy face and was on the plump side, which was possibly one of the reasons why she had so many suitors. In the Maramureş, it is a boon to be buxom. The men of the Maramureş like the women about them to be fat, or at least stout and well built, since such women are thought more able to put up with the long, hard days working in the fields.

The girl's mother, who sat scowling with arms folded high on her chest at the end of the room, was certainly large. Next to her was the rounded mud and plaster stove which she slightly resembled, and next to that the wooden loom which for the moment lay idle. Her eyes slowly surveyed the assortment of suitors in front of her, and if the look on her face was anything to go by she was entirely unimpressed. There can be little doubt that I was the very least impressive.

Soon after we arrived the mother stood up and went out for a minute. As she left the room she looked around menacingly as if to imply that we had better behave ourselves while she was away. The lads, however, were not to be so easily intimidated. The instant she was out of sight those sitting next to her daughter began to tickle, tease and kiss her in a race against time. The girl took it all in good humour, though allowing them only to a certain point and no further. When the mother's looming presence was seen again in the doorway the lads immediately settled down like naughty school-boys, straightening their hats.

The middle of the room was an expanse of scrubbed pine boards, empty of furniture. Instead of furniture there stood a boy holding a bottle and a glass. His job was to fill the glass and hand it to each of the boys on the benches in turn. 'Să trăiţi!' – Long may you live! – they said, drinking it down in one and handing it back. It was then refilled and given to the next boy, round and round the room over and over again. Only the girl and her mother did not partake. Whenever a bottle was finished one of the lads would produce another from an inside pocket of his sheep's wool waistcoat. Since the pourer himself drank in between presenting the glass to the others he very soon became entirely incapable of continuing and stood swaying in the middle of the room like a tree about to fall.

As he staggered, the bottle and glass were swept out of his hands, he was helped to a seat, and another youth took over.

While this ritual inebriation continued one of the boys stood up and went over to the girl. He took her by the hand and led her to the middle of the room, and there, without any hint of awkwardness, as naturally as if they were just going for a walk together, they began to dance the *Învîrtita*, the whirling dance of the Maramureş, to music coming from a little tape recorder on the windowsill. They started turning slowly, then stopped, and the boy began to stamp out a rhythm on the white pine floorboards which shook the benches beneath us. They then changed grip and the two of them swirled around, the wind from the spreading skirt brushing our cheeks. But then, as suddenly as they started, they came to an abrupt halt, both of them stamping on the floor, perfectly in time, as though to attention. The girl's face, even when they were spinning at their fastest, skirt and headscarf flying, remained impassive throughout.

As soon as they returned to their seats Vasile stood up. He signalled to the girl who, without question, joined him in the next dance. By the time we decided to leave she had danced five times. Vasile and Petru stood up to go and walked out without saying a word to anyone. I remained behind alone, feeling distinctly uncomfortable. I thought at least one of us should be polite enough to say goodbye. I thanked the mother and the girl from the middle of the room as though on stage in front of a silent, staring audience. The girl and her mother looked at me without saying a word. The lads all sitting around the room did the same. Not a word was said nor gesture made. They simply stared at me.

'Well, goodnight then and thank you very much,' I said, and walked self-consciously across the room and out of the door.

'You took your time, what on earth were you doing?' asked Vasile.

'I was saying goodbye,' I replied.

'You're not supposed to say goodbye,' he said as though it was the most obvious thing in the world. At this moment the girl walked out on to the veranda. Vasile pulled her towards him, threw his arms around her and kissed her on the lips.

'This is how it works, you see. She comes outside and you have a chance to meet her out of sight of her parents. Here you are. It's your turn now,' he said, swinging her over to me.

Not knowing what to do, I shook her awkwardly by the hand. Then I remembered that girls in the Maramureş generally do not shake hands, and feebly repeated my thanks for their hospitality.

Vasile and Petru looked on, unimpressed.

'I suppose it is only his first time,' said Vasile.

WITH ALL THESE visits to the girls, my thoughts would often turn to the Gypsy girl from the Saxon village, but I had still not heard a word from her, and the weather continued as cold and as snowy as ever. For the meantime I would have to watch others courting and think wistfully of the spring when I might be able to travel south once again.

The courting expeditions were a welcome winter diversion. So too were the many weddings. As you are not allowed to marry during fasts, and in the summer there is too much work, the period from Christmas until the beginning of Lent was the season for weddings. Mihai, as usual, had his own view. 'It's quite simple. People are married in the winter because they need someone to keep them warm in bed,' he said with a wink.

After much courting, and after all sorts of formal visits from father and son to the girl's house to exchange compliments and to talk of dowries and such things, a wedding would be decided upon. During this winter the daughter of a neighbour was betrothed and for days beforehand the neighbourhood gathered to prepare the food. The bride's house became a hive of bustling activity. In the courtyard women stirred huge cauldrons of bubbling meat, while others chased squawking chickens soon to be popped into pots and boiled into broth. Men chopped wood to keep the fires and ovens going. Dogs and cats waited for titbits to be thrown to them. In the house there were hempen sacks of flour, baskets of eggs, fifty-litre saucepans full of potatoes, lines of cakes in tins waiting to go into the glowing bread oven, long coils of sausages in wooden bowls, flagons of oil, pitchers of water and buckets of lard. Girls broke eggs, scooped flour from sacks, beat cream in enamel basins to make butter and cracked walnuts with a mallet. Women kneaded dough on pine tables until their elbows ached, sat with bowls on their laps stirring chopped walnuts into jam, or diligently coated fancy cakes with icing.

The nuptials themselves lasted for twenty-four hours. Meticulously attired guests and moustachioed Gypsy musicians gathered in the bride's house at midday amidst tables groaning with cabbage rolls and fancy cakes, and there ensued several hours of toasting, drinking, whooping and singing before the moment came for the bride to depart. Family and neighbours lined up to sing verses of farewell and offer advice on married life.

One girl, recently married, sang of how to preserve harmony in the married household, and keep good relations with the in-laws in whose house the bride would soon be living:

'*Din picioare să mergi uite / Din gură să nu ştii multe* – Let your legs move quickly, and your mouth not be too clever.'

A girl leant over to another: 'Just listen to her,' she said. 'Would you believe it? Her giving advice! She's been married a year, and their rows can be heard all around the village.'

Only twice do you leave the family house: when you marry and when you die. So when the time came for the mother and father each to sing their own personal songs of farewell, the tone changed.

'Do not forget your old parents. We are not rich but we did all we could to bring you up well,' the father sang. 'And if ever we did you wrong, we ask you to forgive us.'

There was a sound of sniffling in the air as those in the room grew ever more tearful. It was almost like a funeral.

Then the bride arose to leave her family home and the first and happiest period of her life for ever. The women of the party wept and dabbed their cheeks, but were drowned out by the men's chorus who broke into a final parting song:

I go from here with pain and longing,
As the moon passes through the clouds.
I go from here in dejection,
Like the moon when it moves through the stars.

Once outside the mood brightened. The bride, with a long procession of guests behind her, set off down the track in the direction of the church. She was surrounded by a group of unmarried men all singing at the tops of their voices, who were led by the violin, *zongora* and drum playing the merry wedding march. The roar of the men singing, and the booming of the drum resounding over the hill, warned the villagers that the wedding party would soon be appearing.

All along the route villagers lined their garden fences to watch the brightly coloured procession curl its way along the twisting paths, in a clockwise direction, following the setting sun, towards the church where the groom would be waiting. Spectators were offered gulps of *horincǎ* from bottles decorated with ribbons and evergreen leaves, and before long guests and spectators were tipsy.

The singers, noticing a girl craning over a fence to catch sight of the procession, immediately all sang together:

Climb upon the midden too,
And you'll have a better view . . .

The primitive rhythms of the drum boomed out across the hills, the lads whooped and sang, shepherds whistled and the wild energy of the music set a fever in the air.

The celebrations continued throughout the night. In the village hall, at the wedding feast, a hundred couples danced the *Învîrtita* in unison, the men holding their hats in the air with one arm as they swung around, the girls always managing to keep their remarkable composure despite the speed at which they were spinning through the air.

At Maramureş weddings it was often the *Lǎutari* Gypsies who provided the music. I used to watch them with fascination remembering the musicians from the Saxon village. The *Lǎutari* played entirely by ear and with such gusto it seemed the strings, or even the violins themselves, might snap at any moment under the strain. With cigarettes hanging from the corner of their mouths they played through swirls and glissandoes, racing through the galloping dances of the Maramureş, as powdered resin from the bow built up in piles beneath the strings.

The music and the dancing continued until eleven o'clock in the morning. Only then did proceedings draw towards a close. The *Lăutari*'s violins now sang a different tune, a slow and mournful melody, while the bride's godparents, each in turn, solemnly presented her with a headscarf. One by one they laid it upon her head and she cast it away. Then the best man, using the tip of the knife which he wore on his belt, picked it up and placed it back upon her head. Again she threw it away, three times. Only on the fourth attempt did she finally accept it, symbolically accepting her newly married status.

During the ceremony of the headscarves the villagers wept as they watched the young girl leaving her carefree youth behind her. In the crowd I saw the faces of Ion and Vasile. They as well, I noticed, had been moved to tears. Little did I know that in two years' time, I too would be shedding tears amidst wild lamenting at their weddings. They were, as it turned out, both to be married on the same day.

FOR MUCH OF the winter, when not courting or going to weddings, I walked about the village, wrapped up in an old shepherd's overcoat, fur hat and the *opinci* Mihai had made for me. I visited friends and together we drank large quantities of *horincă*, since no excuse was ever considered sufficient not to partake. *Horincă* was 'good for every ailment!' they repeatedly assured me. Either way, it was certainly good for passing the time.

Of the many people I visited one was Moş Ilie who, with his wife, lived in a beautiful wooden house in the higher village, up near the cart tracks which led out into the woods beneath the mountain. Moş Ilie still flailed his wheat by hand. He was one of the last in the village to do so.

'I don't have enough corn to make it worth going down to the threshing machines,' he told me, 'so I do it myself in the old way.'

This was how we had met. In the autumn I had asked Moş Ilie to teach me to flail. He tried, with much patience, but I could not master the technique, and only succeeded in bruising my arms while the wheat remained stubbornly attached to the stalks.

In the winter when I passed by their house I used to drop in to see Moş Ilie and his wife. Moş Ilie, who was exactly the same age as Mihai, would tell me about life in the village in Communist times.

'Here the Communists made life better for the poorer people,' he said. 'Before the German War life was hard. People would work for the landowners just for the food they were given as they worked. Sometimes, if they were lucky, they might be given a measure of maize flour to take home, but nothing else. Then after the war we were given land by the Communists and were able to survive off what we produced ourselves. I don't know what life was like elsewhere in the country, but for us the Communists made our lives better.'

I discovered that Moş Ilie and his wife were Greek Catholics. In Romania the Orthodox and Greek Catholic Churches did not see eye to eye, and indeed in Communist times the Greek Catholics had not been permitted to worship. Earnestly endeavouring to understand the differences between the Orthodox and the Greek Catholic Churches, I asked them why they had resolutely chosen to remain Greek Catholics and to go to the illegal Greek Catholic services.

'Well,' said the old lady, carefully weighing her words, 'it is because the Greek Catholic church was closer, and they had chairs.'

Another of those I visited was a delightful old man called Gheorghe a Curatorului. His mother had been the great story-teller of the village, and he had inherited her talent. He lived in a simple house and seemed to wear a permanent smile on his face. The first time I went there a young lamb was playing, jumping and tumbling about with the cat in the middle of the floor. It was a touching scene. The lamb slept under a bed in the kitchen and shared his box with the cat; the cat even had her kittens there, and they all lay in a bundle together in the warmth near the stove, the cat laying her head on the lamb's body and purring as her kittens suckled her.

As he poured me a glass of *horincă* I asked the story-teller about his stories.

'I will tell you one now,' he said, 'if you are ready for me to begin', and off he galloped without a moment's delay. The story was told in rhymed couplets and continued without a break for the best part of an hour. It was about a Romanian hero called Baba Novac, and his son Gruia, and their travails with the Ottoman Turks. The Romanian provinces had lain for many centuries on the frontier between Christianity and Islam. The Turks were the Romanian bogeymen, used to frighten generations of mischievous children, and were even painted into frescoes and altarpieces as the brutal and leering soldiers who had crucified Jesus. On winter evenings Romanian children would gather around the stoves and hear tales of Romanian heroes who, like Irish giants, vanquished vast armies of terrifying Turks single-handed. Indeed the painted monasteries of the Bukovina had been built to celebrate victories over the armies of successive Sultans.

Gruia Novac, in the story I was being told, seemed to have no problem defeating the Turks, and he was always careful to leave at least one of them alive to run back to Constantinople to describe their humiliation to the Caliph. In the end Gruia is somehow captured, and sentenced to death. The Caliph, however, before the sentence is carried out, orders him to tame a beautiful black stallion. Naturally Gruia is the only person skilled and brave enough for such a task. The gates of the palace are firmly closed in case Gruia tries to escape, but this does not daunt someone like our hero. He leaps on to the horse, jumps clean over the walls of the palace and gallops to freedom upon the Sultan's favourite horse. He returns to his country, killing a dragon on the way, of course, and, as they say at the end of all ballads in this part of the world, 'If he has not died, / Then in some place he is still alive.'

Many times I would visit Gheorghe and listen to stories of princesses and dragons, wolves and bears, invincible Romanian heroes and perfidious Sultans. He even told me a story of Attila the Hun who, he said, ate human flesh and made bowls out of the tops of people's skulls.

'He was buried in a golden coffin near the city of Cluj and people are still trying to find it today,' he assured me.

Grateful and impressed by his stories I promised to buy him an Austrian scythe as a present. At last in the summer I managed to find him one and asked someone in the village to give it to him. At half past five the next morning, on his way to the fields, he walked straight into the house and directly into my bedroom. He could not wait to thank me.

'You are a man of your word!' he said with a big smile on his face, scythe in hand. 'You have bought me a scythe. And it is from Austria. I am so happy. I will tell you as many stories as you like, as many as I can think of.'

I was still half asleep, blinking and trying to come to terms with the unexpected presence in my bedroom of this joyful reaper.

'I just hope the scythe will work well,' I stammered.

'Oh yes, it will work well. Austrian scythes are the best. Mowing will be just a game for me now,' he said as he walked out. As he crossed the courtyard I heard him whistling a merry tune.

9

The Thaw Begins

*All things presenting themselves to the mind in violent contrasts and
impressive forms, lent a tone of excitement and of passion to everyday
life and tended to produce a perpetual oscillation between despair and
distracted joy, between cruelty and pious tenderness.*

Johan Huizinga, *The Waning of the Middle Ages*

O NE BRIGHT DAY in March, as the snow in Breb was at last slowly
beginning to melt and forming clear sparkling rivulets running
down the meadows, I had an idea. I was mulling over the strange
matter of the letters and decided it was time to send another. I would
send it by normal post, only on this occasion I would also write a few
carefully chosen words on the back of the envelope. I prepared the
letter, licked up the envelope, and wrote upon it in my best Romanian:

> If this letter is not delivered I will come myself to the village and
> deliver the next one in person.

I then gave the letter to Petrovici and waited.

The snow continued to melt and the stream running by the house
turned into a torrent. When the first strong melt had come, it had come
with sudden violence, the streams and rivers gushing down from the
mountains, the ice crashing against trunks of trees on the banks, gash-
ing them and tearing off their bark. After the initial flood had subsided
thick sheets of ice were left piled up on the banks, some blocks lodged
between trees, and there they remained for weeks afterwards.

Where the snow had gone the lower meadows filled with snow-
drops and bright purple crocuses which the children wove into

crowns to wear on their heads. Mihai slipped a crocus into the brim of his hat. The early spring seemed full of hope. The first green shoots of grass were appearing, and even a few small buds on the trees. I, however, was beginning to lose hope that I would ever see Natalia again.

Then, one afternoon, after a morning spent raking leaves and twigs from the hay meadows so as to allow the new grass to grow unimpeded, Ion, Mihai's young cousin, came running up with a letter for me in his hand. A man who lived on the other side of the village had, he told me, been given the letter by Petrovici in Ocna Şugatag on market day the week before. This was the conventional method of delivery used by Petrovici if there were only one or two letters on any one day, so as to avoid the fourteen-kilometre walk to the village and back. The well-meaning man had put the letter in his hat and had gone to the bar. From there he had walked home across the fields, although not necessarily in a straight line, and, arriving exhausted, had fallen on to the bed and gone to sleep, his hat rolling on to the floor into a corner. Only when his wife was cleaning some days later did she see the letter, and the strange foreign name, and give it to Ion to bring to me.

I opened it, expecting to find more anonymous threats. It seemed, however, to be from Natalia. Indeed it was signed 'Natalia', although after the anonymous letter I could not be entirely sure. It read:

> Meet me at two o'clock on the 24th at the crossroads on the Sighişoara road.

The 24th was the very next day.

The roads were now nearly clear of snow and so I decided to go. Mihai was horrified at my plan to leave so suddenly. He had always warned me to be wary of the Gypsies.

'You should take a gun with you,' he told me.

'Where on earth am I to find a gun, Mihai?' I said. 'In any case I can't go around shooting people.'

'Well then, at least you must take a knife. The Gypsies are unpredictable,' he said.

The car had been out of action all winter and it took a while to persuade it to start, but in the end it spluttered into life. I set off the next day. As I was leaving Mihai solemnly handed me the knife which he had especially prepared and sharpened for me. I had seen him bent over the grinding stone the evening before.

'You might need this,' he said.

Driving out of the village I saw Ion walking to the fields, with a rake on his shoulder, and waved to him. He waved back.

'Take care in the outside world,' he shouted.

WHEN I ARRIVED at the crossroads, just after eleven, Natalia and one of her brothers were waiting for me. Clearly the letter had not been sent by a jealous boyfriend to lure me into a trap. We greeted each other happily.

'This is Nicolae,' she said. 'He was away when you were with us in August.' Nicolae leant towards me, with an open smile on his face, and shook my hand. He had an easy, reassuring manner and in his blue eyes there was a confidence-inspiring calmness.

We found a bar where we drank Turkish coffee.

'How are you?' I asked Natalia.

'I'm well,' she replied.

'And what have you been up to?'

'*Nimic.*'

I should have guessed.

'Something must have happened in eight months,' I said.

'Not really. Life is much the same,' she replied. 'A bit of work, a bit of dancing. We need to keep warm.'

'Did your food last the winter?' I asked.

'No,' she said, 'but my brothers collect wood in the forest and sell it. They have horses. And my parents had a little money left over from working in Hungary during the summer. With this we can buy food.'

I now turned to the perplexing matter of the letters. 'Apart from the latest letter, did you receive any others from me?' I asked.

'No,' she said, shrugging her shoulders. 'I assumed you had forgotten us.'

'I had sent others,' I told her. 'What can have happened to them?'

'They will have been stolen by someone,' she said matter-of-factly. 'I was sure you had sent others. It was a good idea to write on the back of the last one. If you hadn't, that one would have been stopped as well.'

'But by whom? Was it Frau Knall?' I asked.

'No. It might have been the postmistress herself. There are people who wouldn't want you to be our friend. She is one of them.'

'But why?'

'It's a long story,' she said. 'You don't want to hear it now.'

'Yes, I do,' I said.

'The main problem is that we are Gypsies, but that is only the start.' She was going to go on but then she looked at me with her big, gazelle eyes.

'Why don't you come and live with us for a while, and you can find out as much as you like?' she said.

It was a tempting suggestion. I had been thinking of her throughout the long, cold winter days and nights. But I knew Herr and Frau Knall would be appalled, and clearly there were others who wanted to prevent it. There was bound to be trouble. And most importantly there was the delicate problem of the displeased boyfriend who wanted to kill me.

'Oh don't worry about the Lad!' said Natalia. 'We will protect you.'

I admired her sangfroid, but remained worried, and decided for the moment to turn down her kind offer.

'I have to go back up north. I told Mihai I would only be away for a day or two,' I said.

Before we parted, we fixed another meeting, down to the precise day and hour, as letters were obviously not an option.

I RETURNED NORTH, over the rolling hills and rippling mountains, up narrow valleys where half-frozen streams rushed downhill towards the Someş river. These icy waters had a long journey. They would enter the Tisa, then the Danube and from there flow gently into the Black Sea and on warm currents eventually into the Mediterranean.

By evening I had reached the top of the pass and, leaving the outside world behind again, descended into Breb just before dark. Mihai was greatly relieved to see me.

'Weh-hey!' he shouted, 'Willy's back.' Glasses were put out on the table and filled to the brim with *horincă*.

It was the eve of *Blago Veştenilor*, the Annunciation, which in most of the rest of Romania is called the more Latinate *Bună Vestire*. At dusk people began to light bonfires. There were fires in different parts of every garden, and as they were lit leaves twisted up into the air on billows of smoke. The fires, Mihai explained, are intended to keep unpleasant insects, mice, rats and snakes away from the house. It was clearly a custom of pagan origin. I climbed the hill to see the spectacle better. All over the village, and then appearing in neighbouring valleys where settlements lay, always more and more fires were lit until the whole landscape was brightened by thousands of dots of orange flame. Behind the glow of the bonfires was the cold, wild beauty of the darkening forests and mountains.

THE CLOCKS WENT forward on 30 March, but Mihai and Maria took no notice. They continued to use old time. 'We cannot accustom ourselves to city ways,' they said. Besides, time here was rarely told by clocks. In the field it was calculated according to the shadows made by the ricks, or by the aeroplanes whose white trails could be seen high above the village travelling between one great city and another.

Over the next weeks a first few tiny leaves began to appear on the trees, the snow receded further up the hill and new colour, slightly greener every day, gradually spread itself over the landscape. But although we were in April it was dangerous to assume the winter was over, and indeed Mihai told me that in one year they were still collecting haystacks off the hill by sleigh at the end of the month. It was mild enough during the day when the sun was out, but it still snowed from time to time and was cold at night. An old woman who lived alone froze to death in her bed, unable to fetch wood from outside for the stove. When she was buried, the grave was full of water from the melt and the rain, and the coffin had to be weighed down with rocks.

During these days Mihai and I continued to walk out to the fields and rake leaves and twigs into piles which we set alight, so as to prepare the strips for good grass and easy mowing. All over the Breb lands plumes of smoke rose up from amongst the trees. There was something comforting in being aware of everyone busying themselves with the same work.

On the eve of the day of Forty Saints, way back on 9 March, it had frozen at night. Mihai had told me then that, according to the old men, it would freeze for another forty nights. It was now 19 April, forty-one days since 9 March, and the night before had indeed been the first night without frost. The old men had it exactly right. The weather was warm, and on this very day people started ploughing. It seemed everyone in the village went by the same old wisdom. Coming back from the market I saw a team afield; a girl in skirts and headscarf led the horses, the man steered the plough. The crude wooden harrow with its protruding metal spikes, looking like some medieval instrument of torture, lay on the ground by the strip. Once they had scattered the seed they hitched it to the harness, weighed it down with a rock and the horses dragged it over the strip to break up the larger clods of earth.

Our neighbour Dumitru was also making ready to plough, fastening a share to its wooden frame. He had made the share over the winter out of an old piece of scrap metal. Full of admiration I used to watch him at his home-made forge carefully hammering out the beautifully curved blade.

'This is Gypsies' work,' he told me, 'but I know how to do it too. Here we have to know how to do everything.'

The cherry trees were the first to flower. Mihai leant on his rake one day and looked out over the fields. He called to me from the other side of the meadow and pointed out how the hills above the village were now covered with bursts of white blossom.

'It is a wonderful sight,' he said.

Mihai truly appreciated the beauty of the Breb lands, and this was to make it all the harder when a few years later the cherry trees were cut down.

SUNDAY 20 APRIL was *Duminică Floriilor* – Sunday of the Flowers – the Romanian name for Palm Sunday. In the dim light of the church, under the candle-blackened, barrel-vaulted ceiling, a hundred peasants were assembled, all dressed in traditional clothes, and all holding sprigs of willow catkins aloft. The catkins were blessed, then taken home and placed decoratively around the icons that adorn the walls of even the simplest peasant house. Most people, however, used them as a charm for averting storms.

'You just throw a few pieces on the fire and the storm goes away,' they told me matter-of-factly. The priest was continually having to contend with such ideas. On this day he again railed against magic and superstition.

'Magic spells do not work and to do them is a sin against God,' he said. All the villagers shifted uneasily and looked sideways to avoid his gaze. Not one of them saw any incompatibility in believing in God and some pagan divinity at the same time.

I passed the priest later that day on my way to the well to fetch water. Without thinking I put my bucket on the ground. In the village it was considered unlucky to pass someone while carrying an empty vessel of any sort. To mitigate the situation you must put the vessel down and recite a special verse. This I did. The priest gave me a withering look.

'I am a priest,' he said, 'and I do not know about or believe in such superstitious nonsense.' He went on his way without another word.

A few days later, in the morning I noticed birds singing loudly outside my window once again. It was 25 April. In the market at

Ocna Şugatag straw hats were for sale for the first time since last summer. The traders too had decided the cold weather was over.

SINCE THE BEGINNING of the week the signs of Easter approaching were apparent. Eggs were being hoarded, and in the evening horses pulling carts, with sacks of grain aboard, trotted out of the village, off to the water mill in Budeşti; they returned in the dark at a canter, the carts now laden with flour for the Easter cakes, their drivers tipsy and sparks flying off the horses' shoes. As I walked about the village, or to and from the fields, rake on my shoulder, I passed women carrying wicker baskets filled with rugs on their way down to the river to wash them. Newly made shirts, to be worn on Easter Day, were being washed in ash and hung to dry on the shiny, wooden poles which swung out in front of the verandas of the wooden houses. All winter, girls and their mothers had been diligently weaving, stitching and embroidering. Each Easter it was essential to have bright new shirts with all the requisite puffed and smocked sleeves and lace cuffs; if you did not grandmothers would give each other knowing looks.

In the town I witnessed scenes of almost biblical slaughter. It was a massacre of the innocents. The scenes were played out in public, even in the streets and on the pavements. Throughout the week leading up to Easter I saw lambs trotting happily beside their mothers to market. At the market there was a special room set aside. There waited a line of people, all cradling in their arms lambs they had recently purchased. The lambs looked around for their mothers but seemed unaware of what was about to happen, despite the blood trickling into the nearby gutter. When a person reached the front of the queue their lamb was grabbed by the butcher and hooked up on a spike which passed through the tendons of its back legs. This was the moment to look away. Its throat was cut and blood poured like wine down the white-tiled walls.

Others were choosing the cheaper option and slaughtering the lambs themselves on the grass outside their apartment blocks,

Mihai in best bell-sleeved smock and glass of *horincă* in his hand

Marishka

Above: WB on a ladder leading to the 'best bedroom' in a covered haystack by the house. The roof can be raised or lowered

Right: Neighbours in Breb wearing *pinci* shoes

Below: A *Căldărar* Gypsy girl with shells and red tassels in her hair, standing at the entrance to her tent

Girls dressed in their best embroidered smocks during the Sunday promenade

Village lads, wearing Maramureş straw hats, playing cards in an orchard

WB sharpening his scythe, dressed in his brown *pănură* waistcoat

Maria, Mihai and a Gypsy friend having a break for lunch during a day's haymaking.
The wooden forks lean up against the rick

Carts parked during the market at Ocna Şugatag, the horses kept warm
with colourful home-made blankets

In high spirits on the way back from market, the horses wearing red tassels
to ward off the evil eye

Herr and Frau Knall in their cobbled courtyard at Halma

The Saxon fortified church of Archita with its defensive ring-walls and bastions

Natalia

stringing them up on a tree. A dog trotted along the pavement very pleased with itself, a lamb's foot dangling from its mouth.

Mihai bought a lamb at Ocna Şugatag from a shepherd. He chose one carried by an old man who was dressed from top to toe in clothing made from sheep. We took it home in the back of a cart. For a while it skipped about on the lawn. Then in the afternoon a neighbour came round. He tied its back legs together, hung it upside down and it died with a quick stab to the throat.

Wherever I went in the village lambs were being hung on trees and their throats cut in preparation for the Easter feast.

At home the pine floors were being scrubbed, flour was being kneaded, eggs broken into basins, and Easter loaves and lines of cakes in tins were being placed, three or four at a time, on the end of a long wooden spatula and into the glowing bread oven. When Maria had finished, the neighbours came around and baked their cakes in her oven as well. Behind the village so filled with activity the mountains stood motionless, gleaming in the sun, still white with snow.

IT WAS ALMOST three o'clock in the morning and pitch dark as I made my way alone down to the church for the Easter service. I picked my way carefully over the stony track. The stream next to me rushed by, still swollen with meltwater from the mountain.

On nearing the church, above the noise of the stream I could hear the strange, urgent rhythms of the *toacă* being hammered, and saw a hundred memorial candles, lit by each family, flickering in among the trees, spread out on graves all over the cemetery.

Outside the wooden church, on the grass, was assembled a collection of men and women dressed in brown *pănură* waistcoats or white sheep's wool coats rimmed with black. The men were bare headed. I, too, took off my fur hat. They held candles which lit up their faces in chiaroscuro. All around me I saw the powerful and dignified features of peasants, looking more like Greek philosophers.

We stood reverently in front of an icon of Jesus which had been covered by a veil. Above us in the cold night air rose the spire of the church, like a witch's hat, pointing upwards towards the moon, the stars and the planets. All of a sudden the priest, like a magician, cast the veil off with a flourish, and the men began to sing, in their strong bass voices, the beautiful Easter hymn of the Romanian Church:

> Christ has risen from death, and through death has trampled upon death, and given life to those in their graves.

Awaiting their moment, the women joined in, quietly, almost imperceptibly at first, their voices rising in crescendo to give maximum impact to the moment of joy on hearing again the news that Christ had risen from his tomb. The faces of the old men, and of the women, young and old, their heads wrapped in headscarves, looked under candlelight like those of saints in devotion. The icon was picked up by Ion and Vasile. They walked around the outside of the church three times, followed first by the men and then by the women, all to the glad ringing of bells and the wild beating of the *toacă* to announce the Resurrection.

We processed into the church and kissed the holy icon which was now placed at the front of the candle-lit church. The singing continued, incense was shaken to the north, south, east and west, and the priest walked up and down between us announcing that '*Hristos a înviat! –* Christ has risen!' and we all in turn affirmed that '*Adevărat că a înviat! –* He has risen indeed!'

I walked out of the church and into the darkness. It was now half past four. Under the stars the candles were still flickering in the cemetery as though mirroring the night sky. Others were making their way home, but I wandered in among the graves. There, hidden by trees, but just visible in the glow of guttering candles, a few old men knelt in the middle of that chill April night, their hands held upright and together in front of their faces, praying alone beside the graves of their wives.

AT ELEVEN O'CLOCK the next morning I walked down to the church again, this time with Maria and Mihai, and everyone else in the village. Each of the many village families carried an Easter basket filled with Easter loaves, decorated eggs, water and the inevitable magic charms. The charms were well concealed at the bottom of the basket, as nobody wanted to distress the priest unnecessarily. The baskets were placed outside the church and the priest duly blessed and sprinkled them with holy water.

At lunch we ate the lamb.

On Easter Monday, dressed in newly knitted white jerseys of the latest pattern, and newly plaited straw hats with ribbons a-fluttering, the lads gathered at the house of the village violinist. The musicians, with violin, *zongoră* and dogskin drum, had started to play. The drummer beat the drum, whose 'boom' could be heard all over the village, and they set off through the orchards, the lads singing and whooping, their hat bands blowing in the wind. They walked through the middle of the village, past the promenading lasses now dressed in their Easter smocks bright as snow in the spring sunshine, and to the open-air dancing pavilion. There they waited, and as the promenading girls appeared, made a sign to the violinist. Then, leaning on the columns of the pavilion, like sailors leaning out from the rigging of a ship, they beckoned to the girls. Soon everyone was dancing and the pavilion shook to the stamping of feet. The lads became progressively drunker and merrier, dancing with bottles in their hands, and the violinist gave it his all, sweat pouring from his brow. Lent was well and truly over.

AFTER EASTER EVERYONE returned to work. Some were spreading manure, others ploughing with horses, buffalo or oxen, their ploughs slicing silently through the ground like knives, turning up a line of earth so smoothly cut that its surface almost reflected in the sun. Others were digging up seed potatoes from clamps in the garden, ready to be seeded as soon as the ploughing was finished. In some gardens you could see family groups sitting on the grass carefully shearing their few sheep, the sheep lying calmly with their heads on the shearer's knee submitting peacefully to having their hair cut.

'Beatus ille,' I thought, remembering Horace's epode, 'Happy is he who works with oxen the family land . . . stores pressed honey in clean jars, and shears the harmless sheep.' The sun was shining, and all over the village there were scenes of calm and contented bucolic life, as the peasants worked with their usual slow deliberation to prepare for planting and the coming warm weather.

Every tree near the village was useful for food, either apple, pear, plum, mulberry or walnut, and so spring, when it came, came in a spectacular burst of blossom. Everywhere there were trees covered in pink and white flowers. Violets, both purple and white, wood anemones, syringa and narcissus were appearing. Old ladies walked about with posies and children decorated the corners of their houses with sprigs of lilac. In the trees of the orchard outside my bedroom window birds were busily making nests and waking me in the morning with their clamour.

Mihai, on the other hand, was miserable. He was coughing badly and was sitting in a chair looking at the floor telling us he was about to die. He even refused to make a harness because, he informed us, he would have neither the time nor the strength to finish it before his imminent death. I was preparing to leave, as the day to meet Natalia was approaching, but first I went on an errand. I had to visit the vet who lived in the upper village. Dressed in headscarf and skirts like all other village women, she hunted about in a cupboard and gave me a clean needle and penicillin reserved usually for cows or horses; this, over the next few days, we injected into Mihai's arm. In Breb there was a priest but no policeman, and there was a vet but no doctor. It showed where priorities lay. In any case, most people used what they called 'Leacuri Băbești' – Old Wives' herbal and other curious remedies. Maria recounted to me how Mihai had once had hepatitis. They had no money for doctors and so she used fleas, which she picked off the buffalo. She fed them to him alive. Fleas, she assured me, do not die when you swallow them, but eat whatever causes the illness. With the fleas you must eat only potatoes, but without salt.

THE DAY CAME at last for me to return south to meet Natalia. She was at the place we had agreed to meet. In a bar we ordered a Turkish coffee and sat down to talk. She had a cold.

'Our house is rather chilly,' she explained.

'Don't you have a stove?' I asked.

'Yes, but there is no glass in the windows,' she whispered to me under her breath so that the superior-looking couple on the next table would not hear.

'Why not?' I whispered back.

'My father smashed them all.'

'All?' I said, impressed.

'Yes. All.'

'But why?'

'He'd had too much to drink and was cross with my mother.'

'Don't you have *any* rooms with windows?'

'No, he smashed them all. I told you.' This was, I later discovered, entirely in character. Her father, Attila, never did anything by halves.

'So are you going to come and live with us now?' she said.

I demurred. Not only was the Lad still at large, but now their house was barely habitable.

'But you haven't any windows,' I replied.

'No, but . . . perhaps you could help us mend them . . . or even just one room? Anyway we are nearly out of the cold now. Soon we won't need windows.'

'I am sorry,' I told her. 'I really can't come just now. Forgive me. I would like to but I have to go back to my village in the north. Mihai is ill. Here is a little money to mend the windows. It's not much but it should be enough for a room or two.'

'I piss on your money!' she said contemptuously. She was right to be cross. I was indeed displaying a feeble cowardice and lack of Gypsy-like spontaneity.

'Now is not a good time for me to come,' I said. 'In any case the Lad still wants to kill me. We can't live in the village with him around. Write to me. Send your letters from the neighbouring village and they will get through. I will arrange things so that I can leave the Maramureş and we can meet again soon. Then we can organize how I can come and live with you.'

'Other people would do anything to be with me. You just make excuses. And you are afraid of the Lad. Huh!' she scoffed. 'I tell you, if he were just to touch you my brother would kill him.' This last comment was presumably intended to reassure me. It did not.

The meeting was not a successful one. I said goodbye and suggested she write to me. I assured her I would return soon.

10

Scenes of Country Life

Cetera mandru zice, / Inima rau ma strice − The violin sweetly
sings, / My heart with longing wrings.

Maramureş song

I SPENT THE summer cheerfully scything the fields and waiting for
a letter from Natalia. But no letter came and I assumed she had lost
interest in me. I was not surprised. I had shown a spinelessness worthy
of contempt. I did want to go to Halma, and move in with Natalia,
but at the same time I knew almost nothing about her and her family,
and there still lingered an irrational, atavistic mistrust of Gypsies
which made me hesitate to launch myself into the middle of the
apparent chaos in which they lived. Nor did I want to be responsible
for the death of the Lad, or myself, or anyone else. I felt I had made
the right decision, but I missed Natalia and her hypnotic eyes, and the
idea of living with her remained firmly planted in my mind.

The summer days in the Maramureş passed peacefully by, but
now in late autumn a sense of approaching winter hung over the
village and the surrounding mountains. In the spring the green of
the unfurling leaves had risen higher and higher up the mountain.
Now the brown crept slowly downwards as the beech leaves
changed colour and dropped to the ground.

We carried out the last tasks of the year. The pumpkins, cabbages, beans and dried maize stalks were brought down from the
fields on carts. We finished scything the last fields of *otavă* − the
second cut of hay − which was then stacked in the last ricks of
the year. Soon all was ready for another winter.

Many months had passed and I assumed that Natalia must have forgotten me. I did not write to her as I was sure my letters would have been 'lost' en route, and so there resulted a long silence. I was also worried about Mihai's health during the coming winter. The penicillin in the spring had cured his bronchitis but his coughing was still not good.

'You are like a son to us,' Mihai used to say to me. 'We might not see each other all day sometimes, but we are still happy just to know that you are here.'

Although I had thought of travelling south to see Natalia, I knew that I must stay another winter in the Maramureş.

MIHAI HAD NOTICED during my first winter in Breb that I was complaining of cold feet and suffering from not having the right footwear. He had therefore made me a pair of *opinci*. Now for my second winter he and Maria put their minds to organizing proper clothes for me. The few clothes which I had brought from England were entirely insufficient to keep me insulated from the churlish blast of Romania's winter wind, and the old shepherd's coat, borrowed from a friend, was now threadbare.

The thick woolly material used for making coats and the brown, fulled cloth for waistcoats, called *pănură*, was bought in the village from women who had made extra material on their looms the previous year and had a few rolls spare. These we put into baskets which we hoisted on to our backs and walked over the hill to the village of Sîrbi where the best tailor in the area resided.

'*Spor la treabă!* – Strength to your labours!' Mihai shouted as we passed friends still carrying out the last jobs of autumn in the fields so as to leave everything tidy for the winter.

'Where are you off to, Uncle Mihai?' they shouted back.

'To the tailor. We have to kit Willy out with proper winter clothes, do we not?'

There was general agreement.

As we descended through the orchards into Sîrbi the grass under the trees was speckled with fruit and we passed large piles of apples and pears in people's back gardens waiting to be turned into *horincă*.

'Oh Lord forgive us,' said an old lady to us as she piled pears into a basket, 'there'll be some drinking this winter and there'll be trouble – but *horincă* is money and we have to make it.'

The village tailor wore peasant clothes and even *opinci*. Around his neck hung a long measuring tape, the sign of his profession. He set about measuring me as though I was in Jermyn Street.

'And would Sir like the coats to be trimmed with black cord or black velvet?' he asked. I chose black velvet for the coat, the *gubar*, and black cord for the waistcoat, the *pieptar*.

'And would you like an inside pocket?' he asked.

'You must have an inside pocket, Willy,' said Mihai, 'big enough for a small bottle. It is essential to have a bottle of *horincă* with you when you go courting.'

The design decided, we lifted the now empty baskets on to our shoulders and walked back over the hill in the last light before the sun dropped behind the mountain. Dotted everywhere tall ricks cast long shadows over lawn-smooth meadows, and there was such an abundance of pink autumn crocuses that it was impossible not to trample upon them.

'MAY YOU WEAR them in good health, and be married in them soon!' said the smiling tailor when a few weeks later I went to pick up my new clothes, and from then on, apart from having to endure the initial helpless giggles of the village girls, I wore them with pride. Attired in my new *gubar* and *pieptar*, and with Mihai's *opinci* on my feet, I could now almost be taken for a native, and gradually as my grasp of the dialect improved I became always better at blending in. Even though I wore glasses people who did not know me were unable to see beyond the clothes.

Sighetul Marmaţiei is the main town of the Old Maramureş. Sighet, as it is called for short, is surely the last town in Europe where you can still see country people in full traditional dress, and wearing *opinci*, walking down the street. In Sighet there was only one bank, and this was upstairs in a small room of a building near the railway station, and it was from here that I obtained the small amount of money needed to keep myself going in Breb.

Attired in my new garb I handed in my passport and waited to cash a cheque among a crowd of town and village people. A clerk emerged from a back office and, looking straight through me, shouted, 'Where is the Englishman?'

I was at the front of the queue looking directly at her.

'Where is the Englishman?' she shouted again, but louder, over my shoulder.

'I am here,' I said.

The clerk jumped.

'I am so sorry,' she said, 'but I thought . . . well, your coat and hat . . .'

'They are the best thing for such cold weather,' I said.

She then started telling her colleagues with excitement about an Englishman disguised as a Maramureş peasant.

'He is English. He really is. Look at his passport!'

In those days, and still today, most Romanians were trying to escape from life in the country, and those who moved away from the villages felt themselves to be a cut above the peasants; it was hard for them to imagine why anyone should willingly allow themselves to be seen dressed in peasant garb.

ANA, THE WIDOW of Mihai's brother Ştefan, was a white witch, and on winter afternoons I used to trudge up through the swirling snow, dressed proudly in my smart new clothes, to knock at the door of her one-roomed wooden cottage. During the cold months there was little work to be done out of doors, and so villagers were happy to chat away the long evening hours. It was from Ana that I began to discover more about Romanian magic.

Ana was ninety, but her mind was limpidly clear and, in her crackly voice, she could recite poems and songs and elaborate on the principles of magic for hours without tiring.

According to Ana, Romanian magic was practised for two main

purposes. The first was to protect against the power of jealousy or envy, which might be directed towards you by an 'Evil Eye'. The second was for reasons of love.

'If you have a beautiful horse, cow or sheep,' she explained, 'or a beautiful child, bad people will be envious of your good fortune and may want to destroy them. You need to protect yourself against such evil forces which might be directed towards you. You can go to a witch, like me, or simply take a few precautions of your own at home.' She made a list. You can wear a clove of garlic or a phial of mercury around your neck, she told me. Garlic is a well-known shield against evil, and mercury, being slippery, does not allow evil to stick. You can also use mirrors to deflect wicked thoughts, or you can symbolically spit in evil's face, as Romanians do when they see a beautiful child. Or you can wear red. From Naples to India red is the colour used to protect against the evil eye. In Romania red tassels are hung from horses' head collars, or the tips of cows' horns, and sheep have threads of red wool sewn on to the fleece.

When it comes to love, again, you can use a witch, or there are precautions you can take yourself. Once we were making hay and I put my hat on the ground. Mihai warned me to be careful.

'When you're not looking a girl will pass it between her legs, let a drop of piss fall on it, recite a spell and you'll find yourself in love with her,' he said.

'Don't talk nonsense, Uncle Mihai,' said a girl who was raking nearby, 'of course they don't do that.'

He looked at me with a knowing look and said, 'Yes they do.'

'And don't ever accept a drink from a girl,' Mihai told me once.

'Why not?'

'Because they might have put juices in it from secret places in order to put a spell on you,' he replied.

In Romania when they say that a man has been enchanted or bewitched by a girl they mean it quite literally.

Mihai also told me of how girls used to bathe naked in the stream on the eve of 6 January to predict what sort of man their future husband would be. Ana confirmed this.

'Two girls must go down to the stream in the dark,' she said. 'One undresses and stands in the river while the other sprinkles her with water, using sprigs of dried basil, and recites a spell. The basil is then planted in the snow and the future can be foretold according to the shape of the icicles hanging from it in the morning. It is important that when the girls return to the house they must not look back, otherwise the spell will lose its power.

'And of course there is always a wolf's windpipe,' Ana went on. 'After church a girl stands on the edge of the crowd of women, and when the man she desires passes by she blows through the windpipe towards him, pretending she is coughing, and he will be enchanted – *farmecat* – and unable to resist her. The only way to untie the spell is to use the windpipe in reverse,' she explained.

Bat's bones were also effective.

'First you must get hold of a bat,' she said.

'Where would you find a bat?' I asked.

'Oh, the girls know where to go. They climb up the church tower in the evening, or find them in the attic. Then, once caught, they have to kill it.'

I had images of girls in skirts and headscarves clambering up the church tower, somehow managing to catch a bat, and then trying to knock it on the head as it flapped around, snapping its teeth and trying to bite them. Once killed, the bat must then be buried in an anthill, Ana explained, and left until the ants have stripped the bones off the flesh leaving a perfect little skeleton. Among these bones you will find one shaped like a tiny rake. This is the bone you need. Again, waiting for the right moment after church, when there are always crowds, you must pass by the man with whom you are in love and lightly scratch him on the arm with the little rake, so lightly he will not even notice, or will simply think it is a broken button or a stiff piece of material on someone's clothing.

WITH ALL THE talk about spells and the evil eye, and all the mischief girls apparently got up to in order to attract a man, I began to wonder whether Natalia might not somehow have cast a spell upon me. It was, after all, the Gypsies who had brought many of the magical practices to Europe from India. Certainly Natalia did exert a powerful attraction. And although I had not written to her, nor she to me, I often found myself thinking of her, and was planning a journey south to find her in the spring. Mihai was convinced that I had been *legat*, or bound to her by a spell. How otherwise could an ordinary, apparently sensible person like myself possibly be so fascinated by a Gypsy, and keep disappearing off to go and see her? ('Fascinate' is another word whose literal meaning, from Latin, is 'to be bound up' in the sense of having a spell cast upon you.) Frankly I did not mind the idea of being 'bound' to Natalia, but Mihai was adamant. I must go to a white witch to be *deslegat* – unbound. In the end, out of curiosity, I agreed to go. Others, seeing I was not serious, warned me not to.

'You must not mess around with these things,' they said. 'It is very dangerous.'

Nonetheless, Mihai kept introducing me to more good witches in the hope that I might perhaps be converted. One of them, a cousin of his called Ileana, lived in the neighbouring village of Budeşti. I walked over the hill with Mihai to meet her.

As we walked he told me of the ethnologists who had come up from Bucharest. 'People here used to pretend to know spells and incantations because the ethnologists brought presents with them. There was a woman from Manasturi, I remember, whom they all went to see. It was funny. She wasn't a witch at all. She made it all up to get the presents. Ileana, however, is a real witch.'

'But do you really believe in magic, Mihai?' I asked.

'Of course I do,' he replied.

'Why?'

'Because it works.'

Mihai and Maria had told me many stories of how their cow, and neighbours' animals, had been cured by witches. Many people too, who had been made ill by the evil eye, felt better after visiting witches who reversed the spells, sending them back to those who had cast them. Whether or not it was the magic which cured them did not matter. The main thing was that they were cured.

Mihai and I walked into a tall, steep-roofed house, the newel posts of the veranda polished with use. In a room with tiny windows which let in little light an old lady and her three-year-old granddaughter were in bed together keeping warm. Ileana's voice was gentle and clear despite her age.

'Why have you come?' she asked Mihai kindly.

'My friend wanted to ask you about spells and magic,' Mihai replied.

'I'm afraid I can't do spells today; it is Sunday,' she said apologetically. 'It would be a sin against God.' During the week presumably God did not mind.

'But what is wrong with the boy?' asked Ileana. 'Has he had a spell cast upon him, or does he want to find a wife? Or is it some other problem?'

'He just wants to know about the spells, how they work and so on,' he said.

'Oh I see,' she said. 'All the same, he should come tomorrow if he doesn't mind.'

I did return and came to know her, her family and her eldest granddaughter to whom she was teaching her craft. They were always welcoming and always gave me a bowl of soup to give me strength for the walk home through the snow. In the end the old lady did not choose to reveal much about witchcraft, but she did once tell me the outlines of a complicated spell which involved putting into a bottle nine pieces of elder, cut only on Tuesdays or Thursdays, nine different samples of earth from nine graves, and nine small slices of wood from wooden grave crosses, which should all then be buried on the empty ground between villages.

'If you do this in the right way, and I know the right way, no one can harm you,' she said, looking at me with her owl-like eyes.

'But who might be trying to harm me?' I asked.

'Anyone who goes to a Gypsy to put a spell on you,' she said. 'Who knows? It might be anyone, but if you do this it will send the spell back to them.

'But I don't do many spells these days,' she went on. 'People complain about having to pay. It's not fair. People pay doctors, so why shouldn't they pay me? I cure them as well as any doctor. In fact I am better than a doctor. He treats the symptoms, I cure the causes. And if someone comes to me who is just ill, I tell them. They think they have been bewitched. I tell them to go away and take an aspirin.'

I was not persuaded to be 'untied' from the spell which Mihai was so sure had been cast upon me. I heeded friends' warnings to beware of making fun of magic, and in any case I did not really want to be untied. I enjoyed being bewitched by Natalia.

But I also enjoyed walking over the hill to Budeşti and so used visits to Ileana as a reason to stretch my legs.

One day when I arrived on her doorstep she looked particularly pleased.

'Ah, good, I have been waiting for you,' she said. 'I have something to give you.'

Slowly, with a smile on her face, she began to gather things from different hiding places about the room. 'You must take great care of these,' she said, 'they will keep you safe and protect you from all different sorts of evil.' I could not help thinking that Mihai had been talking to her. On the old wooden table in front of me she placed a palmful of earth which she said had come from a holy monastery near Suceava, and some salt crystals which she had apparently 'worked on'. These I must mix together and sprinkle over the threshold of my house and under my bed. There was also a bundle of nine twigs of elder tied with thread, each piece of which I must place at intervals along my garden fence. Nine is the number always used in magic spells. Then there was a piece of wood with nails driven through it which I should fix beside the threshold of my house, then another bundle of slivers of wood chipped off her loom which I must place at the four corners of my house, and then a bent nail passed through a dried onion to be placed near my head when sleeping, and a necklace of dried cloves of garlic threaded on to a piece of string which I should wear around my neck. I was now pretty well kitted out. She swept everything into a cloth bag and put it into my hand, telling me to be very careful with the contents.

The last time I visited Ileana there were tears in her eyes. I was surprised to see them as she had never wept before. I think she knew she would never see me again. Witches are said to be able to foretell their own deaths, even to the hour. Outwardly she seemed as healthy as ever. But I never did see her again. She died within the month.

I WAS UP on the hill. Spring at last was once more upon us. Mihai and I had raked all the hay meadows, and now Mihai's cousin Ion and I were ploughing. I walked along in the sun, whip in one hand, leading the horses with the other, the plough rumbling and creaking behind. The horses, with their calm faces, worked patiently and diligently. At the end of each furrow I turned them and Ion dragged the plough around. I now understood why the fields here were long and thin, just as they had been in medieval England.

Passing on a nearby path, a woman called to Ion to ask how I was managing. Everyone knew I was a beginner.

'He's doing as well as some who have been ploughing all their lives!' he shouted back.

'That was kind of him,' I thought, and beamed with pride.

We finished our work, unhitched the horses and settled under an apple tree to rest. The share and the knife now shone like polished silver. The horses nibbled hay and we drank *horincă* from the bottle which Mihai had put in my hand as we were leaving that morning.

I looked out over the valley to the mountains upon whose tops the snows were now melting. During the winter I had firmly decided to return to Halma when the weather improved. There was now a warmth in the air. I would go in a few days' time. I knew I would be replacing my quiet life with chaos and uncertainty but the Gypsy spell, as Mihai and others would have it, was too strong to resist.

I lay down on my new *pieptar*-waistcoat to read and fell into a doze. A horse had lost a shoe and Ion had taken her down to the Gypsy blacksmith. There was time to sleep. When I awoke it was to all the familiar country sounds of that time of year: the creak of a plough, the call of ploughmen on neighbouring strips, the bleat of sheep grazing the meadows, the high-pitched whistles of the shepherd boys, and the lilting chatter of women planting potatoes in a field on the other side of the valley. People had walked by on the paths while I had been asleep, but of course no one disturbed me. My book lay open where I had dropped it, the pages gently turning over in the breeze.

II

The Moon Wanders Freely

*Then I realized that these people are still intimately familiar with the
art of killing, blood is something they know well, and the flash of a knife
is as natural to them as the smile of a woman.*

Sándor Márai, *Embers*

To MIHAI'S DISAPPOINTMENT, soon after the ploughing, I left
the calm and security of Breb and once more journeyed south
to find Natalia. The night before I departed there had been wild
weather. Last year's hayricks were looking tousled and the now
wispy tails of the night's storm clouds were untangling themselves
from around the pointed peaks above the village and hurrying off
towards the High Carpathians and beyond, eastwards to the rolling
Moldavian hills and the Bessarabian steppes. I wound my way along
the tortuous road up the mountain and crossed the pass heading
south, and descended into Transylvania, where the huge beech
woods were now bushy with leaves, all growth a few weeks more
advanced than in the colder north.

I arrived in Halma in the early evening, and it was not long before
things started to go wrong. I went first to the house of Herr and
Frau Knall, expecting the usual warm and friendly greeting. I did
not receive one. They would not even let me into the house. Only
from behind a half-closed window were they prepared to talk to
me, to tell me that their beloved altarpiece had been stolen from the
church. I was horrified.

'But who stole it?' I asked.

'The Gypsies,' came the answer. They quickly closed the window and drew the curtain across to show that the conversation was firmly over.

I walked into the village square, my head spinning with the news, and headed for Natalia's house, anxious not to bump into the Lad on the road.

I walked into the courtyard and found her barefoot, nonchalantly drying dishes with her skirt.

'You have come back,' she said coolly.

'Yes,' I said. 'Why didn't you write to me? I would have come sooner.'

'Best for you to come in your own time. Anyway you do what you like.'

'Don't you?'

'Yes, of course.'

'Where is the Lad?'

'Still worried about the Lad? You don't need to. He is in prison. You can come and live here now without fear.'

'Do you still want me to come?'

'Yes,' she said. 'If you want to.'

She looked at me with her large almond-shaped and hazel-coloured eyes. '*Ochi căprui, / Fură inima oricui*', as Romanians say – 'Hazel eyes / Will steal anyone's heart.' I was persuaded to plunge myself into the maelstrom of her and her family's life.

For Natalia's part I think she had little more than a playful curiosity about me, an inquisitiveness as to the nature of this difficult-to-place foreign entity, who had suddenly appeared in their midst and who, intriguingly, spoke Romanian with a rather quaint country accent. It might be an amusing diversion for her to have me around for a while. I was infatuated with her, as were many other men. She was prepared to put up with me for the time being.

I asked her how life had been since we had last met.

'Not great. My uncle died. He was only thirty-four and had four children,' she said.

'But if he was so young how did he die?' I asked.

'The police took him in when the altarpiece was stolen and by the time he came back that evening he was finished,' she said.

My head was spinning again.

'Your uncle stole the altarpiece?' I said, appalled by everything I was hearing. I remembered how Herr Knall had shown me the altarpiece with such pride a few years before and had explained to me how it had been specially made for the church in 1513. I had told the Knalls that I would help them protect it, and repair the roof to stop the rain pouring in upon it. Now I was hearing that Natalia's family were the prime suspects for the theft.

Natalia put me right.

'Of course he didn't steal it. Everyone always blames the Gypsies. Didn't you know that?' she said, becoming upset. 'Please let's not talk about it. He was taken to the police station and he died the next morning. That is it. That is how our life is here.'

'But what happened?' I asked.

'Who knows?' she said.

'Can't you find out?'

'I doubt it. Anyway it is for his wife to make a complaint, not me, although here complaining just makes things worse.'

I MOVED INTO the family house. All Natalia's siblings were there, but not her parents who were away working in Hungary. Often during those days I wished I could return to the peace and sanity of Breb. I could hardly believe the situation in which I now found myself. The more I thought about it the more anxious I became. I was in the process of raising money to protect the Saxon churches and their contents. I had written a pamphlet about the situation, and money was already coming in. But now it was possible that I was living with the very family who had stolen the altarpiece. And the main suspect, Natalia's uncle, was now dead. Had he been killed deliberately or was it an accident? What had happened? I knew almost nothing. I had expected surprises, but this one outdid any that I could have foreseen. Whatever happened, for the present I had to remain in the dark, nervously wondering what the truth might be.

★

THE ATMOSPHERE OF *dolce far niente* which I had experienced when I had first been in Natalia's house a couple of years before still very much hung in the air. Sometimes the brothers would work in the fields ploughing the potato patch or planting, but Natalia did not really go in for work. Occasionally she would clean the house or wash clothes. Otherwise she would lie languidly on a bed listening to music from her battered tape recorder, rising occasionally to move about the room, dreamily practising her dancing steps.

Only when evening came around did she start to become animated. Each day, as the sun was going down, everyone assembled in the village square waiting for the village herd, the *ciurda*, to return from the hills. In the square each animal paused for a drink at the water fountain before making its way back to the stables.

This was the time to meet and chat. Almost the entire village was assembled, even those who had no animals. It was a congenial way of passing the early evening. For the Gypsy contingent, and especially for Natalia and her sister Marishka, it was the moment to plan the evening's entertainment. Practically every evening there seemed to be a party, where young and old, almost all Gypsies, danced as if there were no tomorrow. Their lives were so difficult and so uncertain they might just as well enjoy themselves while they could. Certainly for Natalia and Marishka, and all the other Gypsies, it seemed to be their *raison d'être*.

Anywhere was a good enough place to have a party; in the summer on the mound-like hill, the Huiberi, above the village where, from the square, you could see the fire flickering and the silhouettes of people dancing, or in the winter in one of the abandoned and now half-ruined Saxon houses, as long as the wooden floorboards were still there, and as long as a light bulb could somehow be made to work using electricity 'borrowed' by means of a wire hooked illicitly over the nearest passing power line.

At such parties everyone danced the traditional Gypsy dances, the young imitating the old. It was fascinating to watch them, the men especially, their arms and legs moving in such bewildering and mesmerizing patterns, too complicated to imitate, and so fast, with fingers clicking and hands slapping thighs and the heels of shoes, that it seemed as though their feet hardly touched the ground. The girls too compelled attention, but for different reasons. Dancing was something they had distilled to a fine art. During the day, I had noticed that, like Natalia, many of the Gypsy girls would put a tape recorder on a windowsill, and, in the road or in the courtyard in front of their houses, practise their steps, moving their hips in rhythm with the music, always gradually perfecting the rituals of provocation. Now at the dance they moved so erotically, Natalia in the midst of them, that I sometimes felt I ought to avert my eyes, as though I was witnessing something which should have been private between two people. It seemed as though they were making love to the air. To this provocation the young lads would tear off their shirts and dance half naked, showing off their bodies honed by long days scything in the fields, which soon would shine with sweat in the glow of the flickering light bulb.

My memory of the days I spent with Natalia is hazy. They were dominated by a whirl of parties, one following hard upon the other and often continuing long into the night. She and the other Gypsies had extraordinary stamina. The dancing seemed almost never-ending; for when Natalia eventually arose from her bed, she would put a cassette into her faithful tape recorder – which cunning Gypsy hands and judicious use of string, wire and glue had kept going well beyond the end of its natural life – and would dance around the room or the courtyard in a world of her own.

'NOT CARING TO command,' wrote Franz Liszt of the Gypsies, 'they neither choose to obey.' This described Natalia. She was wild and wilful and did entirely as she pleased. I was Natalia's lover, but when the spirit took her, on a whim, she would disappear and have romantic meetings with others whether I liked it or not. At these times I would go to the *crîşma* and ask Marishka if she knew where Natalia had gone. She would shrug her shoulders and cast me a look of sympathy.

Inevitably, in the end I discovered that Natalia did not always tell the whole truth. I had been away for a few days deliberately to escape from the chaos, and while I had been absent she had been with another man. She had tried to hide it from me, but I knew what she had been doing. I confronted her with the evidence. She was not shaken.

'I don't know why, but men are always falling in love with me,' she would say airily, by way of explanation.

'Anyway, I thought it was better that you did not know,' she went on. 'You might have been upset, done something stupid and got hurt.' She had, therefore, done me a favour.

'And you were away. What was I supposed to do?' she said. 'I had no idea when you were coming back, *if at all.*' The justifications of her outrageous lies combined with her disarming truthfulness would make one quite giddy, and somehow in the end she left you thinking that she had barely done anything wrong. Either way, I did not feel it was my place to try to restrict her freedom, and was inclined to agree with the old man in Pushkin's story *The Gypsies* (which he had written when in love with a Gypsy in Moldavia) who advised the outsider, Aleko, about the Gypsy girl, Zamfira:

Do not be sad . . . You are upset unreasonably. You love anxiously and earnestly. A woman loves playfully. Look how in the sky the full moon wanders freely, casting her light equally over all the world . . . Who would point out to her one place in the heavens and say 'There will you stay'? And who is to say to a young girl 'You must love only once'?

Of course Natalia's playfulness did sometimes cause her problems, and as a result she was always on her guard. One day when we were about to enter the *crîşma*, she drew a knife out of her pocket, carefully opened up the blade, and slipped it back.

'Natalia,' I said, 'why did you do that? Is there going to be trouble? If so, it would help to know in advance.'

Her response was laconic. 'You never know. Anyway, it's better to be prepared.'

Judging by what happened on another occasion her advice seemed sensible, but whether anyone was prepared or not, this time it was Marishka who came to the rescue. Natalia was dancing in the *crîşma*, moving her hips in a way that she knew only too well was likely to arouse violent passions. Her intention was to make me jealous. In the Gypsy world, only in this way can you truly tell whether a person loves you. Instead of making *me* jealous, however, she upset someone else. Out of the darkness of the village square there appeared a man in the doorway. To my horror I saw that it was the Lad. It seemed he had not been in prison but only in temporary custody. Striding across the room towards Natalia, he whipped out a knife whose blade glinted in the glow of the lamp. I was sitting next to Marishka, in the shadows. We had been laughing together, but her face changed in an instant, and she jumped to her feet. The Lad, his eyes blazing with anger, swung the knife at Natalia and her dancing partner. As it flashed through the air Marishka threw herself in its path and tried to grab his arm. The knife was moving fast and she caught only the blade. It sliced through the skin right up to the joint between her thumb and forefinger. Pandemonium broke out. Dancers were spattered with blood as together they struggled to wrest the knife out of the Lad's hand. Marishka walked out clutching her wound. At the dispensary in the town they had no anaesthetic and sewed up the gash with six rough stitches. As the needle went in and out Marishka did not once complain.

I KNEW I could not bear all the excitement for much longer, especially as the Lad was now back to liven things up still further. Life with Natalia had been an eye-opening experience, and indeed I had at last learned how properly to 'make fire', but it had been exhausting. I admired her recklessness but could not endure it for long. She was all too similar to Pushkin's Gypsy girl. Like the moon moving through the night sky, she lit each cloud brilliantly, but then inevitably drifted on to others. It was clear that she was already drifting on to another and I saw it was time to leave. I told her one day that I was going to return to the north. Now it was Natalia's turn to be upset. I did not want to hurt her, and was surprised she should care, but I was tired out and did not have the strength to change my mind.

Travelling back to the Maramureş I kept thinking of the death of Natalia's uncle. Often over those weeks I had wondered whether he might have been involved in the theft of the altarpiece, despite what she had said to the contrary. For the moment it remained a mystery. It was only later that I came to hear the horrifying and gruesome details of what had actually happened.

As I reached the top of the pass in the evening and came down towards Breb, I saw the village's ten little 60-watt street bulbs flick-ering. Behind it loomed the vast blackness of mile upon mile of forested hill and mountain which until then had acted as the barrier between the old Maramureş and the 'outside world'.

12

A Double Wedding

The Maramureş is one of the . . . strangest places on earth.
Sacheverell Sitwell, *Roumanian Journey*

I RETURNED WITH enthusiasm to my old way of life. Mihai was overjoyed that I had come back in one piece, once more, to the cocooning safety of the Maramureş, and we went out each day together to work in the fields. I was still very happy in Breb but was sad to see how life there was gradually changing. In 1997 there had been an election and a new Western-leaning government was elected. It was not long before global corporations, in the pursuit of profit at any price, sent slick advertising companies to Bucharest, with the aim of selling the peasants things which they had never needed or wanted before. A new sort of advertisement started appearing on the television. People crowded agog around the few sets in the village and watched in amazement as naked women bathed in showers using some highly desirable new soap called shampoo, danced on beaches drinking Coca-Cola, or in shockingly short skirts sang the praises of coffee percolators. The old were horrified by such improper images evidently intended to trap the young; the young were horrified to be missing out on all the fun and began to question the traditional ways. Ideas from the other side of the mountain began to infiltrate, which would eventually destroy the way of life of the old Maramureş.

IN THE FIELDS we did not see Ion and Vasile any more and I missed their happy conversation. They had gone off to learn a profession in the town on the other side of the mountains. It had been a big step for them. It would be a frightening and disorientating experience for someone from such a village to live in a big and comparatively modern town, but they had not wanted to be left behind, and no doubt they too did not want to miss out on all the excitement hinted at by the new television.

That summer the weather had been particularly hot and on a free afternoon Ion and Vasile had been persuaded by their new town friends to go to a nearby lake to cool down. Everyone except Ion and Vasile knew how to swim. People from the countryside did not learn to swim. Ion, however, did not want those from the outside world to think that he was either afraid or backward, and he jumped in. He might not have done so if he had known how deep it was.

WHEN THE NEWS first started to filter through of Ion and Vasile drowning in the Blue Lake nobody believed it. There were after all no bodies. The two of them lay embraced at the bottom of the lake for three days. Then at last they were found and brought to the surface. They had left the village full of hope for the future, and came back in coffins. The modern world had made short work of them.

'THERE WILL HAVE to be a double wedding,' said Mihai. 'Neither of them was married.'

'A wedding? But they are dead, Mihai,' I said, confused.

'Yes, but they will have to be married nonetheless. It is our custom,' he said.

'But who will they marry?'

'A couple of girls from the village,' he replied.

WHEN THE BODIES were brought back Mihai approached me.

'I must go and see the boys. Please come with me,' he said.

We walked up in the twilight along the paths through the orchards, Mihai in front, bent slightly forwards, straw hat and stick, silent and solemn, very much the village elder on important business.

We passed people returning from the fields, hoes over their shoulders.

'Where are you going, Uncle Mihai?' they asked.

'To Vasile's.'

'Oh what a terrible thing to happen,' they said, shaking their heads and looking grave. 'The poor boys, they were only children.'

As we approached the house in the gloaming through the fruit trees, picking our way over the freshly scythed grass, up ahead in the courtyard we could make out a group of people. The house was on the edge of the village, silhouetted against the mountain and the last blue light of day.

A woman walked about with her head in her hands. An old man, the grandfather, with hair wild and unkempt, like a character out of a Greek tragedy, saw us coming. With arms raised in front of him, as though carrying some large object, he came towards us.

'Oh Mihai, we should all live to old age. Then there would not be so much woe.'

'It is true, Gheorghe. At least when we die there will not be so many tears.'

'They died each embracing the other,' said an aunt, 'that is how they were found at the bottom of the lake! The poor things, two brothers beloved of their mother, clutched in each other's arms. Oh, that such a thing should have happened, both taken at the same time, one would have been bad enough, but both . . . Though perhaps it is better they have gone together for how could one have lived without the other.' Her speech tailed off towards the end into tears.

'Come,' they said, 'come inside and see them.'

We followed into the small wooden house. The boys had been underwater for nearly three days before they had been found. The lake was deep and dark. I dreaded to think what they would look like.

On the floor lay two simple bare wooden coffins side by side. A young man, a cousin, stood at the head of the coffins. With feet astride to give him balance he opened the heavy lid of the first. There Vasile lay dressed in his Sunday best: white pressed smock, black curly sheep's wool waistcoat, and the Maramureşean straw hat tilted over his brow. His skin was waxen and dun coloured, but he was not disfigured and not the shocking sight I had been expecting.

The women in the room began weeping at the sight of the boy.

'Oh, the poor thing, the poor thing,' one of them sobbed, 'he jumped into the water to try to save his elder brother.'

The cousin, struggling to keep the unwieldy lid open, pleaded with us in a loud and urgent voice.

'Touch him, touch him, feel how cold he is! Don't be afraid.'

Mihai leant over and put his hand on Vasile's hand.

The second coffin was opened. I saw Ion's now waxen face. His fingers were wrinkled from being in the water, his lips too. Only recently I had seen him singing and dancing at Christmas. I remembered how he had run up to me smiling with the letter from Natalia, and had wished me luck in 'the outside world'.

We crossed ourselves, and Mihai bent over again and touched the boy's hand.

'May God forgive them and let them rest in peace,' he said.

'They both used to go to church every Sunday. They were good boys,' said one of the women; there was therefore no question of God having punished them.

Outside in the near darkness stood the mother and father. The younger sister, the only surviving child, stood in the veranda of the main house looking down at us, silent and staring.

'She had been so looking forward to her brothers coming home to play with them, but they came back in boxes,' said the mother, through tears.

'This is a terrible happening,' said Mihai.

'God gave them to us and now he has taken them away,' replied the mother.

'May they rest in peace,' said Mihai and we walked away, carefully back down the paths in the darkness leaving the family to their grief.

ON SATURDAY MORNING I went up to the coppices with Mihai to cut hazel wands. We brought them back by cart and stuck them in the ground by each new bean shoot in the vegetable garden. Then in the evening in the orchard I mowed enough grass to last for the next two days, the two Whitsun holidays, as we would not be able to work again until Tuesday. Sparrows followed me, eating the grubs revealed at each swing of the scythe. When I leant over to take a handful of cut grass with which to clean the blade before honing it they all flew away in a flurry and perched on the branches of the plum trees to wait until I was harmlessly occupied in mowing again.

Everyone I met during the day asked me what the drowned boys looked like. In the evening, in the street filled with people chatting on their way home from the fields, a woman told us who would be the wives, best men and maids of honour at the funeral. All afternoon a team of men, all kinsmen of the boys, had been digging a large double grave. They too passed by as we talked, having finished their work, with picks, shovels and measuring sticks over their shoulders.

ON SUNDAY MORNING the village was awoken by bells – two ten-minute-long peals, one for each of the drowned boys. They were rung with especial solemnity.

At midday I walked up the same green paths on the edge of the village as two days before, only on this day I was joined by hundreds of others, all dressed in their sober Sunday best, all making their way in a long line in single file, as the paths across the hay meadows are narrow, up the hill to the funeral. Again today the sun was beating down, the sky was blue and cloudless, almost oppressively so. As we approached we could hear the cries of keening women.

In the courtyard outside the house these women, relations of the boys, walked about slowly in front of the assembled mourners, as though on stage, sobbing and wringing their hands. An aunt with tired, staring eyes sang a rhymed lament:

'Goodnight, Ionuc and Vasile, Goodnight once more I say, but you say nothing, your hearts are of stone and your mouths are cold for you have been so long in the waters of the lake. Hey, come children, beloved of your mother, come in the evening at dinner time and look in at the window. You will see then that, instead of eating our dinner, we shall be crying.'

All around the edge of the courtyard women, some with hair let down underneath their headscarves, as is traditional at funerals, listened and dabbed their eyes. The little sister, Ileana, dressed all in black, her hair coming down below her waist, stood with hands folded in front of her by the entrance to the house where the brothers lay. She seemed strangely calm but the rims of her eyes were red

'Oh little Ileana,' sang one of the keening women, 'left without any brothers. Oh Vasile and Ionuc, how could you have been so cruel as to leave your little sister all alone. Oh Death, Death and Death again, terrible and without justice, you part brothers and sisters without mercy.'

The lamenting continued unabated, fearful and haunting, always to the same plangent tune, the last words sustained in a pitiful sigh, each couplet repeated twice so as to give time to compose the next heart-rending line. One of the women broke down for a few moments and wept with a handkerchief over her face before continuing: 'How beautifully your mother dressed you and sent you off to school, but you went and entered into the water, and the water sucked you to your death, it drowned you and, Lord, how much we are in pain, for Oh Ionuc and Vasile, when you left home you did not properly say goodbye, neither to your mother nor to your father, as you thought you would be coming back.'

Mihai pointed out the grandmother. She was walking about by herself, keening not in the traditional way, but more quietly, staring in front of her, hands clasped on her chest, saying over and over again, 'Oh if only there might have not been such a great calamity.'

When she neared the veranda she leant her head against the wooden columns among the leaves of the young vines which curled their way up to tangle themselves in the eaves. Up here in the north by the mountains the grapes will never ripen.

'Oh beloved of your mother, sons,' the lamenting verses went on, 'you will be married young to the daughters of an Emperor, the brides of the sky, but when you leave with your betrothed you will never come back. When Sunday comes around we will look for you but you will not be there, so we will look for your hats to remind us of you, all decorated with flowers, but you will have taken those with you too.'

Before long two girls dressed as brides, posies in their hands, could be seen walking across the fields towards the house, their faces covered by white veils, and followed by their maids of honour. When they reached the house they proceeded straight into the room where their dead 'future husbands' lay and took their places solemnly at the head of their respective coffins.

In the Maramureş the similarity between weddings and funerals is unmistakable. Both involve irreversible departures, hence the many tears shed at weddings as a beloved son or daughter leaves the family home for ever. Marriage is, however, one of the main purposes of life. So when a person dies unmarried, but is of marriageable age, he must, without fail, be married before he is buried. For this reason a symbolic marriage was about to take place, between two young girls and two boys who were already dead, dead in fact for nearly a week, three days of which had been spent underwater; it was verging on the macabre, but it had to be done, for the boys must not be given any reason for feeling that their lives had been unfulfilled.

In Romania there is an ancient ballad called *Miorița*. Everyone knows *Miorița*, but it is so old that nobody knows its origin. It tells of a young shepherd who discovers he is about to be killed by his two envious companions and so begs one of his lambs to pass on a last message to his mother. 'Ewe lamb, small and pretty, for her sake have pity,' he whispers. 'Let it just be said, I have gone to wed a princess most noble on the threshold of heaven.' The shepherd of

Miorița dignifies his death in the same way as the peasants of Breb who marry their dead children to the daughters of an Emperor. 'The sun and the moon held our wedding crown,' so the shepherd goes on, 'the mountains were our priests, the birds were our musicians, many thousands of birds, and the stars of the sky were our candles.' The shepherd accepts his fate. In Breb the two drowned boys must be persuaded to accept theirs too; if they do not, their unquiet spirits, or *strigoi* as Romanians call them, will be tempted to return.

The Church of course does not go along with this idea, but nor does it try to stop it. For the missionaries of the Byzantine Church, when they first reached these remote valleys sometime in the Dark Ages, were forced to make compromises if they were to have any hope of convincing the local people to worship their new God. Perhaps one of the effects of these compromises was the extraordinary theatre I was witnessing that day. The priest performs a conventional Christian funeral service and the peasants reinterpret it for themselves as a wedding. In their gold-braided robes the priests, holding crosses and swinging censers, look on impassively as the peasants weave their pagan rituals in and out of the Orthodox obsequies.

The room where the lads lay was full of people, most with looks of horror on their faces and crossing themselves. The women held handkerchiefs or walnut leaves to their noses. Since Friday there had been two sweltering summer days. There was a sweet, sickly odour in the room and the boys' hands were beginning to show signs of decay. The two waterlogged corpses were now wearing finest wedding clothes, their smocks intricately stitched and embroidered, and their waistcoats covered in multicoloured tassels with tiny round mirrors sewn on to them to deflect evil. Scattered over them was every sort of wild flower from the fields, and sprigs of evergreen box were stuck into the bands of their straw hats. Their arms clasped round loaves of bread, and in them were pressed, presumably to pay the ferryman, not just one coin as in Roman times, but as many coins as they could possibly have fitted; no expense was to be spared.

Back out in the fresh air the courtyard was now crammed full of people. The best man, carrying the ritual wedding pole bedecked with bells and strands of headscarves, hurried about among the crowd organizing matters just as he would have done at a wedding. In the corner of the yard stood a violinist next to a group of ten teenage girls, all dressed in white. He raised his violin to his chin and played, and the girls began to sing to its sorrowful tune:

'Oh Ionuc and Vasiluc, look how well you are to be married, to the daughters of an Emperor, the brides of the sky. Raise yourselves up and see what beautiful wives await you. Your brides will want to have children, but you are leaving us only to make black earth. Your brides will want to enjoy themselves but you are leaving us only to putrefy.

'On the edge of a lake a big wind blew, and soon after they brought us the news that we should put on black clothes and come to a funeral. But instead we have come to your wedding, and dressed ourselves up in our wedding clothes, and we have not let down our hair.

'Look how troubled are your mother and sister, but it is not only they who are upset, the girls will be too, and so will the place where the flowers grow, for no longer will you come to pick the crocuses, buttercups and marjoram to decorate your hats when you go to the dance.'

Mihai took my arm.

'The priests are coming,' he said.

On the path below the house I could see the ecclesiastical party making its way across the fields carrying black church banners. As they approached we could hear their solemn chants carried up to us on the summer breeze. They walked into the courtyard and straight into the house. When the Breb priest came out he was visibly moved, running his index finger across each eye and flicking away the tears. Then, taking a deep breath, as though to give him strength, he proceeded into the second house where *horincă* and food were served.

Now the moment for the coffins to be taken out of the house had come. One of the aunts sang imploringly: 'Hey Ionuc, Hey Vasiluc, awake! Do not sleep! Your brides as beautiful as flowers have arrived. They came in one by one but you did not say a word to them. Bridesmaids and best men have come but you do not want to talk. Beloved of your mother, Ionuc! Vasile! Get up! Do not sleep! Put yourselves behind the table and play the host, get up and talk to us for straightaway we have to part.'

The mother then sang for the first time since I had arrived: 'Hey Ionuc and Vasiluc, beautiful were your names but short were your days, you were as beautiful as blossoms, but now you will melt like the dew of the morning when it goes from the flowers.

'With much hardship we brought you up, many nights we did not sleep, many tears we shed until you had grown, but now I will cry for as long as I live, and my heart will be full of pain. Hey Ionuc and Vasiluc, I do not know for which of you I will cry the more. Sit up just one last time and kiss me, kiss me on the cheek, and this kiss must last me for the rest of my life.'

The coffins, still open, were lifted up and carried out through the crowd of mourners who craned their necks to see. Each coffin was followed by its party of bride, bridesmaids and best man shaking the wedding flag up and down and left and right, its bells jingling and its headscarves flapping.

They were carried into the orchard where they were placed on trestles and the family gathered round them. The grandfather stood motionless, staring fixedly at the boys, his old face betraying a battered stoicism. Flies were settling on his grandsons' faces and from time to time he would flick them away from their lips with a white handkerchief. The mother bent over the boys each in turn, all the time mumbling, 'Mother's chicks, mother's dear boys', and the sister stood impassively, her big eyes staring ahead of her, red from the gentle, constant flow of tears. All around people pressed in to catch a glimpse. There was a grim curiosity to see the lads who had lain underwater for so long.

For well over an hour we stood in the heat as the priests led the service and tried to find comforting words.

'God's thoughts are not our thoughts, God's plans are not our plans. Just as women take great care to plant their garden and then pick their most beautiful flowers for the church on Sunday, so the Lord did with these two boys . . .'

Most mourners could find shade under the apple trees but the coffins lay in the sweltering sun and the boys' faces looked worse and worse as the minutes passed and all three priests, one by one, gave their long addresses. Flies continued to gather. The family brushed them away. When they could no longer keep them off, transparent white muslin was laid over the boys' faces and the flies trapped underneath were flushed out one by one. From time to time the brides looked down at the steadily deteriorating faces of their 'husbands'.

At last the orations were over and the pagan wailings against an unjust world resumed. Twelve unmarried boys hoisted the coffins on to their shoulders and the violinist once more raised his violin to his chin. But this time the music took me by surprise. It was no longer the mournful dirges of before. All around people were weeping and wailing. But the violinist had struck up the merry wedding march of the Maramureş. It was a contrast which confused the senses. The atmosphere instantly changed; having been heavy with tears and grief, suddenly, at the suggestion of the lilting music, it became lighter and people began to talk. The best men shook their wedding poles and the procession, headed by the coffins, followed by the brides and their maids, set off along the narrow paths across the fields to the church, the violin music swirling, the drum booming and the bells on the poles rattling in rhythm.

As they left the courtyard I heard a woman sing, 'Hey Ionuc and Vasiluc, as you leave break off a flower from the magic elder tree and stick it in the eaves of the veranda. Leave it there for your parents so their grief will pass more quickly.'

Three shepherds stood on a little hill above the house. They blew a long blast on their horns which resounded about the hills and valleys. Then as the procession wound along the village lanes, women wailing and the violin playing, the shepherds ran on ahead to position themselves on other knolls and mounds above the path to the cemetery to blow their last salutes.

At all crossroads and bridges, places which historically are charged with spiritual energy, and where evil spirits are said to lurk, the procession stopped. The violinist dropped his violin, the best men ceased rattling their bells, the keeners hushed, the men bowed their heads and the Christian world was allowed its prayers for a few moments. Then the shepherds blew a blast on their horns and the pre-Christian world took over again.

All the people by the roadside were in tears. An old lady, bent with age, stood in the garden of her wooden house with her hands together in front of her face, like a saint in prayer, occasionally moving them back and forth imploringly. Her husband stood with his hat held to his chest and head bowed.

Now the church bells added their tolling to the great swell of noise as the hundreds of people approached the graveyard and pressed in around the gaping double grave, at the head of which the coffins were laid. The brides came to a halt next to them, looking down upon their soon-to-be-buried 'husbands'. On top of the pile of newly dug earth stood a group of children peering into the coffins with expressions of both horror and fascination upon their faces.

'Be happy, Cemetery!' sang the wailing women as they wept and beat their brows. 'We have brought beautiful flowers to plant in you, but we have not brought them to blossom, but to decay. Oh Ionuc and Vasiluc, look where you will now be living, at the bottom of this hole where there is never sun, where it never snows, rains or freezes, where there is never dew and there is never morning. Oh Ionuc and Vasiluc, in the summer where will you mow, in the summer where will you make hay? Here in the cemetery under a walnut tree. There you will be working, and your grandmother, who is also here, will make the haycocks, the grandmother who loved you so much, how surprised she will be to see you so soon.'

The mother was now distraught. 'Oh how I am destroyed. You, Death, have taken both my sons at the same time, why did you not take me instead?' She flung herself down on the ground and threw her arms about as though washed over by waves of grief. The men tried to put on the lids of the coffins but she brushed them aside several times before they managed to lodge them into place and drive long blacksmith's nails through the tops and into the sides.

As the coffins were lowered slowly by men straining on ropes the women became hysterical and the keening reached a fever-pitch. Gheorghe son of Petru, who had been with us all at Christmas, was looking down into the grave with tears pouring off the end of his nose on to the coffins. Ion and Vasile's little sister stood upright in the same pose she had held all day, hands together on her lap, but now tears were coursing down her cheeks.

Then, in sudden contrast to the violin which had been playing the merry wedding tunes ever since we left the house, there came the loud hollow thudding of stones and earth upon the lids of the coffins as the grave began to fill. The violinist lowered his bow.

'Well,' said Mihai, who I found to be standing next to me, 'they have gone, they have been married to the earth.'

Now was the time for the funeral meal. But the mother would not leave the graveside.

'No, no, let me be with my children,' she shouted.

'Come,' the men said firmly, 'there is work to be done at the house.' They lifted her up and she let herself be led away.

We ate on long tables set up in the orchard, a rich lamb broth followed by cabbage rolls and then cakes all washed down with many swigs of *horincă* passed round from one person to another and drunk straight from the bottle. Every time we drank we raised the bottle and said, 'May God forgive them and let them rest in peace.' The Gypsy basket-makers who had camped on the edge of the village had joined the gathering, the whole family of eight. They, like others there, had not known the boys, but the food at funerals is too good to miss and is given to all comers.

After the meal the funeral once more became a wedding as the violinist lifted his violin to play music for dancing. The young stood up and, as at a wedding, danced the rushing *Învîrtita* and the *Sîrbi* in a big circle, arms over each other's shoulders, laughing and smiling.

Mihai and I left while the music was still going on, the evening sun lighting up the orchards and spreading its glow over the blue distant hills. The neighbour's children followed us chasing each other through the long grass, falling over when they were caught and tumbling about giggling. From a distance we could still hear the violin playing and see the silhouettes of the dancers among the apple trees.

'Well, what a thing,' said Mihai as we walked slowly homewards. 'I have seen my two cousins married, and both of them on the same day.'

DURING THAT SUMMER, autumn and winter, Mihai mentioned to me many times how much he would like it if I were to settle down and marry in the Maramureş.

'Think what a wonderful wedding you could have here,' he said.

'And when we die you could have our house – after all we have no children to give it to,' he added.

'I would like to, Mihai, and it is such a kind offer. But I can't marry just anyone,' I said.

So each Sunday Mihai would take me down to watch the promenade, and on Saturdays he would try and persuade me *să merg la fete* – to go courting. At other times while walking around the village we would drop in to visit the white witches so as to accustom me to the idea of magic in the hope that one day I might consider untying myself from the Gypsy spell.

When we met girls Mihai did not beat about the bush. If he thought they were suitable he instantly began to stir things up. He considered me too shy and retiring, what he called *moale*. I needed to be more forthright or *aspru*. As a result there ensued a series of embarrassing incidents. Mihai would arrange meetings with fat ones, thin ones, tall ones and short ones, simple down-to-earth girls, and others with airs and graces. Of the slimmer ones, who seemed to me to be the perfect shape, Mihai would say, 'I don't know what is wrong with her – she must have some illness.' Of the plumper ones he said, 'Now *there* is a proper girl. She would be able to help you in the fields lifting the hay right on to the top of ricks.'

There was one girl, called Ana, whom I had met a year or so before and liked more than the others. Mihai had noticed. She was hard working, slim and elegant. While the other girls would boast about their family's accomplishments and property, she simply said, 'Well, we are poor. We have nothing.' I laughed at her frankness. 'No, really,' she said, 'we have nothing.'

One day when passing their wooden house Mihai suggested we go in. It was winter and the loom was set up, taking up the usual third of the room. Ana and her mother were there. Ana who had been bent over the loom stood up, stretched and straightened her back.

'We praise Jesus!' said Mihai as we entered.

'And may He be praised for ever, Amen,' said Ana. 'Uncle Mihai. How nice to see you.'

Glasses of *horincă* were handed around.

'We have come *a peţi*,' said Mihai smiling. I could not believe what I had just heard. *A peţi* means to ask for her hand in marriage and talk about arrangements for a wedding. It was a joke of Mihai's, and I was praying Ana and her mother had realized, but even so it was close to the bone.

'You are a fine-looking girl, Ana,' said Mihai. 'You would be well suited to Willy. The only trouble is Willy is too *moale* with the girls.' I could not silence Mihai as I did not want to offend anyone, so I had to sit there and endure.

'I feel sorry for Willy all by himself in the main house. We sleep in the smaller house in the courtyard,' Mihai continued.

'If you are lonely I will come to keep you company,' said Ana. I went red.

'Oh, I'm all right really,' I said, and added, 'Besides, there is only one small bed.'

'That doesn't matter,' said Ana, as quick as a whistle, 'I'll sleep on top of you.'

Everyone roared with laughter. It was all in good humour, and I laughed too, but I blushed all the more. I would not have minded if she had come, as I *was* lonely, but had things got out of hand I was sure I would have been expected to marry her, and I did not want that.

When we left and were out of hearing I turned on Mihai.

'I was only joking,' he said. 'Anyway she is a wonderful girl and you need someone like me to get you moving.'

THEN AT THE market fair one day I saw a beautiful headscarved face floating through the crowds. The face belonged to a tall, graceful girl who lived in a nearby village. I talked to her and asked if I could visit her. She gave permission. From then on, I went more seriously a-courting, with my tailored *pieptar* and the half bottle of *horincă* which Mihai would always put in my inside pocket before I set off. Năstafă, for this was her name, was delightful and intelligent, and her family always welcomed me with great kindness. When I visited we would dance the Maramureş dances and talk and laugh about the world. But when I left each evening I repeatedly failed to remember to depart without uttering a word, as was the custom. I would politely say goodbye to one and all, and they would stare back at me silently. I always forgot that I was supposed to walk out and leave the door slightly ajar as a sign that I would like Năstafă to follow me.

In the summer I would go and work with Năstafă's family in the fields on the hill, and at sunset we would walk home in the golden light of evening, our wooden tools over our shoulders, weaving down between the trees of the orchards, plucking apples from overhanging branches as we went, motes of dust from the haymaking floating in the air and catching the light as the last rays of the sun burnished the leaves of the trees along the edge of the paths.

I became quite carried away. I imagined myself settling down with Năstafă and living in a little wooden cottage surrounded by fruit trees on the edge of Breb. I would scythe and she, dressed in her skirts and headscarves, would rake and turn the hay.

In the kitchen at home Mihai would catch me deep in thought.

'You are very quiet, Willy. You are thinking of Năstafă,' he would say. He generally knew what was on my mind.

'Yes, I suppose I am,' I would reply.

'You should marry her,' he would say. 'It is time you were married. You cannot always be alone.'

'Yes, I suppose I should,' I would reply.

Mihai was expecting to hear good news soon. But the news did not come. Perhaps she noticed a hesitation on my part. Perhaps by mistake I closed the door too many times when leaving her house. Or perhaps she saw that I was also in love with the old way of life, whereas she had had quite enough of sowing and hoeing potatoes and wanted, with open arms, to welcome in the modern world that was now peeping over the horizon. Whatever the reasons she sensibly decided that our lives and backgrounds were too different for any settling down to be successful. Once again dear Mihai's hopes were dashed.

13

Gypsy Musicians and Hungarian Counts

In every village there are Gypsies who make the music for the people,
swarthy rascals with music dancing in their blood, who can make their
instruments say everything that is in the hearts of men, the birds and
of the very earth itself.

Donald Hall, *Romanian Furrow*

THE SNOW PILED high in the courtyards that winter, so much so that we had to take it away in sleigh loads and dump it outside the village. As always the freezing time passed slowly, but at last the melt came in April, and for a month or so the meadows glittered again with trickling rivulets. Travelling came to mind and so I decided once more, for a change of scene after the long cold months, to make a journey south. I packed my bags and set off in the direction of the Saxon villages. Now that money had been raised to help preserve some of their fortress-churches and old village houses I needed to go there to identify buildings which were in special need of protection. Again Mihai stood at the gate with tears in his eyes, and waved until I was out of sight.

Over the winter my mind had often returned to Marishka and her courage in the bar. There was something intriguing in her combination of beauty and bravery. She was different to Natalia. Natalia was obsessed with men, just as they were obsessed with her. She did not have time for other considerations. Marishka, being the eldest and having borne much of the burden of bringing up her brothers and sister, seemed more thoughtful.

'We must not laugh *too* much,' she once said to me, checking herself after we had been sharing a joke and tears of laughter were running down our cheeks, 'or something sad might happen.'

It was inevitable that while I was in the Saxon lands I would not be able to resist returning to Halma. I stopped first at the house of Herr and Frau Knall. I knew they were relieved that I was no longer with Natalia, and I was hoping that by now enough time had elapsed since their altarpiece had been stolen for them to be able to bring themselves to talk to me. They greeted me, dressed in their work aprons, with smiles. They were able to tell me the happy news that the altarpiece had been recovered somewhere in Hungary and had been returned to the Saxons. The panels were now being looked after in the city of Sibiu. I told them of the money available to repair their church. As we said goodbye they shook my hands warmly and thanked me.

But they added: 'We do hope you are not going to visit the Gypsies.'

There was a sternness in their tone, and in their voices I could sense the many years of frustration at living beside and putting up with the chaos of the Gypsies' lives.

'I might just pass by and say hello,' I said tentatively.

'You must not go and stir things up there again,' they said. 'Natalia has another boyfriend. You must leave. The Gypsies are not for you.'

It did not take me long to disappoint them. I walked into the village square and there were Nicolae and Marishka sitting on the wooden bridge over the stream which flowed along the village green. The stream was now swollen, swirling and eddying with meltwater. I went over to them. They were pleased to see me.

'So what has happened since I last saw you?' I asked.

'*Nimic,*' they replied.

'Yes, of course . . . *nimic,*' I said. 'And not too many more fights, I hope.'

'No, no, not too many, just the usual,' they said.

I told them how impressed I had been by the way Marishka had saved Natalia.

'Marishka is always doing that sort of thing,' said Nicolae.

'No I am not,' she said. 'Shut up.'

'How is your hand now?' I asked her.

'It's fine,' she said and stretched out the thumb and the forefinger to show me the scar between them.

From the village square we followed their two cows and their horse along the road to the house. When we arrived the cows were standing outside, their heads facing the gate, waiting to be let in. They knew where they lived without having to be told. Nicolae opened the gate and the cows made their way into the stables and stood waiting patiently to be milked. Again, they knew what to do. Marishka gathered the buckets from the house, one filled with warm water, and settled down on a milking stool. She washed and rinsed the milk-swollen udders, then placed the empty buckets beneath them and pulled at each of the teats in turn. The milk squirted in a jet into the bucket, creating a froth of tiny bubbles on the surface.

That evening Marishka and Nicolae made up a bed for me and told me I could stay as long as I liked. Natalia was by this time living elsewhere with another boyfriend. We ate a mess of eggs with bread, drank a mug of milk, and were ready to return to the square.

From the house we made our way to the *crîşma*, and as we walked down the track Marishka and Nicolae sent runners to ask their uncles to bring their instruments. Ovidiu and Gabriel appeared half an hour later, trumpet and accordion in hand. Ovidiu puffed out his cheeks and began to play the Gypsy dances, and Gabriel leant into his accordion with a beatific smile on his face, his fingers rolling over the notes. Another man beat out the rhythms on a dogskin drum.

The music was exhilarating and within moments half the occupants of the bar were on their feet. Like all Gypsy bands they had the knack of making people dance and soon dust was jumping from the floorboards. As usual everyone danced in the Gypsy way, and the room overflowed with a feeling of undiluted enjoyment, faces smiling, fingers clicking, and thighs and heels being slapped at speeds which dazzled the senses. The dances had a magic to them and you could sit and marvel at them for hours. Those not dancing clapped their hands, whooped, crying '*Zii Merrrrr! –* Play it, boys!' and raised their glasses and bottles in the air.

Marishka came over during a break in the music, laughing and gasping for breath. She placed a bottle of beer in my hand, and leant over to ask if I was all right. 'It is wonderful,' I told her.

'Yes,' she said, 'it's fun, isn't it, except that Andrei is not here. You remember him, another of our uncles, the violinist.'

'Yes,' I said. 'I am sorry about what happened to him.'

'So are we,' she said as she walked back to the dancers.

IN ABOUT THE year 1010, the Persian poet, Firdausi, wrote an epic poem called *The Book of Kings.* In it he related how the good King Bahram Gur of the Sassanid dynasty, concerned for the welfare of his people, was dismayed to hear that they drank wine unaccompanied by music – a circumstance apparently so uncivilized as to persuade him to dispatch forthwith a diplomatic mission to India to ask King Shangul to send to him without delay several thousand musicians, specifically players of the lute. The musicians duly arrived and the King tried to settle them in Persia; but they did not take to sedentary life, and so he set them on the road again to wander the country earning their living as travelling minstrels. The musicians were called *Luri*, and still today *Luri* exist in that part of the world. In the nineteenth century the English traveller, Henry Pottinger, bumped into a band of *Luri* in Baluchistan. Pottinger, who later became the first governor of Hong Kong, and whose nephew was the celebrated Hero of Herat, describes them as having a striking affinity with the European Gypsies. 'Their favourite pastime', he writes, 'is drinking, dancing and music.' According to Angus Fraser and others, many similar groups of nomadic musicians and metalworkers left India and travelled in the direction of Europe in the early Middle Ages. Some remained in Persia, others travelled further west.

As I had discovered when I first met Marishka, and as I had seen on several occasions since, many of her relations were musicians, or *Lăutari* as they are called in Romania – literally 'players of the lute'. During the days I had spent with Natalia, and now over the coming months in Halma, I learnt more about the story of their family.

Marishka and Natalia's maternal grandfather was called Valentin, and he had for much of his life lived in a small blue-washed house on the margins of the village; and it was from there, before he was married, that he and his brother Vergil used to set off over the hills with their violins and accordions slung over their shoulders, accompanied by their grandfather who had taught them, to play at dances and weddings in all the different villages of the neighbourhood.

Music was their first profession, but they had another particular skill. During the day Valentin and Vergil worked with their father cobbling the pavements and courtyards of the village, and lining wells with stone. Their father, who had never learnt to play music, was an accomplished stonemason who had, according to Vergil, cobbled many of the streets of Sighişoara. As they worked together he taught his sons all he knew, and it was this skill which had saved them during the Hitler War. For in 1942 the music had come to an abrupt end. The Romanian Jandarmes arrived and Valentin, Vergil, their father and other members of their family were arrested. Their gold, two cups full, was confiscated, and they, along with large numbers of other Gypsies, were herded into cattle trucks and sent to concentration camps in an area called Transnistria, many hundreds of miles away on the bleakest shores of the Black Sea. The few members of the family who avoided deportation did not know if they would ever see them again.

When in July and August 1942 the first transports of Gypsies arrived in Transnistria, some still with their horses and carts, some by train, no one seemed to know what to do with them. There were so many families and there did not appear to be a proper plan. One group was housed temporarily in a barracks in the Oceacov district. The concerned local constable described their predicament:

> Winter conditions will make it impossible for the Gypsies to remain in these barracks. First, the roof which they damaged for its wood threatens

to cave in on them; secondly they will die of cold because they are so poorly dressed that if you saw them it would bring tears to your eyes.

When the winter came it was decided to move the Gypsies to another settlement near the Bug river. The constable described the journey:

> . . . the Gypsies are so thin and frozen that they die in their wagons. On the first day 300 died on the road. In the barracks they had lived in an indescribable state of misery, they were insufficiently fed and due to the poor quality of the food they lost so much weight that they shrank into mere skeletons . . . they were full of parasites . . . they are naked, without any clothing . . . there are women with their lower parts completely naked in the true sense of the word . . . In general the Gypsies' situation is terrible . . . because of their misery many of them are reduced to mere shadows and are almost wild . . .

Among those suffering were many old men who had fought for Romania in the First World War. And many of the women were wives of men who were at the time fighting in the Romanian army. While their husbands were risking their lives for their country they and their children were dying in the camps of starvation, cold and typhus. It was an injustice of staggering proportions. Constables from the areas of Balsaia and Karanicain wrote that the Gypsies 'died worse than animals and are buried without a priest'.

In August 1944, as the Russian army was about to enter the country, amid the chaos of war the Gypsies escaped from the camps and made their way back towards Romania. It was a hazardous journey. Many of those who encountered retreating German soldiers were shot. Of the more than 25,000 Gypsies deported to Transnistria only around 6,000 made it back to Romania.

After the war Marshal Antonescu, who had ordered the deportations, was tried and found guilty of war crimes. He was executed on 1 June 1946.

VALENTIN AND VERGIL's family had been settled in Halma for as long as anyone could remember; at least a hundred years, maybe two. The *Lăutari* had to be settled in order to gain a reputation and to be available when required to play at local weddings and dances. But they were as Gypsy as the nomads. When Antonescu started the deportations he arrested the nomads first, but then turned his sights on the settled Gypsies.

Vergil is now old and ill and talks little about what happened in Transnistria.

'We were treated much worse than animals, but then that was their plan,' he said. 'They did not take us there to work, they took us there to kill us. We survived only because we knew how to pave roads and were given slightly better rations.'

I remembered an old Gypsy woman I had met in Moldavia clutching her thick hair and telling me: 'As many people died as there are hairs on my head.'

But Vergil shrugged his shoulders.

'These things happen. We are Gypsies. What can we do?'

He had a fatalistic attitude. Indeed few of the Gypsies whom I met during the years I spent in Romania ever expected compensation. They had survived, they were lucky; others had died. The deportations and the camps had been just another episode in the long history of their suffering.

THERE WAS ONE aspect of the story which was reassuring. Most ordinary Romanians, who were humane country people, were not happy about what was going on. In Transylvania villagers had protested: sometimes whole communities signed petitions against the deportations, though to little effect. The Gypsies were their friends, and as village blacksmiths, musicians, brickmakers, dairymen and manual labourers, they provided valuable services. The leader of the National Liberal Party too, Constantin Brătianu, begged Antonescu to stop the persecutions which, he said, turned back the clock on several centuries of history.

In late 1944 the camp gates were opened, and among the few survivors Valentin and Vergil set off to walk home, with only rags wrapped around their feet as makeshift shoes, dodging the German and the Russian armies as they went. The journey took three months. At last they arrived back to their simple blue-washed house on the outskirts of their village in southern Transylvania, and gradually the music began again.

One evening a few years after their return Valentin and Vergil had walked over the hills to the village of Daia to play at a wedding. They kept fiddling all night long, playing their violins behind their heads to show off, and in the morning, when they set off to return to their village, they took a young girl with them. Valentin had 'stolen' her. Her parents would not have allowed her to go with him, so he took her, with her consent of course, but not with theirs. This was often the way these things were done with the Gypsies.

Having fiddled and fought his way through most of the inns and taverns of Transylvania, Valentin now settled down, after a fashion, with his new 'wife', and together they had an array of children. There were several boys, Ovidiu, Gabriel and Andrei amongst them, who were all taught to play different musical instruments, and several girls, one of whom was the mother of Marishka and Natalia.

It seems there were also other offspring which the grandmother, and perhaps the grandfather as well, did not necessarily know about, conceived by accident in the course of one musical jaunt or another. Half a dozen or more were said to be scattered in various nearby villages, but nobody seemed to know for sure. Indeed there was at all levels of the family a surprising vagueness as to how many brothers, sisters, uncles, aunts or cousins there might be at any one time. When I asked the grandmother how many siblings she had she seemed genuinely unsure, but guessed at seven. Then she remembered another and it was eight. Then someone reminded her of a couple more and it became ten. Who knows how many there really were? Probably nobody.

Valentin's sons all learnt to play instruments when they were young. They learnt in the old-fashioned way, by ear, as did all musicians before the invention of musical notation a thousand years ago. They did not know how to read music. Ovidiu played the trumpet,

Gabriel the accordion and Andrei the violin and saxophone. If all was well, with their father and uncle they made up the village band for wedding dances, Christmas and Easter celebrations and funerals. Only occasionally did others have to fill in when an instrument might 'accidentally' have been broken during a previous outing. Indeed most Gypsy violins in Romania have been glued back together, some of them several times, and most trumpets and saxophones are dented or twisted. At parties there was always a fight of one sort or another, and in the confusion musical instruments often had to be used as weapons. But when there was peace, the music flowed as much as the drink. Andrei's bow rolled across the strings, Ovidiu trumpeted out his staccato notes, red in the face, and Gabriel's fingers flowed over the accordion keys accompanied by the usual happy smile upon his face.

THAT NIGHT I returned to sleep at Marishka and Nicolae's house and met their mother, Clara, and their father, Attila, for the first time. Over the weeks that I had been with Natalia they had been away, working in Hungary. Clara was a dark Gypsy. Attila was, to my surprise, a fair-haired, moustachioed Hungarian, and not a Gypsy at all.

'Come in, come in,' said Attila with arms outstretched.

So this was the man, I thought, who had smashed all the windows.

Attila wasted no time bringing out his home-brewed apple wine from under the table with a flourish. Marishka and Nicolae made signs to warn me not to drink it, but I could not refuse. Glasses and mugs were filled to the brim and we talked into the night.

'Everyone here in the village is mad,' said Attila. 'Have you noticed?'

'Yes, and you are the maddest,' said Marishka.

'Every now and then you have to be a bit mad to protect yourself from the madness of others,' he said.

I asked Attila what it was like to be a Hungarian married to a Gypsy. How did people react?

'Very badly,' he replied, 'but what the hell, people are stupid.'

'You should ask what it is like being a Gypsy married to a Hungarian,' said Clara.

'What is it like?' I asked.

'There is never a *dull* moment,' she said, raising her eyes to heaven.

'Have another drink!' said Attila. 'We like to enjoy ourselves, though others don't approve. I am sure they are right but we cannot help it. Life is too short.'

As we became drunker the music from a tape recorder was turned up and Attila grabbed first Clara and then Marishka and whirled around the room. At one point he started singing snatches of Italian opera.

I climbed into the bed they had made up for me, befuddled with apple wine, at two o'clock in the morning. It had been an enjoyable evening but a nagging and disturbing thought kept recurring in my head: were these Gypsies, however innocent they might seem, actually responsible for the theft of the altarpiece, the altarpiece which I had been trying to protect? Opening one eye before I sank into a coma-like sleep I saw again, pinned on the wall above my head, the old Saxon embroidery, '*Gebet und Arbeit* – Prayer and Work', looking down and admonishing me.

THE MORNING SUN coming through the slatted shutters sliced across the room, and motes of dust were intermittently illuminated as they floated in the warm air. I lifted myself lazily out of bed and washed my face and hands using the jug and basin the family had left for me on the bleached-pine wash stand. I was becoming intrigued by Marishka and her family. There was something different about their manner and bearing. They seemed somehow superior to the other Gypsies of the villages. Having now met Attila I assumed it must have been because of him. He was the one who seemed to be most out of place. I wondered what could be the history of his family?

There was a smell of smoke wafting into the room. Outside in the middle of the courtyard breakfast was being prepared on an open fire and the Gypsies were all squatting barefoot on the ground around it. Some concoction made of beans, mashed and mixed with caramelized onions, was being eaten from bowls with bread, but without spoons or forks. I, however, with great ceremony, was presented with a bent aluminium fork.

All finished their food and departed. Marishka remained, squatting on her haunches by the fire, poking up the embers. I watched her. She seemed every inch a Gypsy. She had the fine Eastern lineaments so characteristic of Gypsies. She behaved like a Gypsy, she had the wild look in her eyes that one expected, and she described herself as a *Ţigană*. When I had first met her and Natalia it had not crossed my mind that they were anything but Gypsies. But now it transpired that their father was Hungarian.

I asked her about Attila. 'Your father seems different from the other people in the village,' I said.

'He *is* different,' she said. 'He is not a country person. He is from the town. From Sighişoara. That was where we were born.'

THE OLD TOWN of Sighişoara has stood on a rock in the middle of Transylvania for 850 years, and its medieval towers and spires have for centuries soared upwards high above the Târnava river. Still today, from their beetling parapets, if you dare to climb up to them, you can see the rolling hills and forests of the Transylvanian plateau stretching for miles in all directions. In places the forest comes close up to the edge of the town, people's gardens disappearing into trees, and sometimes in the middle of winter from the houses nearest the forest you can hear the wolves howling into the night.

Clara, at the age of seventeen, had run away from the village to Sighişoara and had met and 'married' the dashing though considerably eccentric Attila, with his aquiline nose, drooping moustache, and penchant for *palinka*, the Hungarian schnapps.

Although Attila, by some chance, bore one of the most noble and illustrious names in Hungary, his origins were obscure. Born immediately after the war he had been brought up in straitened circumstances by his mother. Then, as a young boy, he had been sent by the

Communist authorities to a correctional school many miles away in the south of the country near the Bulgarian border. As a result, he had hardly known his father who had been shot in the legs by a machine gun on the Russian Front in 1943 and died of his wounds a few years later. Nor did he know either of his grandfathers. His maternal grandfather had been eaten by a bear in the Korund mountains when Attila was still a boy. His paternal grandfather was well into his sixties when Attila's father was born and had died soon after the Great War. Attila one day revealed to me that his mother had told him that this grandfather had been a Count, or *Graf* as he called it.

'But how could that be true', he said, 'when I don't even have enough money to buy a packet of cigarettes?'

Clara and Attila set up home in Sighişoara. They had four children. The eldest of these was Marishka. There then followed Nicolae, Natalia and the youngest, Eugen. To begin with all went well. Attila doted on his delightful children. But as the years went by he became a less and less attentive father. Increasingly he preferred to spend his evenings carousing in the drinking houses of the town and it was not long before he had run out of money. Little by little the apartment in which they lived was emptied of furniture, all sold by Attila to help finance his nightly excursions to sing and dance into the early hours of the morning. When there was no furniture, or almost anything else, left in the house, for Attila was never one to do things by halves, Clara finally decided it was time to leave. One day, when Attila was out enjoying himself in his usual exuberant fashion, she and the children quickly gathered the few clothes left to them, wrapped them up in blankets and put them over their shoulders. They walked out of the house, mother followed by four young children, and set off along the railway line, past the hovels on the edge of town and out into the countryside, leaving the pointed fairy-tale spires and towers of Sighişoara behind them.

After passing several village railway stations, where in the style of Eastern Europe and Russia there are no platforms and people climb up into the trains from the ground, they arrived at the village of Floreni. Here they left the railway line, walked through the dirt streets of the village and then up the hill along cart tracks towards the forest. People scything the hay meadows rested from their work for a few moments to wish them good day and shepherds hailed them in the friendly way of the country while calling off the ferocious dogs who guarded their flocks from wolves and bears.

When they reached the edge of the forest on the top of the hill, they entered into a cool world beneath a covering of glittering green leaves. It was a relief to be in the shade after the hot sun in the meadows but as they wound their way in the silence between the towering trunks of the beech trees Natalia and Eugen clung to their mother at every crack of a branch or hoot of a bird. After what seemed an age, they saw light at the edge of the forest ahead of them and before long they emerged on the other side, from where they could see overlapping hills rolling away for miles into the distance and stretching as far as the dark, jagged silhouette of the Carpathian mountains on the furthest horizon.

Below them, at the meeting of three valleys, was a small village whose Gothic steeple was clearly visible from where they were resting under the trees. The village was surrounded by hills, the lower parts of which were covered with grassland, the upper parts with forest which seemed in some directions to have no end.

This was Halma, the village where the children's grandfather Valentin lived, and it was with him they hoped to be able to take refuge. Valentin still lived in the little blue-washed house on the edge of the village and here the children knocked on the door.

Valentin received them with open arms and tears in his eyes. He adored his grandchildren, and was only too happy to have them to stay. The children's grandmother, however, was more practical. How could so many people possibly fit into such a small house?

So the next day Clara and the children set off again, but this time only as far as the neighbouring village. There they asked the mayor to let them lodge in one of the empty houses in Valentin's village. The mayor was busy, and not pleased at being disturbed by this ragged bunch of Gypsies. 'No,' he told them, 'there are no houses available.' But each morning the little collection of wide-eyed homeless children returned with their mother and sat on the door-steps of the village hall. At last, when people began to gossip, the mayor relented. The house he gave them was dilapidated, but at least it had a roof and walls. They begged panes of glass and planks of wood off people in the village, and managed to make windows and doors. They scrubbed and cleaned, whitewashed inside and borrowed a couple of beds. Valentin made them a stove.

And so began the children's life in the country. They were very poor. They had nothing except the few blankets and clothes they had brought with them, but the young children helped their mother to make a little money in the different ways they could. They worked in the fields, hoeing, raking and collecting hay, or tending sheep. They picked wild raspberries and cherries in the forest in June, wild strawberries in July, hazelnuts in August, walnuts in October, gathered acorns for pigs in November and mistletoe for goats and sheep during the winter. All these things they sold to the Saxons who lived in the village. As the Saxons were so hard work-ing and well organized, they usually had a little money to spare and so were able to buy from the Gypsy children, or at least to give them a bowl of soup or some potatoes, eggs, cheese or bread to take home for the family supper.

Valentin also worked hard to help the children. He scythed all day long in the fields, sold firewood to the Saxons, cobbled court-yards and played music. Occasionally in the evening he would pick up his accordion and play songs for the children, or tell them fairy tales of Sultans and princesses, and milk-white Arabian horses.

Then one evening Valentin did not feel well. He had had a carting accident a few months before and ever since had been suf-fering. He told the children to take care of themselves, to be well behaved and to listen to their mother, and during the night fell asleep and never woke up. He was carried along the streets to his grave on the edge of the Romanian cemetery accompanied by music played by musicians from a nearby village. His sons, and his brother with whom he had spent the long years in the camps in Transnistria, carried their instruments in their hands but, as is the custom, they did not play.

And so it was that Clara and the children came to be living in the village of Halma. A few years later Attila joined them. He had discovered their whereabouts and had, for better or worse, persuaded Clara to allow him to live with them.

'May I be struck down where I stand if I ever cause you any trouble again,' he had said. These were empty words, of course, for wherever Attila went, trouble was never far behind.

14

Red Flags and Renaissance Altarpieces

The Omens at times seemed full of happiness keeping him awake half the night like a sweet, bewildering caress, but often they were dark and terrible.

Hermann Hesse, *Narciss and Goldmund*

ATTILA WAS BUSY heating coffee on the fire in the courtyard. 'If you would like milk, or perhaps *café au lait*,' he said with a flourish, 'be kind enough and go to the cowshed and fill this up. Marishka is milking.'

He handed me a battered enamel mug.

Entering the semi-darkness of the cowshed, warmed by the animals' bodies, I saw Marishka settled on a three-legged stool by the cow.

'I just need some milk for the coffee,' I said.

She took the mug, filled it direct from the cow and handed it back.

Attila lodged the cup on the edge of the fire and set to preparing fried eggs. Marishka appeared five minutes later with a bucket full of frothing milk half of which she poured through a sieve into a saucepan and put it on to boil. Attila then brought up a chair for me, so that I did not have to squat, and handed me an enamel plate of fried eggs, a piece of bread and a mug of *café au lait*. He then put his finger in the air, to show he had forgotten something, and rushed indoors, to return with the fork, which he carefully straightened out and presented to me with great formality.

'There you are! Like in a restaurant!' he said.

He was relishing having someone else in the village whom he considered to be from the city, and who would be able to appreciate his snatches of Italian songs, or his few French words. When he discovered I played chess he embraced me and kissed me on the cheek.

'I am so happy!' he said.

It was a beautiful sunny day. There was a warmth in the air, all the more blessed to those who have lived through months of freezing temperatures. I went for a walk in the village. Blossom was on the pear trees by the track, white and perfumed, and ducks and geese were sitting on the bank of the stream or floating in the pools. Every now and then a horse and cart would clatter by, the driver wishing me good day.

All about me were the solid Saxon houses, painted different shades of blue, green, yellow and pink, but they were crumbling from neglect. Some were falling down, others had collapsed already, gradually sinking back into the earth from which they had been made. I was determined to start work as soon as possible to save those still standing.

Walking across the square, however, I found myself face to face with Barbu, the severe, ex-Communist policeman whom I had met at the time of the incident with the Lad, and who had warned me to keep away from Natalia's family. He was on a visit to Halma from his headquarters, and stared at me coldly.

'I see you have taken no notice of the warnings,' he said.

'I am just here for a short time,' I said. 'I live in the north, in the Maramureş.'

'All the better,' he replied. 'This is not a place for people like you, with all respect.'

As we talked the postmistress approached along the track and joined in our conversation.

'They are the worst Gypsies in the village,' she said. 'You mustn't believe a word they say. They will rob you and cheat you. You must be very careful.'

I retreated to the house. Eugen was playing with the dog, Nicolae had gone off with the cart to collect wood for the fire, and Attila was trying to mend an old radio, wires and transistors all over the table.

'I love to listen to Hungarian music, and Italian, of course, *Italia, Italia . . .* but it has blown up again,' he said.

Marishka had been washing clothes. Now she was hanging them out to dry in colourful display on every available space in the courtyard. Some were laid over the fence, some hung on nails in the barn where the sun occasionally put in an appearance, and some on the wooden rail of the veranda. Her hair shone and the brown skin of her arms glowed in the sunshine as she reached up to arrange the clothes on the line.

When she had finished she poured some milk into a bucket and disappeared into the barn. Looking around the door I saw her squatting next to a young, tawny and white calf of soft velvety coat, which was shoving its head into the bucket and drinking.

She returned with an empty bucket and went indoors, took a rug off one of the beds and told us she was retiring to the orchard behind the house. She then went into the barn and appeared with the calf, still licking the milk off its nose, on a leading rope.

'*Hai!* – Come!' she said to me, beckoning with her head. 'Do you want to come? I am taking the calf to the orchard. It is such a lovely day.'

She spread the rug in the shade of an apple tree and let the calf munch at the grass nearby. Every now and then it would come and poke its small wet nose into our faces, sniffing, or jump about, rejoicing like us in the warmth of the spring day.

I asked Marishka about Barbu.

'I have just seen the policeman in the street.'

'What did he say to you?'

'He said I should leave.'

'He is an idiot. But leave if you want.'

'He doesn't seem to like you very much,' I said.

'No,' she said, 'he doesn't. We are Gypsies.'

'But your father is Hungarian.'

'Yes, but we are Gypsies. We are nothing else but Gypsies. That is how others see us, and that is how we are.'

'But you are theoretically half-Hungarian,' I persisted.

'So what? Our father is wilder than any Gypsy. And he is proud of it. The Gypsies here are afraid of the Romanians and the police. He is not. As a result we constantly have problems. Being half-Hungarian in our case only causes us trouble.'

THE TROUBLE, IT seemed, had begun in the late 1980s, during the last and darkest days of the Communist regime, soon after Attila had traced Clara to the village and had managed to persuade her to let him live with them again.

Life had been difficult for Clara without a husband and for the children without a father, but they had managed. There had, at least, been a degree of peace. It did not take long for Attila to blow that peace to oblivion. Unable to control his rebellious spirit, he did something which marked the family out as troublemakers for years to come.

One crisp winter's evening, having consumed a considerable quantity of *rachiu* in the village *crîşma*, Attila emerged in benevolent mood into the frosty night air. To his right the Communist flag fluttered provocatively outside the village shop. He glared at it out of the corner of a dewy eye, and saw red. Its mere existence was an affront to his pride and disturbed his good humour. In his inebriated state he felt it quite right and proper that it should at once be removed. He walked over, took hold of it, ripped it down, and tore it in two, flinging the two halves disdainfully on to the ground in the snow. Attila was either very courageous, very drunk or very stupid, or possibly all three.

The police came the next day. Someone had informed them that the flag was no longer where it should have been. Attila was walking along the quiet track leading to the village when they found him. They beat him to his knees, apparently with a spanner, and took him away. He was driven to the town of Făgăraş, thrown in a cell and there the beatings continued day and night. What, they kept asking, did he have against the Romanian state? It did not help matters that he was ethnically Hungarian. Every time he fainted they threw water over him to revive him and the beatings started

all over again. This went on for seven days and nights until suddenly the door was opened and he was told to leave. The owner of
the shop had heard what was happening and had made a declaration
to the police: Attila had, he said, slipped on the ice on the steps and
grabbed the flag to save himself from falling; the flag was torn in
half but this was unintentional. Attila came home, but everyone
knew the real story, and from then on the police, and their friends
in the village, kept a close eye on him.

AFTER THE REVOLUTION a degree of peace had returned to the
family, but then there was another unfortunate incident. Marishka
told me about it while milking the cow a few evenings later. It happened at one of the dances and involved a Romanian called Ion.

Ion was the son of a man named Goga. Goga was a huge bear of
a man who, some years before, had beaten the living daylights out
of Nicolae. Nicolae was twelve years old at the time, little more
than a boy, and was tending sheep in an orchard near the village
when he saw Goga walking towards him across the grass. Goga was
smiling and Nicolae was not alarmed. This was, however, Goga's
usual trick since, being as fat as he was, he was unable to run. So
he approached, smiling, to put the young Nicolae at his ease, but
when he was close enough, with a swift grab he took him by the
collar and beat him about the head.

'You Gypsy scum,' he shouted, 'I saw you grazing your sheep on
my land this morning. I'll teach you to be more careful in future.'

Nicolae returned home bloody and bruised, frightened and left
permanently deaf in one ear as a result of the slaps across his head.

In the village Goga boasted of his son Ion's strength. Ion was big
and had a mad look in his eyes. When he started drinking the
Gypsies knew they had to be careful, and, because his father was
good friends with Barbu, and he himself was Barbu's godson, he
could do almost as he pleased.

The Gypsies of the village were excluded from Romanian
dances, but the young Romanian men often came to the Gypsy
parties. The Gypsy parties were wilder, and there was of course

something irresistibly fascinating about the Gypsy girls and the way they danced. The Romanians, however, often behaved boisterously. They would have a few drinks and, to impress the girls, would start fights with the weaker Gypsies.

At a party in the early nineties Ion was drunk and picked on one of the Gypsies. Nicolae, who was then sixteen, saw what was happening and told him to leave the boy alone. Ion was not used to being told what to do, especially not by a Gypsy. He saw Nicolae's impertinence as another opportunity to show everyone how strong he was. He slapped the boy in the face and Nicolae intervened. There followed a crucial fight. Ion who had been so sure of himself could not match Nicolae's strength and speed. Before long he found himself on the floor, his face covered in blood. Nicolae picked him up and threw him out of the door.

MARISHKA HAD FINISHED milking the cow. We returned to the house with a pail of frothing milk. She poured some into a saucepan, and stoked up the fire in the stove.

'So Barbu and his Romanian friends don't like you because Nicolae beat Ion Goga,' I said.

'Yes. And because we are Gypsies. And because of our father's "eccentricity" and because of other things. There is no shortage of reasons,' she admitted.

'What other things?' I asked, secretly hoping, but also dreading, to discover the truth about her uncle Andrei, and whether he had had anything to do with the theft of the altarpiece.

'Why do you ask so many questions?' she said.

'It interests me to know about your family. I like you, all of you, Nicolae, your mother, father, Eugen, even Natalia,' I said.

Marishka looked at me long and hard. I felt she did not know whether to trust me. Nonetheless little by little the stories came out.

NICOLAE'S BEATING OF Ion had humiliated and infuriated the Goga family. Up until then few Gypsies had dared to stand up to

Romanians. Attila, Nicolae and their family were different, and now, it seemed, it was essential that such difference should be crushed. Nicolae was singled out for special treatment. Whenever the Gogas or their friends saw him in the street, they threatened or attacked him. There were many incidents.

In the end, out of desperation, Clara made a complaint to the police. It was not a wise idea but she did not know what else to do. The result was that the police sent an officer to bring Attila to the station for questioning. Attila refused to go; he knew from bitter experience what questioning at the police station meant. In any case, he had done nothing wrong.

'You would refuse to go as well if you knew what they do at the police station,' said Marishka as she told me the story.

A group of villagers gathered as an argument started. The policeman was being made to look stupid by Attila's defiance. He drew out his pistol and pointed it at Attila. 'You will come with me now,' he said, and then, in a quick movement, he hit him with the butt on the side of the head. Attila fell, the policeman jumped on him and put him in a stranglehold. As the policeman tightened his grip Attila's tongue hung out of his mouth and his face began to turn purple. The policeman then put the pistol to his head. Things were getting out of hand, especially as the policeman was clearly drunk.

At this point stories differ. Perhaps to protect Nicolae, some say that the policeman lost his balance and fell; others that Nicolae, seeing that his father could no longer breathe, punched the policeman with all his strength. Either way, the policeman flew backwards, the pistol fell out of his hand, and Attila picked it up. Roles were instantly reversed. Suddenly the policeman became curiously friendly. He begged Attila, in the nicest possible way, to give back the gun. He would lose his job, he explained, if he returned to the police station without his pistol. If Attila were to give it back he assured him the story would end there; nothing further would happen. He even went down on his knees to beg and to promise. It was as a result of promises like these that Nicolae and Marishka learnt not to trust the police. Attila, however, handed the pistol back, and the policeman slunk away.

Nicolae, brother of Marishka and Natalia, driving down from the hill in the evening

One of the Breb threshing machines. The sheaves are fed in from the top.
Dust from the threshed wheat fills the air

At a neighbour's funeral in the snow in Breb. The keening woman walks around
the coffin with her hands clasped. A candle stands in a jar filled with wheat on the coffin

The market at Ocna Şugatag in the winter. The women on the right peer into a
blanket-covered box containing piglets

Right: Death and Devil. Two of the Breb mummers, wearing animal skins, horns on their heads and cow-bells hung on their front and back. The Devil, on the right, has a ruffed rat on his head

Below left: Mihai rakes the straw from around the blackened body of Grigor the pig who has just been slaughtered and singed

Below right: Ileana, the White Witch of Budeşti

Năstafă and her father harrowing the fields in the spring

The girls and lads of Breb dancing the *Învîrtita* at Easter

Above: Mourners dance at the Death-Wedding. One of the brides is in the middle of the picture, with the musicians behind her to the right playing violin and *zongora*

Below: Marishka stands by the coffin of her cousin Florin at his wake

Below: Nene Niculaie and one of his shepherds, wearing the traditional Transylvanian shepherd's hat and waistcoat, milking the goats at the sheepfold

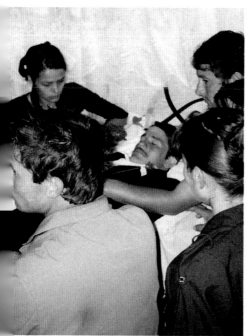

The Blue House. Behind it is the orchard, and beyond that the start of the forest

WB's sleigh is driven out of the gates of the Blue House pulled by the horses
bought from Nicu

ove: Marishka drives the cart on the way back from a neighbouring village in the evening

low: A *Corturar* Gypsy with distinctive hat
l beard at a Transylvanian market. The long
rd is a sign of his importance

Below: A *Căldărari* Gypsy encampment.
The man in the background is working on
a pole-anvil finishing the copper pot-still
beside him. The women prepare food

Mihai, WB and Constantin, late summer 2007

Maramureş shepherds blow on their horns at a funeral in Breb

That evening people in the village came and warned Attila to leave. But he did not. Although aware of the consequences he had decided upon a nobler course of action. Instead it was the sixteen-year-old Nicolae who left the house before daybreak and walked away, up into the forest. He had been warned as well. In hushed voices in the shadows friends had told him he should leave at once. They had heard talk. He went, and not a moment too soon.

The police came at first light. There were, some say, almost a hundred of them. So as not to leave room for escape they came down from the hills with dogs and surrounded the village. They found Attila in the house and dragged him out. Marishka and her mother were milking in the stable. They too were dragged out by their clothes and hair, and the milk pail was kicked over. In a few minutes the courtyard was filled with armed Jandarmes – the Romanian assault police – with wolfhounds, and with them, of course, was Barbu. Marishka told me what happened next:

'They swore at us, called us stinking Gypsies, and let their dogs jump at our faces. "Where is Nicolae?" they kept demanding. My mother was terrified and screaming, so they sprayed her in the face with a paralysing spray. Then they looked at me. "Where is Nicolae?" they shouted. Of course I didn't tell them and they hit me on the head so hard I fell flat on the ground. Then I saw the Commandant. He was holding a photograph of Nicolae. He took it between his teeth and tore it in two pieces. "When we catch him I will eat him!" he said.

'They then took us and threw us in the back of a lorry and we cowered there among the Jandarmes and their dogs. The lorry set off and, on leaving the village, passed the house of my uncle Andrei, the violinist. He shouted out of his window at the police, telling them that they should be ashamed of themselves. The lorry stopped abruptly and before long Andrei was thrown in with us. From there to the police station, a distance of seventeen kilometres, the Jandarmes took turns to beat him with their fists and with their guns. When we arrived at the station he was only semi-conscious. He had wet himself and urine was trickling out of the back of the lorry, the whites of his eyes were blood red, and they had even pulled out his moustache and forced him to eat it. They hit me too as I begged them not to beat him, but thankfully one of the Jandarmes protected me. At the time I was seventeen.'

Nicolae, who had left during the night, was to remain on the run for six months, an outlaw living in the forest, occasionally coming down to the village for food during the night, always on the move, sometimes setting off to other parts of the country when things became too hot. The police continued to search for him. They did not give up. They knew it was Nicolae who had knocked down the policeman with one blow and were determined to catch him. Sometimes the police would be informed of his whereabouts. He had been seen in the village. They would then appear, at dawn, coming down to the house through the orchard with their dogs sniffing for tracks, to try to catch him unawares. But they never did catch him. The dogs searched the house, the stables and the barns but they never found him. Nicolae was always one step ahead of them; he too had his informants.

In the meantime Attila was kept in custody. At the trial he told the judge that he had hit the policeman. He took the blame upon himself to protect Nicolae and was sentenced to seven years in prison. It was a noble thing to do. He was the one person who had not hit anybody. As he was led away he made a gesture of encouragement to his family.

Clara went home in determined mood. She sold the few cows they had and with the money hired the best lawyer she could afford from the city. The lawyer lodged an appeal. In the meantime she went to see the King of the Gypsies to ask for help. All the King's teeth were of solid gold, he had huge armchairs into which Clara sank deep down, enveloped by cushions, and the women and girls of the family stood around, their dark plaited hair coming down to their knees. Clara reported all this full of admiration. It was the stuff of fairy tales. The King, having heard the story, graciously said he would do what he could.

A date for the appeal was set. The police had no trouble finding witnesses. If the police asked a favour it was better not to refuse, and with Attila locked away for seven years there was little to fear from him in the near future.

One of these police witnesses went by the name of Arpi. On the day of the trial, he stood up and told the judge how Attila had attacked the policeman, viciously and unprovoked, how he had even grabbed the gun from its holster, and the policeman had narrowly escaped with his life. Clara could stand the lies no more. She rose to her feet and pointed to him with her arm outstretched. 'Arpi!' she shouted, and the courtroom fell silent, 'Arpi! God will punish you for the lies you are telling.' The judge shouted at her to remain silent. Clara's lawyer then pointed out the inconsistencies in Arpi's evidence.

It is not clear whether Arpi was more afraid of God, the police, or of perjuring himself. Whatever it was, slowly he began to speak again, looking down at the floor: 'What I have just said is indeed not true.' He then went on to relate how the policeman had drawn his gun and put Attila in a stranglehold.

The judge looked at the prosecutor, and the prosecutor at the judge and they knew the case was over. After such a public admission the judge was unable to do anything but dismiss the case. Attila was immediately freed. Arpi's evidence had turned the case. The police put their heads in their hands. Attila had had a tremendous stroke of luck. If Arpi had told the truth from the start his testimony would not have had nearly the same dramatic effect – it was the admission that he was lying in mid-flow which made it impossible for the judge to continue. He had his reputation to think of. Lawyers from the city were there. He had no choice but to free the proud Attila. A few days later Nicolae, too, was able to come down from the hills.

IT WAS ANOTHER bright, warm spring day. Marishka, the calf and I were again in the orchard in the shade of an apple tree. Marishka lay on the rug with her eyes closed and dappled light flickering across her face. As she dozed I explained to her my plan to save the eighteenth-century houses of the village.

'People have no money to pay for such work,' she said sleepily.

'They don't have to pay. I will do it for free,' I replied.

'Then you are stupid and people will just laugh at you,' she said.

'But the money is not mine. It has been given by others.'

'Well, I suppose those who do the work will be happy to have a job,' she said, shrugging, 'and those whose roofs are mended will be happy too. But everyone will still laugh at you.'

'Come with me for a walk,' I suggested. 'We can find a few houses which need repairing and people can have a job right away.'

She reluctantly agreed to disturb her rest, and we set off down the road, leaving the calf to graze alone in the orchard.

We strolled lazily down the village tracks. On all sides there were houses which needed urgent repairs. We entered through broken gates into abandoned courtyards, and as I poked about I discovered any number of intriguing details among the ruins. I saw the forms of tulips carved on the huge oak beams of the creaking barns, found gently curved columns topped with primitive capitals holding up now wobbly verandas, and came across eighteenth-century dates, framed by outlines of flowers, sculpted on lintels, half hidden beneath layers of lime. Marishka found it hard to understand how I could possibly be interested in these rotten and dangerously tottering buildings.

Gently we meandered along the tracks, exploring houses as we went, and soon found ourselves in the Romanian part of the village, equally beautiful, and almost as crumbling as the Saxon part. Clearly there was work to be done here as well. Marishka showed me the Orthodox church whose roof, I noticed, looked as though it needed patching.

She pointed out a new-looking fence cutting across the graveyard.

'The Romanians put that up recently,' she said, 'to separate "their" part of the cemetery from ours. They told us that Gypsies can only be buried on the other side of it. Even when they are dead they cannot bear to be near us.'

We walked on and passed yet another crumbling house. Outside were a group of young dark-skinned Gypsy children playing a game with a few sticks and stones. Marishka waved and smiled at them.

'This is my uncle Andrei's house,' said Marishka. 'Although now he is up there on the hill,' she said, pointing towards the cemetery, 'on the other side of the fence, of course.'

'How did he die?' I said, asking her the question I had been wondering about for a long time.

'He had a heart attack,' she said. 'Look. These are his children.'

It was now, and during the next weeks, that I discovered from Marishka and others what had really happened when the Saxons' beloved altarpiece had been stolen.

IN SEPTEMBER 1998, if you had been especially attentive, a tiny story in the British press concerning the disappearance of two valuable sixteenth-century altarpieces from two churches in Transylvania might have caught your eye. The story took up just a few lines, and could have passed almost unnoticed. For Marishka and her family, however, the consequences of the theft were to change the way they looked at the world.

One of the altarpieces was, of course, the grand, old winged Gothic-Renaissance altarpiece from Halma, made especially for the church in 1513, which Herr Knall had shown me with such pride several years before.

On one warm and fateful September night a year and a half before, when I had been in the Maramureş, thieves had scaled the ancient walls of the castle-church. Once inside, with saws, wrenches and axes, they dismantled and cut the altarpiece into sections – they intended to sell the panels separately – and carried it away in sacks across the fields and into the forest.

The next morning Herr Knall came as usual to ring the bells, but noticing splinters of wood near the church door, he walked hurriedly into the church. To his horror he discovered that their precious altarpiece was no longer there.

Herr Knall was shocked and frightened. Only a year before the Lutheran Archdeacon from the city had visited the village. The altarpiece, he had told them, must be removed from their church; it was too valuable and there were too few Saxons left to protect it. The Knalls, however, and the few other remaining Saxons who had resolved not to abandon the village of their forefathers, had stood in the road when the authorities came to take it away.

'This is our altarpiece,' they said, 'you cannot remove it. We decide what happens to it and we wish it to remain here. Without it our church would be like a person without a heart.' They had right on their side. According to Saxon law each parish is autonomous. There is no overall Saxon temporal authority, only a spiritual one in the form of the Bishop who resides in his splendid Baroque palace in the city of Sibiu. The Archdeacon remonstrated, but the villagers stood firm.

So the altarpiece had remained in the church. Now, within a year, it had been stolen. Herr Knall realized what this meant. Though they had been perfectly correct in keeping it, and it was their right as the remaining villagers to decide whether it should stay or go, its loss was in some way their fault. Herr and Frau Knall were distraught and wept and wrung their hands.

Then the police came. They asked many questions. Herr and Frau Knall told them they knew nothing.

'But Mr Knall is the only one with the key of the church,' they pointed out, 'and the door was not forced.'

'Yes, but we leave the door open to keep it aired,' they said, 'and we are old and it is a long way up the hill for our old legs to carry us, so we do not close it every night.'

The Knalls were frightened by the way the police questioned them, although it was obvious they had nothing to do with the theft. As a bizarre finale to their interview the police made Herr Knall stand in the middle of the room, holding a candle in one hand and a Bible in the other, and swear he knew nothing of what had happened to the altarpiece. They then marched out to proceed with the questioning of other suspects.

One of these was Marishka's uncle Andrei. He was a suspect

because his back garden ran up to the edge of the defensive walls of the church. He had at the time some extra money to spend and the police wondered from where he had obtained it. In fact the money had come from a calf he had sold, but this detail did not deter Barbu, who was now able to report that they had a proper suspect – and, better still, he was a Gypsy.

Andrei was taken to the police station. For many hours he was questioned. At last, in the evening, he was released and he stumbled back along the dirt track to the village. He was feeling dizzy. His left side was numb. His legs were trembling and he had a strange look in his eyes. To his wife he seemed like a different person.

When he saw his children he tried to pretend that all was well, but later alone with his wife he told her what had happened, and how they had beaten him. They had wanted him to confess to the theft, he said, but since he had not stolen anything he was unable to do so, so they hit him harder.

Andrei had been ordered to come to the police station again the next morning for further questioning. At supper, however, he could not eat. Then overnight he complained to his wife of stomach pains, and in the early hours of the morning he died. He was thirty-four, and father of four children, the eldest of whom was nine.

A few minutes before he lost consciousness he said to his wife: 'I am dying. Look after the children.'

When the police arrived at Andrei's house his wife barricaded the gates and refused to let them in. She did not trust them. They would, she was sure, take the body away in order to hide evidence of his beating. Only later, when two separate doctors arrived, did she relent and allow them in to carry out an autopsy. Many people, however, later suspected that the doctors had spoken together and had been sent there by Barbu.

There followed a scene of medieval gruesomeness. Andrei's body was carried out of the house and laid on the kitchen table which had been placed in the middle of the courtyard. Everyone present was told to leave, but Andrei's eldest son was hiding in the barn and, looking through the slats, was a witness to the whole scene. The doctors sawed off the top of his head and took out his brain. They then cut out his tongue. Then they sliced Andrei open from the neck down to the groin using the axe from the wood shed to hack open his ribcage. The intestines were, according to Andrei's son, covered in blood. This, the villagers later whispered, was a clear sign of internal bleeding. The good doctors, however, took the innards to the well, filled a basin with water, and washed and rinsed them before examining them. They then put them back into the basin, along with the brain and the tongue, and with a huge curved needle and thick black thread sewed up the hole in the stomach. They wiped the body clean of blood with a cloth, which they threw into the basin, and then left. The distraught family returned into the courtyard. Andrei's elder sister saw that the skin of his scalp and face had been peeled forwards and was hanging down in front of his eyes and nose. She could not bear the sight and walked away. Those remaining had to clear up the mess the doctors had left. They put his face and scalp back as best they could, and with difficulty managed to dress him in his best clothes and lay him out in the house for the wake. The basin full of his intestines, heart, tongue and brain was buried in a hole in the corner of the courtyard – they did not know what else to do with them – and there his wife and children still light a candle every year in his memory.

A few days later the doctors presented their official report. Andrei, they wrote, had died of a heart attack, and there were no signs of violence to be found on his body.

The real thieves were never caught, but by a curious chance several months later in Hungary the panels of the altarpieces were found concealed in a pool table. It was said they were about to be taken across the Hungarian border to their respective buyers in Western Europe. At the same time, a 'shopping list' of everything else the thieves had intended to steal came to light. A similar list had been given to collectors, and these collectors had then placed orders for whatever would be most suitable to adorn the walls of their luxurious villas. That these altarpieces had been sculpted and painted for the churches in which they had stood for nearly five hundred years was of little concern to these connoisseurs of fine art.

Following the doctors' report the investigation into the circumstances of Andrei's death was closed. Of the villagers, however, whether Gypsy, Romanian or Saxon, few believed what the doctors had written, and thereafter nobody, not even the police, ever claimed that Andrei had had anything to do with the theft.

'ANDREI WAS MY favourite uncle,' said Marishka as she milked the cows that evening. She sat on her three-legged stool and began to wash the udders. When she turned towards me the whites of her eyes shone out in the half light. 'He was always good to my brothers, my sister and me. But Barbu hates us, and he can do what he likes, and nobody does anything. They will try to get Nicolae next, you can be sure of it. It is just a matter of time.'

Marishka's life seemed in many ways to be so carefree, but since Andrei's death, just below the surface, there was concealed a deep and deadly seriousness.

15

Moving in with Marishka

L'amour est l'enfant de Bohème, il n'a jamais connu de loi – Love is like a Gypsy child, it knows no law.

Henri Meilhac and Ludovic Halévy, *Carmen*

IN THE HISTORY of the Gypsies there has never been any shortage of suffering. It is something to which they have become accustomed. In any case, life had to go on, and so, on the surface, despite the troubles, the daily round in Halma proceeded as usual. Andrei's children played in the streets with all the other children. The cows went out to pasture in the morning and ponderously returned in the evening, lazily rubbing their heads against the pear trees, before retiring to their respective byres. The *crîşma* filled with people after milking time, carts stood outside, the horses shifting and stamping in the darkness, or falling asleep in the traces, and Gypsy music floated across the square carried on the warm evening air.

There always remained, however, the menace, and the feeling that another crisis could be precipitated at any moment. I should have left there and then, but I was horrified by the story of Andrei and worried about the predicament of Marishka's family. I felt I could not abandon them, and perhaps even that my presence might help to protect them.

IN ANY CASE I felt drawn to Marishka. Not only was she beautiful, but she was funny and I could not forget or help admiring her courage in protecting her sister from the knife attack. So I stayed. I lived in the family house. Marishka was usually doing jobs around the courtyard. I would sit reading in the orchard. Marishka, when she had finished cleaning, would come and doze under the apple trees, vaguely keeping an eye on the calf.

Over those days I must have been looking at her frequently, and one afternoon on the rug in the orchard she noticed me watching her for the umpteenth time.

'Why do you keep looking at me?' she asked.

'I am sorry,' I said. 'It is because you are beautiful. I will try not to do it any more.'

'I don't mind, you can do what you like. Anyway I am not beautiful. I am a dark-skinned Gypsy. Beautiful are the blonde-haired and fair-skinned ones,' she said.

'Yes, I suppose you're right,' I replied.

'You are not supposed to agree!' she said, laughing.

At a party a few evenings later Marishka was trying to teach me to dance. We had both had a few drinks and were having a good time.

'Do you really think I am beautiful?' she said as we swung around arm in arm.

'No I don't,' I said. 'Gypsies are too dark skinned to be beautiful.'

She gave me a look of exaggerated crossness.

NATALIA WAS NOT amused. She noticed that Marishka and I were becoming friendlier and realized there was a danger that love might soon occur. Her game was to taunt me in the *crîşma*, dancing in a deliberately provocative way, and then, when she saw me glancing at her, returning me a look of contempt. One evening as she walked past she leant over and whispered in my ear.

'*Eşti un cacat!* – You are shit!'

'Why?' I replied. 'You did what you liked and went with whom you pleased when you were with me.'

'Yes, but you are going with my sister!' she said.

'What do you want me to do? To leave?' I asked.

'*Da!*' she said.

I did not leave, however, although perhaps I should have, and before long, one evening after a few drinks, all barriers were broken down and what Natalia had feared might happen, happened.

WEEKS PASSED. IT was now early summer. The fields were spread over with a rich array of wild flowers. The trees in the forests were covered in soft new leaves, and in the glades wild strawberries grew in abundance. The cherry trees too were in fruit and one day Marishka and I decided to go up to a tree on the edge of the forest which she knew had particularly sweet fruit. We took a basket, borrowed Nicolae's mare, and set off up the hill in the direction of Floreni.

We creaked and rolled our way up, high above the village, from where we could see the blue Transylvanian hills rippling into the distance for as far as the eye could see. The cherry tree stood by itself, decorated all over with dangling red bunches of fruit. We spread out a rug on the grass under the tree. I clambered up and threw down the cherries to Marishka. When we had half filled the basket we sat down to rest. There was no one around. There was silence. Even the birds seemed to hold their breaths.

Marishka lay down looking upwards through the branches. The sunlight flickered through the leaves and on to her hair.

'You are looking at me again,' she said.

I pulled her to her feet, we walked into the forest, and once again caution was thrown to the wind. Now lying contentedly on the margins of the trees in the silence of that warm June afternoon, we talked from time to time about nothing in particular.

She lay with her shirt half open. In between her breasts I noticed a small scar, no more than a centimetre long. This and the scar on her hand were the only blemishes on her body. The scar on her hand I knew about. I put my finger on the scar on her chest.

'What is this?' I asked lazily.

'That? Oh, just a little scar.'

'What is it doing there?' I asked.

'When I was about fourteen', she said, 'a man, another of the village musicians, attacked my father with a scythe. I ran in between them and the point of the scythe hit me right in the middle of my chest and stuck itself into my chest-bone.' She then laughed. 'I remember the look of horror on the musician's face when he realized what he had done. Of course he hadn't meant to hit me, but there I was with a scythe planted in my chest, and a patch of blood spreading over my shirt. He thought he had killed me, as did everyone else, and there was a huge fight. It all ended when my uncle Ovidiu hit the musician, *clonk*, on the head with a hammer, and knocked him out cold. Ovidiu is also a musician. He plays the trumpet. You have met him.'

I should have known that there was never going to be an ordinary, banal reason.

'Is that really true?' I asked her.

'Of course it's true.'

I looked at her and laughed. Her sleepy appearance on the rug and the reality of her stormy life were somewhat at odds.

By the time we were ready to return to the village the horse had disappeared. She had moved away gradually, still attached to the cart, munching the grass as she went. We sauntered idly across the fields looking for her, the sun warm on our faces, each holding a handle of the basket of cherries. Eventually we came across her in a dell by a stream where she had found a patch of especially delicious wild flowers.

Marishka took the reins and covered the seat with the rug. We hopped on board, and trundled back down to the village. As the cart creaked and swayed, I looked at Marishka, the reins held loosely in her hands, the fine fingers of the breeze gently stroking her hair, and asked her if she thought it a good idea for us to live together.

'We can,' she said.

MARISHKA AND I became, according to the way of speaking amongst the Gypsies, 'married', although this did not have the same meaning as in the *gajo* world. There was no wedding, no ceremony, we simply lived together and this they called 'marriage'. Some said this marriage would last a few months, others a few years. Even some of the most traditional *Corturari* Gypsies accept that people cannot always live happily together, however happy they are to begin with. There are reviews every two years. If either the man or the woman wishes to end the arrangement then it will be ended, dowries returned, and each person will look for a new 'spouse'. If there is a child it will be looked after within the family by the mother and one of the grandmothers. Marishka's family were not *Corturari*, they were settled *Lăutari*. There were no dowries, but it seemed that similar rules applied.

Indeed Marishka had had a baby some years before, and this boy was looked after among the extended family; sometimes he slept in our house, sometimes with the grandmother or with Natalia, Nicolae, Eugen or with one of his many cousins or aunts. He was a friendly boy and added to the rabble of delightful Gypsy children running about the streets of the village. Marishka's having a child, given the informality of their lives, seemed quite normal and natural. There were indeed so many little dark-skinned children in Halma that I was often reminded of a line from Hemingway in *For Whom the Bell Tolls*: 'Hast thou ever seen a Gitana who was not about to have, or just to have had, a child?'

So Marishka and I were 'married' and the saga of the letters had resulted, in the end, in my 'marrying' not Natalia, but Marishka. I felt more at home with Marishka. She liked having me around, not just for some of the time but all of the time. There were no mysterious disappearances and we spent all day every day together.

Herr and Frau Knall, who had so disapproved of my being with Natalia, and had been so relieved when I had left her, once again shook their heads in disappointment. 'If you have been with a Gypsy you will never be able to return to the normal world,' they had often said to me, repeating an old Saxon adage, presumably intended to prevent Saxon men from being tempted away, and thus risking being permanently expelled from the Saxon community. 'You will become entrapped by the Gypsy girls and their magic,' they said. To me this had the ring of a recommendation. For them it was a dire warning that I would be cut adrift among the outcasts for ever.

The Romanians and Barbu were even more disappointed with me. But in those blissful first days with Marishka, when the hills were carpeted with wide sprays of wild flowers, so colourful that the meadows seemed as though they were part of a huge garden, when the air was warm and the evenings long, I did not notice any of the sideways glances or hear any of the barbed comments.

We lingered in the orchards and ambled to the *crîşma* where we danced to the Gypsy music evening after evening. I was happy and at ease and I did not hear any murmurings or any of the plans being hatched. Everyone was my friend. I bought drinks at the bar for whoever was nearby and basked in the glow of my new and contented life.

THERE WAS A beautiful but dilapidated, blue-washed house, with holes in the roof and in the floor, and no glass in the windows, which stood beside one of the bridges running over the stream. In front of it were three pear trees which, in the spring, were white with blossom. In the cobbled courtyard of the house vines tangled themselves around the columns of the veranda and behind, beside the orchard, stood huge barns, constructed from vast oak beams with rounded terracotta tiles on the roof, laid in the form of fish-scales. I discovered who owned it and was able to buy it. It was the perfect house for us, but to begin with it needed to be repaired.

The main room had long been used as a grain store and so the floorboards were rotten and full of holes eaten through by mice. I bought planks of mountain pine and re-floored the room. I had windows made by the local carpenter, a rosy-faced Saxon called Herr Wagner who, like the Knalls, had decided not to emigrate, and with terracotta tiles we mended the many holes in the roof. Next it was necessary to see to the plasterwork, which was flaking and falling off.

Up in barns by the Saxon church there were some old lime pits. When I had first arrived in the village I had identified many buildings which I had wanted to rescue, and as slaked lime is necessary for any building work I had the pits mended and refilled. Using this lime I patched the crumbling plasterwork both on the façade and on the interior of the house. Then, once this new plaster was dry, several coats of lime wash, dyed blue, were splashed on to the walls, and finally the door and window recesses were painted white.

When I first bought the house I had never actually been inside it, and so it was a great joy when, for the first time, I walked into the main rooms and looked up at the ceilings. They were the finest ceilings I had seen in any Saxon village house, made of smoothed and chamfered oak beams, one of which had the date 1770 inscribed upon it, and another 1835, with the initials of the owner carved in old Gothic lettering beside them. In between the beams were coffered panels of mountain pine. The woodwork resembled that of an officer's cabin in an eighteenth-century ship of the line.

The oak beams of the house and the barn would have been cut from the surrounding woods. The pine had been brought from further afield, from the forests over the hills to the east in the land of the Székely (the *Székelyföld*, as it was called by the Hungarians, the *Ungherime* to Romanians). The Székely are believed by many to be descendants of the original Huns of Attila who settled here in the early Middle Ages. They speak Hungarian, but should not be confused with the Hungarians who came from the east with Árpád and who arrived and settled in central Transylvania and the Pannonian plain in the tenth century.

Marishka's village was Saxon in foundation, and until the Saxons departed the people in the streets would predominantly have spoken either the Saxon dialect or an eighteenth-century version of High German. Ride a few kilometres over the hills to the east, however, and in the first village you reach everyone will be speaking Hungarian; even though they live in Romania, and are now Romanian citizens, some of them do not even understand the

Romanian language. Going over the hill is like travelling to another country.

It was a while before Marishka and I were able to move into the blue house, and so to begin with I had the pleasure of sharing a house with a real Transylvanian Hungarian – this was of course Attila, Marishka's father. Living with Attila was not, however, an experience for the faint hearted, for although full of life and energy, he was also exhaustingly and exasperatingly eccentric. At one moment he would be in the *crîşma* dressed in white suit and tie, in convivial mood, kissing ladies' hands in the courteous old-fashioned style of Central Europe, and the next, bottles would be swept off tables and glasses hurled to the ground, as a glove might be thrown down in a challenge.

'When I pulled down the Communist flag in the square the police hit me on the head with a spanner,' he said, by way of excusing his latest excesses, 'and I've never been the same since.'

Shortly before I moved in, Clara, Marishka's mother, had moved out. Several years before Attila had smashed every last window in the house. Now there had been other incidents and she had had enough. Thereafter the peace was disturbed by strange noises coming from the street outside in the early hours of the morning. I was awoken and asked Marishka what it was.

'It's my father,' she said wearily.

'What is he doing?' I asked.

'Singing,' she replied, half asleep.

'But it's four o'clock in the morning!'

'Yes, I know.'

He was walking through the village railing at the moon and singing sorrowful Romanian *doine* and Hungarian laments. It went on night after night.

Attila could not live without a wife for long. So one day he begged me to accompany him to the *Székelyföld* to search for a new one. There were, he told me, several possibilities, all of them Hungarian. We set off over the rolling hills, arrived at a small village in the remote valleys of the eastern Carpathians and went to the bar with the first candidate. She ordered vodka. Attila looked happy. She then bought a packet of *Carpaţi*, the cheapest and roughest of Romanian cigarettes. None of those fancy Western cigarettes for her. Attila was glowing. She was perfect. Attila wanted to carry her away with him straight away, but she said she could not come until the following Saturday. A week passed, Attila was in high spirits, the drunken songs in the night were now of joy, and on Friday he set off to pick her up. A week later he returned . . . alone.

'What happened?' I asked him.

'She wasn't suitable after all,' he said, shaking his head. 'One evening, she drank a litre of *rachiu*.'

'Oh dear,' I said. 'She really was a drinker.'

'Yes, but that wasn't why I was upset,' he said, seeing I had not understood. 'She drank it when I was out! She could at least have waited for me!'

In the meantime, Clara had found a new 'husband'. His name was Horatiu. Clara, however, was a dangerous choice for any man. A man previously suspected of being Clara's lover had had a narrow escape. Attila had crept through their bedroom window and plunged a knife down into his head. The knife glanced off the lover's skull, and sank into the pillow, leaving feathers floating in the air and the bed drenched with blood. Sure enough, in time, Attila stabbed Horatiu as well, although only in the arm. I met him walking down the track out of the village on his way to hospital to have the gash sewn up and he showed me the gaping wound.

Attila was as wild as any of the Gypsies. Indeed often they would gather and look on in amazement at his antics. He was proud and if anyone crossed him it was not long before a glass was flying across the *crîşma*. Certainly no one had broken quite as many glasses there as he, nor had anyone made it a habit of challenging people to so many duels and with such aristocratic disdain. Marishka would sometimes despair of him, as she was obliged to break up yet another fight.

I often wondered where his eccentricity came from and I would ask him about his family, but he assured me he knew nothing more than that his father had been wounded in the war and had died soon after, and that his grandfather had been killed by a bear in the Korund mountains. The only additional information he provided was that this grandfather had been killed because he did not run away, but had, rather unwisely, stood his ground.

Attila, too, had had a close encounter with a bear. Late one evening Nene (uncle) Petru had rushed breathlessly into the *crîşma*. A bear had taken Attila's pig, he said, and made off with it along the bed of the stream towards Floreni. Attila ran out, grabbed a stick and headed off in hot pursuit. After running and splashing through water, and brushing branches aside, he caught up with the bear who was moving slowly carrying the pig. Attila pulled off a gumboot, put it on the end of a stick, and set it alight. He waved the flaming boot towards the bear, which raised itself up on its hind legs and spat and roared. Bears are afraid of fire, and it backed away and lumbered off. The half-flayed pig was lying on the ground, wide strips of fat torn from its back. Attila turned it over. He looked at it with horror. It was not his pig. It was Nene Petru's.

'Everyone thought I was a hero. I just thought I was a fool, and wearing only one gumboot,' said Attila, swigging back his brandy as he finished the story, and everyone roared with laughter.

NICOLAE, MARISHKA'S BROTHER, was also different from others in the village. For a start he did not drink or smoke, and although he had a browner complexion than the Romanians or Saxons, he had the clear blue eyes of his father. He also had an air of calm and confidence. When there was trouble he was not afraid, and such fearlessness made the bullies uneasy. When he walked into a room people noticed. They continued to drink and pretend to be oblivious, but everyone noted his presence. As a result fights usually occurred when Nicolae was not around. Indeed, so many fights were avoided I often thought Nicolae should have been employed as an unofficial keeper of the peace.

Where Nicolae was not known, he did sometimes have trouble. There was a story going about, when I arrived, which had elevated him to legendary status. He had been in the *crîşma* in a neighbouring village. Marishka, Natalia, and a friend called Petru were with him. In the *crîşma* there were ten or twelve local lads and they kept looking at the girls. As Petru was the weakest he was the first to be picked upon. They mocked him, then slapped him and the girls became frightened, knowing that men in Romanian villages carry knives. Nicolae, Petru and the girls should have left the *crîşma*. Instead, there was a deafening crash as bottles and broken glass were scattered across the floor. Everyone jumped around to see Nicolae standing in the middle of the room. He had raised a table above his head and thrown it with all his strength on to the floor. He now stood there waiting for the local lads to take up the challenge. But not one of them moved. They stood nervously waiting for someone else to be the first. Nicolae glared at them and one by one they left the room mumbling, '*Te aranjăm* – We'll sort you out.' Nicolae, however, sorted them out first. Later that evening he found the man who had hit Petru. It was weeks before the man and his friend, who had tried to help him, came out of hospital.

There were many similar stories and, as a result of Nicolae's reputation, when he was with me I felt safe. I was protected from the blows, but not always from the sights. I still had to watch as beer bottles were smashed over heads, blood poured down faces, and knives were thrust quickly into guts. The stabbings were so fast you often hardly noticed what had happened until afterwards. If the fight took place in the winter the next morning the scene of the fight was evident from patches of scarlet blood spattered over the bright white snow. The dogs which roamed loose in the village licked at the patches until eventually they disappeared.

When Nicolae was not around, others looked after me. One evening in the *crîşma* Aurel, the father-in-law of the Lad, asked me to buy him a drink.

'Don't give him one,' Marishka whispered. 'He is drunk enough already.'

I refused him and he started to raise his voice. I was, he said, responsible for his son being put in prison, and now I would not even buy him a drink. Marishka and Eugen tried to calm him down. They did not succeed. Instead he drew a knife and declared that he was going to cut my throat. Everyone took a step back, except Marishka. She went straight up to him, took the knife out of his hands, and told him he should be ashamed of himself.

'Don't you understand Romanian,' she said. 'You've already had too much to drink. *Du-te acasă prostul Dracului!* – Go home, you Devil's fool!'

I thanked her.

'Don't worry,' she said, laughing, as though nothing had happened. 'You have to show you are not afraid, otherwise things only get worse.'

I DID NOT see Natalia often but inevitably sometimes our paths crossed. One Sunday she and I found ourselves together in the Orthodox church. Nicolae had asked Marishka and me to be godparents to his daughter. It was not, however, a suitable time of the month for Marishka, and in that condition she was not supposed to enter an Orthodox church, so Natalia stood in.

The priest was occupied with prayers by the iconostasis at the front of the church. Natalia and I stood by the font holding cups of holy water in our hands.

'Look at you standing there pretending to be all pious,' said Natalia, 'and you ran off with my sister.'

She was half-joking, I could tell. In any case she had a new boyfriend with whom she was much in love. But it was fun to needle me.

'Shut up, Natalia!' I replied. 'We are in church. We are supposed to be baptizing Nicolae's little girl.'

Natalia elbowed me, and my cup of holy water, which the priest had filled and blessed, spilled on the floor.

'Oh, for goodness' sake! Now look what you've done!' I said crossly.

'It doesn't matter. There is plenty more,' she said, picking up a jug near the font and refilling the cup.

Then an amusing thought entered her mind. The priest's back was turned and she emptied her entire cup of holy water on to the top of my head. The water trickled over my face and down my shirt, dripping on to the floor. She then reached across to the font again and filled up her cup from the jug.

'Thank you for that, Natalia,' I said mopping the water off my face and hair with a handkerchief.

'Serves you right!' she said, a most satisfied expression on her face.

16

Blissfully Unaware

One learnt to expect anything, but was always surprised.
Evelyn Waugh, *Black Mischief*

AT LAST THE blue house was ready and Marishka and I began a contented life together in our new home. We planted a vegetable garden, moved in furniture, and lived happily and comfortably without running water or a bathroom. The lavatory was a wooden hut, with a wooden seat over a hole in the ground, situated near the hay barn, which had a glorious view of the hill and the forest beyond. The bath was a large tin and brass tub made in Hungary before the Great War, which hung from a strong hook on the wall when not being used. Water came in buckets from the well. All stoves, for heating and cooking, were fuelled with wood.

Bath time was one of the most pleasurable moments of the day. For an hour before, water hissed in huge steaming saucepans on the wood-burning stove until at last it was near boiling. The bath was placed in the middle of the room and the water was poured into it using smaller saucepans with long handles. As I wallowed, Marishka would keep topping up the bath with hot water so that I did not become cold, and I did the same for her. We each emerged as scrubbed and clean as a priest's wife. The water was then poured over the edge of the veranda into the courtyard and it drained away out of the front gate. In the summer we would heat up the water in the sun, lock the gate, and bathe in the courtyard.

Marishka's chickens and ducks were brought down from Attila's house, and Marishka's cow was installed in the cowshed. The ducks had originally come from ducklings bought by Natalia. One day in the town a few years before I had given her money to go to the market to buy lunch. She came back hours later, by which time I was starving. She was carrying a small box. Inside it were five fluffy yellow ducklings with tiny pink beaks. She took them out of the box one by one and kissed them each lightly on the tops of their heads.

'They are so sweet, aren't they?' she said.

'Yes, they are charming,' I said, impatiently, 'but what about our lunch?'

'Oh, I didn't have any money left for food,' she replied.

First thing each morning Marishka collected the eggs from wherever the hens had laid them in the hay barn, and picked up the pail of milk on the veranda left by the boy who milked the cow. She then blew into the embers in the stove to bring it back to life, tearing out a few pages from the latest book she was reading to help it on its way.

I had persuaded her to read books, and had given her a copy of *Pride and Prejudice* translated into Romanian – *Mîndrie si Prejudecată*. At first she thought I was joking.

'Try it,' I said. 'You might enjoy it. Anyway, you will learn something about us ridiculous English people.'

'I don't read books,' she said.

But she knew how to read, and one day she picked it up, turned it over in her hands and started to read. After a few days she was making comments. I enjoyed her indignation.

'Darcy is so arrogant,' she said as she finished a chapter, throwing the book down.

But as she read, the volume became always thinner as she tore out the pages to light the fire. The travelling and transitory nature of things was in her blood. She travelled through books like a journey, and when she had finished them they were no longer there. Books as heirlooms for future generations were for settled people. For her they were passing moments of pleasure, like dancing.

Once the fire was alight, with Darcy's latest outrage consigned to flames, Marishka set down to preparing scrambled eggs, toast and coffee. I had taught her how to make scrambled eggs in the English way. With the freshest of eggs and milk I had a feast every morning.

Marishka looked after me with great care. I was not even allowed to bring in the water or chop the wood. These tasks were carried out by assorted helpers who would appear morning and evening. After a while, however, this easy life, though pleasant, did not suit me.

'Can I not chop the wood and bring in the water?' I asked Marishka. 'Do we really need others to do that for us?'

'No, not if you don't want them. Go ahead. Do it yourself.'

So I tried, but every time I went outside with axe or bucket a figure would appear as if from nowhere and insist on helping me. Then in the evening in the *crîşma* they would stand in strategic positions, where I would see them, and look at me with soulful eyes. I had no choice but to buy them a glass of *rachiu*, a beer or a packet of cigarettes.

As a result I was rarely able to chop our own firewood or collect water. Marishka had let me find out for myself. No doubt she had known already. It was unfair not to allow people to help us. They would sometimes wait for hours outside just so as to be able to have the chance to earn a drink or a few lei to buy bread for their families.

To counteract the delightful torpor into which I was being lulled by Marishka and her many helpers I threw myself into efforts to preserve the old buildings of the village, which continued gently crumbling on all sides. Halma was a beautiful place, but it was steadily becoming an extensive romantic ruin, and many of the houses, without help, would soon be piles of rubble.

All over the village roofs were collapsing and houses falling down. With my faithful helpers, mostly Gypsies, but also a few of the poorer Romanians, I tried to put things right. Given the tools, materials and encouragement they did wonderful work to repair the damage caused by ten years of neglect. Gradually the abandoned look of Halma began to change, and it was the Gypsies with their extraordinary skills as craftsmen and their hard work who were largely responsible. Broken rafters, laths and tiles were replaced, and the lime I had prepared in the pits was invaluable for patching up many a teetering wall and filling holes in the plasterwork on any number of crumbling façades. Most villagers thought I was not quite right in the head to be repairing such ruins, but I was happy to see the old houses saved, or at least their lives prolonged, and those who worked were happy to have a job.

After the day's work, Marishka and I would stroll into the centre of the village to meet the animals ambling back from pasture. The slow dreamy pace of the cows seemed to mirror the pace of our life. Although we worked hard, Marishka cleaning, washing and cooking, I overseeing the building, it was not the same work as in the north where the villagers arose before dawn and were in the fields before the sun had risen from behind the hills. As the early morning milking and the sending of the cow to pasture were looked after by a boy employed by Marishka, we were able to lead a much more leisurely life.

IN THE EVENING the cow found her own way back to the stables and was milked and fed for the night. Then, once Marishka had delivered the milk to the dairy, we would retire to the *crîşma* where most of the rest of the village assembled every evening to catch up with the events of the day.

After milking time all paths led irresistibly to the *crîşma*, and, as if to proclaim this fact, outside the door there stood an array of different patched-up milk pails and battered churns. The bar, the only one in the village, was a gathering place for gossip, an arena for arguments, and a venue for vigorous dancing. It was a place full of much sound and fury, of music and fights, which ultimately signified nothing, or at least very little – but then who cared about anything signifying anything. It was a glorious and thrilling chaos, and a pillar from which the poorer villagers lurched from one evening to another and made their way for better or worse through their tempestuous lives.

The bar was a single long thin room with a few sticks of furniture scattered about, and a good metal stove of Gypsy manufacture in one corner. All the furniture had been broken over the years in the course of one difference of opinion or another, but no matter, for a table with three legs can stand if put against a wall, and a chair with only three legs can support a man if he sits on it in the right way.

Marishka enjoyed going to the *crîşma* more than anything. It was the vibrant hub of village life, especially for the Gypsies, who, because of their more light-hearted attitude to life, spent more time in the bar than others. It was here sitting on broken chairs that I began to pick up a smattering of the Gypsy language.

'*So ca mes te pes?* – What would you like to drink?' someone would say to me as Marishka and I strolled into the bar. The Gypsy speakers were most amused at a *gajo*, a non-Gypsy, wanting to learn their language.

'*Ma pau edgy bere* – I'll drink a beer,' I would reply, and a bottle was opened in someone's teeth and placed in front of me on the three-legged table.

'*Te te as bachtalo!* – I wish you luck!' they said as they raised their bottles in a toast.

'*Te jivez ke bud birsch!* – May you live for many years!' I would reply.

'*So kergeas ages?* – What have you been doing today?' they asked.

'*Canj* – Nothing,' I might reply, in time-honoured fashion, or '*Uiliam co orasi* – I was in the town' . . . and so it went on, until an inevitable argument arose as to the correct form of speaking Gypsy. There were so many dialects. Marishka's uncles (some were blood relations, others married to Marishka's aunts) spoke a variety and were always at odds.

'*Mo pralo!* Oh brother! You don't know what you are talking about. You speak *Corturăreşti*, I speak pure *Ţigăneşti*.' (The word *pral* reached English Romany as *pal* and is one of the few Gypsy words to have entered the English language.)

'Shut up! *So dillo manuşi sinyal!* You speak mongrel Gypsy. Every line you say is littered with Hungarian and Romanian words . . .'

Fortunately they did not actually come to blows.

I had dipped into the occasional book about the Gypsy language, although I had never studied it closely, but sometimes I would pick up hints about its origins by chance. While in Romania I happened to meet a woman whose family came from north-west India. She was intrigued how similar the Gypsies were to Indians. You can see the similarity in their faces, in their clothes, in their jewellery, in the way they stand, sit, and especially squat, and you can hear it in their language. When the Indian girl spoke to the Gypsies in her Indian dialect they were able to understand her. I was intrigued and tested her with some simple Gypsy words and phrases.

'So what does "*So keres?*" mean?' I asked. Without hesitating she replied, 'It means "How are you? What are you doing?" Something like that.' I tried other phrases and she guessed them. Then I tried the word *bacht*. In Gypsy *bacht* means 'luck', and I knew it to mean the same in both Afghanistan and Persia.

'No,' she said, 'I don't know that word.'

I had experienced first-hand what philologists will tell you: that the Gypsy language is based on a dialect from north-west India, but that many words were picked up on their great migration through Afganistan and Persia en route to South-East Europe.

OFTEN THE TWO surviving members of Marishka's family band, Gabriel and Ovidiu, were to be found in the *crîşma*.

'We don't play much any more,' they told me. 'Since the Revolution we haven't been able to make money as musicians. The factories in the towns closed, jobs became scarcer, fewer people were married, or even had the money to marry, and so less and less were we asked to play. We got out of practice. Nowadays we play mostly just for fun, at New Year, Christmas, or the occasional party, or for you if you ask us,' they said, smiling. 'Anyway with Andrei gone – may God rest his soul! – we are not a proper group any more, only two of us and a drum. Our uncle Vergil is still alive in Sighişoara but he is old now and doesn't have a violin. His son used to play the violin masterfully, but he has had to give it up too.'

'Life was better for us before the Revolution,' they said – a line I had heard so many times before.

WHEN NOT CHATTING about the ways of the world I played chess with Attila or Nicolae or anyone who happened to be available. While having a quiet game with Attila one evening a bearded man who had been sitting in the corner, his head swaying over a glass of *rachiu*, came over to me. This was, apparently, the priest. He had heard that Marishka and I had moved into the blue house and asked if we might like to make our church contributions. Marishka made urgent signals from the other side of the room for me not to give him anything and so I made excuses. He walked away. Marishka came over.

'He's drunk,' she said, 'and just wants to buy another drink. You should give church contributions to the church wardens. If you give them to the priest they will all go on alcohol.'

'Anyway', said Attila as he arranged the chess pieces for a new game, 'he should not talk about money in the *crîşma* and that's that.'

Later in the evening as we were about to return home the priest beckoned conspiratorially for me to come over to him. In hushed tones he asked whether I would like to buy an old and valuable icon.

'What did the drunken fool want?' asked Marishka as we walked home along the moonlit track.

'He wanted to sell me an icon. Do you think he's trying to sell me the contents of the church to pay for his drinks?'

'Probably,' she said. 'It doesn't surprise me.'

'Is the icon from the church?' I asked her.

'Almost certainly. Where else would it come from?' she said.

The following evening the priest again came up to me while I was sitting with Marishka by the bridge waiting for the cow to come home.

'Oh no, what does that prick want now?' said Marishka when she saw him coming, not perhaps using quite the correct terminology for referring to a man of the cloth.

'Marishka!' I said. 'Please don't cause trouble.'

'Don't worry, I won't,' she reassured me, 'but later on I will tell you a few stories.'

Again he asked me for the church contributions. He explained that the church roof needed mending. I told him I did not have any money on me, but that I would repair the church roof for him myself. He walked away looking deeply disappointed.

'So what has the priest done to upset you?' I asked her later in the evening.

'I believe in God,' she said, 'even though sometimes it is difficult when you see the things which happen to us. This man is a priest and so I should respect him, but how can I when I see what sort of man he is? In Romania there is a saying "Do as the priest says, not as he does", but surely there must be a limit to how badly a priest can behave. Any money he receives from the people here, any donations to the church, he spends in the *crîşma* on drink. Then one evening, when drunk, he suggested I go back alone with him to the parish house as his wife was away. I couldn't believe what I was hearing, but in order to teach him a lesson I told him to go home and wait for me. As he walked off he said, "You promise you'll come, won't you?" I promised, and went back into the *crîşma*. Half an hour later he returned, glared at me, and tapped his cheek in the way Romanians do to suggest I had treated him badly. I just laughed at him, and made a rude sign, which is all he deserved. He tried to seduce Natalia as well. Ask her. And now he is trying to sell you the contents of the church.'

MARISHKA WAS NOT one to shrink from confrontation. She may not have had any proper education, but she did have a refined sense of justice and like her father she was not afraid of telling anyone, no matter whom, the truth to their faces. When she sensed an injustice, instead of withdrawing into the shadows as others did (much the wiser course of action) she would jump to her feet and intervene on the side of the weak without a moment's thought to the consequences. It was a noble quality, but, as Hungarians say, one can fall

off the other side of the horse. Sometimes she went too far, and in her fearless crusade against injustice she made many enemies, and these enemies were usually those with power and influence.

One evening there was an argument in the *crîşma*. A Gypsy had shouted at one of the policeman's friends. Barbu arrived promptly the following morning to take statements from selected witnesses. Marishka went over to him. I sensed there was going to be trouble.

'You are a policeman,' she shouted at him, 'but you know nothing about justice! If a Romanian had insulted a Gypsy, would you have rushed here this morning? No, you would not. All you know is that Romanians are innocent, especially if they are your friends, and that Gypsies are guilty. That is all. But go and look at yourself in the mirror. You will see that you are as Gypsy as anyone. You are so dark it looks as though the stove has emptied its soot over your head!'

I was standing near Nicu, the *Băiaş* Gypsy whom I had known when I first came to Halma.

'I enjoyed that,' he said to me in a whisper. There was a rebelliousness in the Gypsies, but few of them ever dared to confront the police in this way.

I could not see that such outbursts were helpful and tried to take Marishka home, but in vain. She would not be prevented from venting her wrath, and in public, against the man she felt had been responsible for so many of the family's woes.

'Marishka, you really must resist the urge to tell everyone what you think of them,' I suggested afterwards. She cast me a withering glare.

Of course I knew about the injustices against the Gypsies, and was horrified by what I had seen and heard. Andrei's death had been shocking enough for anyone. But I did not want to have an argument with the police or with anyone else. All I wanted was to be able to live in peace with Marishka, and to that end I tried to keep as low a profile as possible.

But just by moving in with Marishka I had raised my head well above the parapet. Not only was Marishka uncontrollably outspoken, but also she and her family were Gypsies; they were no longer nomadic, nor wore the traditional Gypsy clothes, but they were clearly Gypsies. 'The wolf changes its fur but not its nature,' was the Romanian saying. And siding with the Gypsies was not something that could be easily forgiven. In the streets the Romanians made their feelings abundantly clear.

'How can you live with the Gypsies? The dirt and the lice,' they said. 'They will rob you and cheat you'; 'Why don't you make friends with proper people? They are not even half-educated. Marishka is not suitable for a person like you,' they would say.

'Well, I don't know,' I would say, and shrug my shoulders, 'they seem to be very clean to me.'

In the evenings I told Marishka what people had said.

'Why don't they just mind their own business? What have we done to them?'

Despite all the comments, however, and the obvious upset, I did not feel threatened. I assumed the moment would pass. In any case I had recently mended the roof of the Orthodox church, as I had promised the priest, and of the Saxon church, and of any number of village houses. More importantly, I had repaired the water trough in the centre of the village, the only place in the current drought where water was now flowing and where the cows and horses could drink. This was something which everyone, Romanian, Saxon and Gypsy, must be grateful for – or so I thought.

In the meantime, therefore, I lived blissfully unaware of what was brewing behind the scenes. I was happy with my brown-limbed Gypsy girl and she was happy with me. That was all that mattered. There were many warnings, but they drifted away unheeded on the warm summer's breeze, of no consequence when compared to the pleasure of being entwined with Marishka and her way of life.

17

Transylvanian Markets

There is nothing of its sort left in the West that is as picturesque as a Roumanian fair.

Sacheverell Sitwell, *Roumanian Journey*

THE SEEMINGLY ENDLESS woods and sweeping pastures near Marishka's village, where not a fence disturbed the flow, and where rough cart tracks spread off in all directions, made horses the perfect form of transport. There were few roads suitable for cars, and so riding over the hills was often the quickest and easiest way of reaching neighbouring villages. Almost every family in Halma, however poor, had a horse. I was living in a country where horses easily outnumbered cars, and where, after the cow, the horse was a family's most treasured possession.

In the 1990s there were almost certainly more horses in Romania than in any other country in Europe. This was despite the modernizing policy of the Communist government of the 1950s and 60s, which aimed to rid Romania of horses. Horses were, it was decided, a sign of backwardness. Peasants were accordingly obliged to hand over their faithful animals for slaughter. Hundreds of thousands were killed, and in their place tractors rolled into the villages accompanied by flag-waving maidens singing patriotic songs reminiscent of a scene from an Eisenstein propaganda film. But for all the theatre the policy was not successful; in many parts of the country tractors were simply not a practical alternative, horses were more suited to the terrain and to the tasks, and they needed only hay for fuel which the peasants could produce themselves. Gradually the horse made a comeback. By the time I came to live in Romania there were only a few tractors left, but horses were to be seen everywhere, both in country and town.

We had a cow and had bought a pig, and there were a few chickens and ducks clucking and waddling about the yard. But from the moment I moved in with Marishka I dreamt of having a horse as well, or better still a pair of horses, both for riding and for carting.

Dreaming of owning a horse was easy, but finding a good one to buy was a challenge. I was lucky to have Nicolae as my guide. He was a consummate horseman. Riding always bareback, he had a calming influence on even the most fearsome animals which others would not dare approach, let alone mount. Any wild horse he could tame, and any sluggish nag he could coax into a gallop moments after jumping on its back. He had an aura they respected.

Buying at the Transylvanian markets was particularly hazardous. It was not long before the obvious fact dawned upon me that any horse or cow that was any good, and was selling for a reasonable price, would have been snapped up long before it ever reached the market. At the markets people sold what they had not managed to sell elsewhere. The best they kept for themselves; the second best was sold in the village to people who knew what they were buying. What reached the market was likely to be of poor quality, and possibly something the owners were desperate to be rid of.

The horses kicked, nipped or would not pull. Others shied away from motor vehicles (and were thus very sensible, but not useful). So it was with the cows: nobody would keep a cow which produced less milk per day than would pay for its keep, and everyone in the village knew which cows these were; such weak animals could only be sold in the market. The cunning sellers would not milk their cow in the morning, or even the night before, so that by the time it reached the market milk was dripping out of its swollen udders. Cows with milk dripping from their udders, Nicolae informed me, should be avoided at all costs.

It is true that some magnificent horses did reach the market, but these were more for show than for sale. The *Geambaşi*, as the Gypsy horse-copers were called, would gather at the markets to display their best horses to each other, and to the peasants from the surrounding area. It was a way of advertising their wares, just as the Gypsy metalworkers, the *Căldărari*, would wander about the market with a copper pot in their hands, or the tinsmiths carry a sample piece of ornate drainpipe or guttering under their arms. The *grei* or the *semi-grei*, the heavy cart horses, stood with lustrous coats, long flowing manes, huge hooves and rippling muscles, to be admired by marketgoers. Combed, brushed and manicured to perfection, these were exhibition animals, two of which could have pulled against a tractor. These horses were for sale in theory, but the asking prices were so high that they almost never sold. They were brought there to show what an eye the Gypsies had for horses and how splendidly they looked after them.

There were other horses for sale, and at reasonable prices, but when I heard of the tricks the *Geambaşi* played I was amazed that anyone ever bought at the markets. There were a whole variety of ruses to make a horse prance and look alive as though walking on hot coals, from stuffing paprika up its rear end, to giving it a good swig of *rachiu* for breakfast, or prickling it with a hedgehog in the morning so that you only needed to touch it at the market to make it go wild. One heard countless stories of how the *Geambaşi* would buy weak horses and do everything possible to spruce them up, make them look lively, just for the period the market lasted; the horse would sell but then after a few days the new owner would discover he had bought a dud. One of the most unpleasant of these tricks was to fasten a safety pin into the flesh underneath the horse's tail just before market. The horse sold, but over the weeks, from the increasing pain of the pin, grew thinner and thinner until the owner took it back to the market where it was bought for a snip by a friend of the same wicked *Geambaşi*. The pin was then removed and the process could be repeated as many times as they could get away with.

EVEN THOUGH I knew of such tricks it was still tempting to buy, as some of the animals were especially handsome. Hay carts travelling along the tracks of Transylvania were often pulled by horses of superior bearing, who held their heads high, and raised their hooves in a most aristocratic sort of way. They were finer and more classically beautiful than the ordinary draught and mountain horses of the area. These were the Lipizzaners, or Lipizzaner crosses, descendants of the horse created by the Emperor Maximilian II of Austria from crossing the Carsian horse of antiquity with a Spanish stallion in the 1560s, and whose more courtly cousins pranced and pirouetted at the Spanish Riding School in Vienna. In Romania, not far from Halma, there were several Lipizzaner studs. The most important was at Sîmbăta de Jos. Indeed, at the time of the Revolution, Sîmbăta de Jos was said to be the biggest Lipizzaner stud in the world, with over six hundred horses, all lined up in their boxes according to age and colour – Lipizzaners gradually change colour from black or dark brown to white (grey) as they grow older. Sîmbăta de Jos was bigger than all the famous Lipizzaner studs in Austria, Slovenia or Spain, and there were, it was said, more Lipizzaner horses in Romania than in the rest of the world put together. With the Lipizzaner studs nearby, Lipizzaner blood inevitably leaked out into the surrounding countryside, and at the fairs, there were always some horses of Lipizzaner extraction.

The Lipizzaner studs had been set up during the nineteenth century when it was decided that the breeding stock in Transylvania should be improved to provide good remounts for the Habsburg cavalry. At the time of the Napoleonic Wars, to escape the approaching French armies, the stallions from Vienna had been removed to Mezöhegyes in Hungary. From there, some years later, a number were sent on to Sîmbăta de Jos at the foot of the Carpathian mountains where they stayed until 1919. Then, just before Transylvania became a part of the Romanian kingdom, the last imperial officers remaining at Sîmbăta de Jos after the Great War, realizing the Romanians were on their way to take possession of the horses, left in the direction of Hungary with as many of the horses as they could manage. The horses that were left were taken on with pride by the Romanian royal family and the studs survived.

Even after the Communists took over in 1948, the studs were preserved, and so, ironically, for over forty years the Marxist state was heavily subsidizing the breeding of 'the horse of kings'. Indeed, during Communist rule the studs flourished. The great beauty of such a horse as Tulipan XIV, now of an advanced age, is evidence enough.

Only after the Revolution of 1989 did the studs begin to deteriorate. The state stopped supporting them, and the stud managers started selling horses to make ends meet. The Gypsies, from families who had settled at Sîmbăta because of the stud, who generation after generation had looked after the horses, were told they had to leave, and went to beg in Poland. Gradually the prize Lipizzaner studs of Transylvania fell into debt and disrepair, and before long were sold off to private buyers.

ONE OF THE techniques the *Geambaşi* used to sell horses were the *probe* or 'tests'. The first time I saw the *probe* was in the Maramureş. I was pottering happily about the market, admiring the harnesses and head collars for sale and comparing them always unfavourably with Mihai's beautiful creations, when suddenly a cart loaded with people came bursting through the crowd. Standing, clutching the reins with one hand and wheeling a long whip above his head in the other, was a wild-eyed, moustachioed Gypsy. 'Haaa!' he roared as he cracked his whip, and bystanders jumped out of the way. It was then I noticed that the wheels of the cart appeared to be jammed. 'Idiots,' I thought, 'look at the poor horse trying to pull with such a heavy load and they have forgotten to take off the brakes.' I was about to walk forward to point out to the Gypsy the obvious reason why the horse was only managing a burst of a few yards at a time and with tremendous effort, when Mihai took my arm and said, '*Sînt probe* – They are tests.' The Gypsy was demonstrating the strength and determination of the horse he was trying to sell. 'Haaa!' he bellowed again and this time the horse reared up on its hind legs with a frenzied look in its eyes.

At one market the *probe* flew out of control. The tested horse, driven by a Gypsy, barged into a horse standing quietly by its cart. This horse reared up and fell over backwards, and landed in the cart with its legs flailing in the air. The owner of the horse, also a Gypsy, flew into a rage and before long a fight erupted involving stones, whips and fists, during which another horse nearby, attached to a cart, took fright and bolted, galloping at terrifying speed through the market, scattering people and animals. One of the Gypsies, who had previously been fighting, stood in the way to try to stop it but was trampled under the hooves and wheels. The man lay on the ground, as bystanders rushed to see if he was still breathing. He lay there unmoving for several minutes and then, quite suddenly, picked himself up, brushed himself down, pushed the worried crowd aside as though nothing had happened, and immediately rejoined the fray. Nobody tried to stop the fight. As long as the Gypsies did not attack anyone else, nobody cared. Everyone just stood by and watched, tut-tutting. 'Gypsies!' they said. 'What do you expect?'

As THE MARKET days drew on, the marketeers would slowly begin to disperse. Gypsy women in their red floral dresses hauled themselves on to the carts, and arranged themselves and their skirts on rugs and hay. The children ran behind and jumped on as the carts turned out of the field and headed for home, and the streets of the village burned as they galloped down the roads, the drivers standing up, crying out to those following, whip in hand, the horses' shoes striking sparks on the stones. They then left the road and set off over the fields and through the forest to return to their villages, their route unrestricted by fences or hedges, the simplicity of the countryside resembling and enabling their roving lives.

The markets were picturesque affairs with Gypsies of so many different sorts, the old *Corturari* with their long grey beards flowing down their faces and on to their chests, and Transylvanian shepherds wearing their distinctive chocolate brown *loden*-cloth breeches and waistcoats, with their black velvet round-topped hats, like bowler hats, but taller and with smaller brims, perched on top of their heads. The atmosphere was exhilarating with so many people and animals crowded together, and the noise of the *probe* echoing in the background.

But it was better not to be lured into buying a horse. Much better to find one in the village, where you would know the horse's provenance, whether it had been treated properly, and whether it had any bad habits. The Gypsies knew every detail and defect of every local horse and recognized horses more readily than they recognized humans. If in the distance a cart was approaching they would identify the driver according to which horses were pulling it. When I found myself riding or driving borrowed horses through neighbouring villages people would ask me: 'How is life in Halma?'

'How did you know I come from Halma?' I replied. They simply pointed at the horses.

NICU, THE *BǍIAŞ* Gypsy who had accompanied me on walks about the village when I had first arrived, sold me my first horse. He needed the money to pay a police fine. From much pulling during the winter, and not having been given good quality hay, the mare was now thin and ill. Nicolae assured me that, despite appearances, she was a good horse, so I gave Nicu the money he asked, fed her some worm powder and better hay, and within a month or two she was fit and strong and almost unrecognizable as the horse I had bought.

Before I had bought her she had been used to pull cartloads of scrap metal to town – one of the ways Gypsies at that time made a little extra money. Most would gather metal door to door, asking people if they had anything that needed taking away. Others were more inventive, and more ambitious. In the newspaper we read of Gypsies who, one night, when no one was looking, had cut down a hundred-foot-high electricity pylon. Others removed the new shining, and rather kitsch, stainless steel county sign, which had been erected with much ceremony only a few weeks before.

Stainless steel fetched a good price. It was, however, another touch-
ingly incompetent crime, as it was perfectly obvious where the
lumps of stainless steel had come from, and the scrap metal merchant
when he saw the goods, not wanting trouble, immediately rang the
police. The thieves were caught, and the sign replaced with one of
inferior metal.

Burețoică, as the horse became known, was a courageous puller,
but she was too small for me to ride. Nicu, however, had another
larger filly which he had bought as a foal. She was now tall and fiery,
with attentive eyes and ears pricked forward, but she had never been
ridden. Nicolae offered to try her. There was no saddle but in one
movement he jumped on to her back, and threw her into a gallop
along the track, stones flying up behind, through the village square
and back at full speed, hooves hardly touching the ground. He
pulled her to an abrupt halt in front of us, the horse leaning back
on her haunches, almost in a sitting position with her front legs in
the air. 'She seems all right,' he said calmly as he jumped off. I tried
her out myself, but in a rather more English way, with a saddle,
attempting to trot and canter in a controlled manner. For an
unbroken horse she seemed to understand what to do, if a little
erratically, so I paid the asking price, and at last had the riding horse
I wanted.

I had never broken in a horse before, but Nicolae assured me
it was not a complicated matter. She tossed her head as we tried
to put on the bridle, and as we placed the saddle on her for the
second time, her eyes looked nervously backwards, to see what
tricks we were up to. She shifted and started, but, holding her
tight under the chin, we fastened the girth. As she was strong and
difficult to hold I jumped immediately on her back. I had to keep
her on a tight rein, her head upright, to stop her galloping off
through the square. She pranced all the way to the village margins
where I let the reins slacken and she flew across the fields. The
saddle disturbed her, and she swerved unnervingly, but over the
days she became accustomed to it, and we went on many a happy
gallop over the hills and through the forests. In whichever village
I found myself, as I drank beer at the *crîşma* and the horse munched

the grass of the village green, all the local Gypsies, and especially the children, would gather. 'Where is she from?' they would ask. 'How does she ride?' 'Where did you buy her?' 'How old is she?' They never asked where I was from. The outside world was a glorious irrelevance. They were only interested in the horse.

18

Distant Whistling of Shepherds

This evening wolves surrounded the sheep before they were put back into the fold and Nicolae was left alone on the hill with them. The cry went around the village and everyone ran towards the forest. It was pitch dark, but from the village you could hear the shouts, whistles, barks and the fighting of dogs. They managed to get the sheep back into the fold but the wolves took one young goat.

Notebooks, 2001

I N THE MIDDLE of Piazza Colonna in Rome stands the magnificent marble column after which the square is named, put up to celebrate the two invasions of Dacia by the Emperor Trajan in the first years of the second century AD. Dacia was the ancient Roman name of an area which included most of what is now Transylvania. The Dacians, who fought courageously against the Roman invaders but were eventually defeated, are said to be the ancestors of present-day Romanians. It is not easy to see the details of the reliefs which curl helically upwards over a hundred feet, but if you visit the Victoria and Albert Museum there is a plaster cast of the column, conveniently displayed in two pieces. Here you can see more easily the Dacians wearing the long shirts and skin-tight trousers which are still today traditional Romanian dress, and if you look up to the topmost panel you might be able to make out a scene of these Dacians, now defeated, retreating into the hills accompanied by a small flock of sheep and goats.

The raising of sheep and goats and the making of cheese had been one of the main occupations of Romanians even before the Romans arrived. Stories of shepherds and their sheep are the subject of many of the legends, songs and ballads of Romania, the most famous being the *Miorița*, and in the Middle Ages a considerable part of the tribute paid by Transylvania to the Ottoman Turks was paid in sheep and lambs.

In the north, in the Maramureş, I had helped the villagers with their farming. In Marishka's village there was much unused land, and there seemed an opportunity now to have my own animals and crops so as to try to provide our own food. Marishka's brothers, Nicolae and Eugen, were willing to help. Sheep seemed the obvious animals for us to keep, and so before long I had bought a small flock to provide us with cheese and meat.

That summer we set up a fold on the hills, took the sheep up to it, and persuaded an old Gypsy shepherd called Nene Niculaie to look after them. He arrived, his leathery face wizened by years of sun on the hills, carrying his thick sheepskin cloak, and followed by three ferocious dogs.

In Transylvania the keeping of sheep involves constant vigilance and a pack of large and well-trained dogs. The dogs are not for herding but for protection against wild animals. In the British Isles bears were wiped out by the sixteenth century, and the last wolf was said to have been shot by Sir Ewen Cameron of Lochiel in 1686. But here wolves still carry off sheep by the scruff of their necks and bears tear pigs in half like loaves of bread. As Gregor Von Rezzori wrote in one of his beautiful memoirs of Romania, 'The poetic gentleness of the flowery slopes was all too deceptive in obscuring the wildness of the deep forests.' You cannot leave the sheep alone even for a few hours. A shepherd I once met told me ruefully how some years before he had been unable to resist the urge for a drink in a nearby village. He returned to the hill to find he no longer had a single sheep to look after; in a frenzy the wolves had killed every one.

Often Marishka and I would pass by the fold and sit down with the shepherds. One evening outside Nene Niculaie's simple shepherd's hut on the edge of the forest, we talked about wolves and bears. Nene Niculaie, sitting on a milking stool, stirred up the fire and placed another cigarette into its home-made wooden holder.

Marishka and I sat upon his shepherd's cloak which he had laid out for us on the ground like a rug. Marishka leant against me, her head resting lightly on my shoulder, watching the moon, a tracery of branches silhouetted across its surface, rising slowly behind the forest.

Wolves, Nene Niculaie told me, holding an ember to his cigarette and puffing upon it until the tip glowed, operated in such a way as to suggest they had previously agreed a plan of attack. A group might come from the front, he explained, but just as in human wars, this was only a feint to draw off the dogs. Others had been creeping along the wooded gullies quietly towards the lower side of the fold, not letting even a twig snap beneath their paws. When they saw that the main attack had drawn off enough dogs they would move in from the rear. The shepherd would be standing in the middle trying to work out what was going on. It was not easy as the wolves usually came at night, especially when it was raining or better still misty. However, the shepherd has much experience of the wolves' cunning. To begin with he knows from the tone of the dogs' barks whether they are being attacked by wolves or a bear. And the dogs are well trained. When they bark to announce an attack the shepherd shouts out the orders. 'Roata meeerrrr! – Make a circle!' he yells and his voice tails off into the darkness. The dogs instantly position themselves at equal distances around the fold. As the wolves approach from the front, the dogs facing them attack. The wolves then draw back, and the dogs pursue them for a short distance but no more. This is the dangerous moment because younger and less experienced dogs, like raw recruits, break from their positions at the back of the fold and join the chase. Then one of the wolves who had crept silently along the wooded gullies, or the bed of a stream, would leap forward, and before anyone had even noticed, jump over the hurdles, grab a lamb or a kid and run off with it in its mouth.

Bears used different tactics. They were not afraid of the dogs, which could never really hurt them and could be swatted aside like flies or mosquitoes. A bear would stroll across the field on the chance of finding an easy snack. If there were too many dogs he would leave, but otherwise he would wander in, help himself and lumber off, swatting the snarling dogs aside as he went. One of Nene Niculaie's biggest dogs had a limp, his back leg having been torn open by the swipe of a bear's claw.

The bears were enormously powerful. They would sometimes attack horses, cows or even oxen. In Breb a friend had told me how one day his horse had been killed by a bear up on the mountain.

'I didn't realize bears attacked such big animals,' I said.

'Oh yes, they do,' he replied, and went on to tell me how the summer before, on St Peter's Day, he had been on the hills near Hărnicești. There he had seen with his own eyes, otherwise he would not have believed it, a bear attacking a pair of oxen. The bear, in one swing, had torn open the throat of the first ox, whereupon the other ox attacked the bear with its horns. The bear struck out at the attacking ox, wounding it, and then ran off. The first ox died, the second was so damaged it had to be slaughtered. The man lost his most precious possessions within a few minutes.

The bears were not afraid even to come into the village. People would hear their dog barking at night and go out to find the pigsty doors broken in pieces and the pig no longer there, or still there but with a leg missing. When the attacks became persistent villagers would push their pigs down in the cellar of the house, something to which the pigs took great exception. The villagers would then take it in turns to patrol in groups all through the night, with lighted sticks wrapped round with paraffin-soaked cloth to scare the bears away.

Nene Niculaie, taking another swig of the wine which I would always take up to him, told me how once he saw a bear tear the leg off a pig and throw it to the pursuing dogs in order to hold them up. 'They're not stupid,' he said. To emphasize further he told me how they take away their kill and bury what they have not managed to eat. If when they return to their larder the earth has been disturbed they will not touch the remaining meat. They have learned that humans sometimes find their hideaways and poison what they had stored. For the same reason a bear will only eat the meat of animals that he has killed himself. If he comes across a dead animal by chance he will not touch it. When, therefore, you see a bear approaching, it is said to be a good idea to lie down and pretend to be dead, as the bear will leave you alone and pass on by. This, however, takes a cool nerve.

As we sat in the gloaming, the yellow moon climbing up over the Transylvanian hills, mist in the valleys and the Saxon church steeple just visible on its mound above the village, you could sense the nearby forest coming alive. It seemed to awaken, to be alert, listening.

I asked Nene Niculaie how often he heard wolves howling in the forest.

'Oh we hear them often,' he said, 'but most especially in November. This is when they call to each other to bring the packs together.'

This reminded me of how in the Maramureş St Andrew's Day, 30 November, was said to be the day when wolves had their meetings in remote and hidden parts of the forest. On this day the village women tied up the jaws of their scissors and any other snapping instrument they possessed, in order symbolically or magically to tie the mouths of the wolves shut for the following year. Wolves, so the Maramureşeni informed me, are only dangerous if their jaws are hanging open. If they are shut they will walk through the middle of a flock and not touch a single sheep.

A medical officer by the name of Hans Carossa, with the German army fighting the Romanians during the Great War, wrote about the time he spent on the Eastern Front among the forested foothills of the Carpathian mountains. He too mentioned how, towards the end of November, sitting in his trench, even as the shells hissed overhead, he could hear the haunting sound of the wolves howling into the night.

'And do wolves ever eat people?' I asked Nene Niculaie.

'Of course they do. Why should they not? They are wary of humans, but if they are hungry they will eat them,' he said.

'Our mother told us of the village schoolteacher here who was eaten by wolves,' said Marishka. 'She had been walking along the road to the village at night. In the morning in the snow they found only her boots with her feet still in them.

'But perhaps it wasn't true,' she added. 'Maybe they only told us that to keep us straying too far from the village.'

'I heard of a man in the Maramureş', I recalled, 'who was returning from Ocna Şugatag to the village of Corneşti one evening a few years ago. He saw a pack of wolves on the track ahead and climbed up a telegraph pole. All night in the freezing cold he stayed up there as the pack circled below waiting for him to fall off. But he managed to cling on and was at last able to come down when a cart drove along the road in the morning. The carter found the snow around the bottom of the pole trampled by hundreds of wolf prints.'

This reminded me of a book I had recently been reading which describes how wolves had set upon a group of horses near the Black Sea. The horses had formed a circle on the shore, with their heads in the middle, and when the wolves approached they kicked out at them furiously. The horses kept their formation all night and in this way had survived until morning, when the villagers saw what was happening.

'Yes, it is true,' said Nene Niculaie. 'Wolves attack horses. They will even eat earth to make them heavier so that when they grab a horse by the neck they can, using their extra weight, swing it around until it falls over from dizziness. Wolves have many tricks.'

THE MOON WAS now up in the sky, and clouds passed slowly in front of it, each in turn illuminated for a brief moment as they drifted by. Marishka and I climbed on to the cart.

'Be careful on the way back,' Nene Niculaie warned us, 'it's two weeks before St Peter's Day, the worst time for bears.'

As we made our way down to the security of the village we left him shouting across the hills to the other shepherds out with the sheep for their evening pasture on slopes beneath the forest. Whistles responded from a distance and Nene Niculaie knew all was well at present. We cantered across the fields, the moon shedding its glow over the darkening blue landscape.

'*Chea! Gyeh neah!*' Marishka shouted to encourage the horses, and we rushed past the first village houses, and back to the tall wooden gate of the blue house which swung open as we approached; Nicolae had seen us coming. The horses clattered into the cobbled yard, where they were unharnessed and led into the stables. Marishka and I retired to supper, bath and bed, from where every now and then we could still hear the distant whistling of the shepherds on the hills.

19

Violins on the Fire

Whenever any poor Gipsies are encamped anywhere and crimes and robberies etc occur, it is invariably laid to their account, which is shocking; and if they are always looked upon as vagabonds, how can they become good people? I trust in heaven that the day may come when I may do something for these poor people.

Queen Victoria, *Diaries*, Winter 1836

B Y DECEMBER SNOW lay thick on the ground, the streams had frozen, and the ducks were sliding about on the ice. The boards of the veranda creaked and cracked in the cold and when we opened the door of the house there was a swirl of mist as the freezing outside air met billows of warmth from the kitchen. Long icicles hung off the eaves, and ice jammed up the windows and even the lock of the door. The cold air came through the keyhole, condensed and then froze, creating little icicles even on the inside. Every now and then cascades of snow would slide off the steep roofs into the courtyard and had to be shovelled off the paths.

The sheep came down from the hill and were gathered in pens in the open air just above the village. All winter they stayed outside and were given hay and maize to eat. At night they stood motionless, munching hay while snow piled silently upon their backs. The shepherds wore their thick, shaggy woollen coats, consisting of several sheepskins sewn together, which hung right down to the ground. At night they lit fires and slept wrapped up in these same coats, even when it was minus 25 degrees Centigrade outside. In the morning they too, like the sheep, woke up covered with snow.

The cow was kept in the stable. She could not endure the icy cold like the sheep and so had to stay inside until the spring. She went out only for water, walking slowly down the snow-packed road, to drink from the stream where holes had been broken in the ice. The horses were in the stables too. They and the cow warmed each other with their combined body heat. When they came out to drink, they trotted briskly across the yard, scattering the ducks and chickens in all directions, and galloped down the road, snow flying up from their hooves, to the village watering trough. They then galloped back, tossing their heads and manes, pleased to be out in the fresh air even if only for a short time.

WINTER, DESPITE OCCURRING regularly each year, always seemed to catch the Gypsies by surprise. The Romanians and Saxons had been piling up wood, bottling vegetables in vinegar and fruit in syrup, filling the barns to the rafters with hay, and the cellars with potatoes. The Gypsies had usually been helping them. But when it came to their own preparations they had a distinctly Micawberish attitude; something would always turn up.

Marishka certainly took the Micawberish line. Since I was with her it was particularly likely that something would turn up. I would simply buy all the extra food we needed from the market in the town, saving us all the frightful bother of having to produce it ourselves. Life was short, so why spend half of it seeding and hoeing when you did not need to? This attitude made good enough sense, except that I had the idealistic notion of wanting to eat food that we had produced ourselves.

Thanks to Marishka's lackadaisical attitude, when winter arrived we had plenty of sheep's cheese, courtesy of Nene Niculaie, but little else. Imbued as I was with the Maramureş work ethic, and accustomed to putting aside money and food for a rainy day, like the Saxons, I was not best pleased. I tried to persuade her to think about the future but with little success.

'We have run out of potatoes,' Marishka said, coming up out of the cellar one winter's day.

'If we had spent more time hoeing in the summer and less time dancing we might now have potatoes,' I said. For this I would receive a withering look. She did not like rational explanations.

'We are Gypsies. If you wanted less dancing and more potatoes you should have chosen to live with a Romanian or a Saxon girl,' she would say, as exasperated by my inability to understand their shortcomings as I was exasperated at being deprived of my supper.

There was not enough food, nor was there enough hay, or even stoves. We had made hay, but it was not enough to last all winter long; more would need to be bought at always higher prices as the winter progressed. Food too I had to buy, with weary resignation, from other villagers or from the markets.

At least the stove problem the Gypsies were able to solve. Marishka's metal-working uncle Gheorghe was able, within a few hours, to make us a stove which kept us so warm that we slept with the blankets off even as the temperatures outside fell to glacial levels. The Gypsies have always been well known for making things out of metal. Legend even has it that it was Gypsies who forged the nails for Jesus's crucifixion and and so were condemned by God to wander the world in perpetuity.

EVEN THOUGH MOST of the Gypsies of Halma were no longer nomadic and had been more or less settled for the last one or two hundred years, they had still not accustomed themselves to conventional settled living. They hoped to survive the winter with occasional jobs, by borrowing or begging, or simply by not eating very much. Some of the poorest families would even put blankets over their windows, partly so as to keep out the cold, but also to keep their children sleeping longer and so eating less.

Any food the Gypsies might have stored was generally finished by the end of January. Then came the dreaded *Fe'Martie*, the month named by the Gypsies — February and March rolled into one because they cannot bear to pronounce the very syllables of those accursed months. Said quickly, they hope it might pass equally quickly. It was eight weeks characterized by miserable weather, by mud, slush, rain and sleet. This is the 'month', or so the saying goes, when the Gypsy throws even his violin on to the fire to keep warm.

This was also the time when some Gypsies were tempted to supplement their meagre diets and depleted wood piles with petty thefts.

'How can you look into the eyes of your children and tell them day after day that there is no more food and no more wood?' a young Gypsy asked me once. 'You can't just stand and watch them starve or freeze. Of course in such circumstances if we see a chicken wandering into our yard we grab it and put it into the pot. But be sure, we steal a lot less than others. We might steal a chicken or a few fallen branches of wood from the forest or from an abandoned garden. The richer people steal a cow or a hectare of trees, not because they are hungry, but to make themselves even richer. And when they are caught they are forgiven because they are friends of the right people. When we are caught we are beaten and then sent to prison.'

'But surely if you worked harder during the summer, and were more organized, you would have food and would not need to steal anything over the winter.'

'But there are no jobs to be had, nobody employs us, or at least all too rarely, and when they do they pay us almost nothing.

'Might you give me a job mending the houses?' he continued. 'You know you should give jobs to the poorest people. If we don't have jobs we have to steal. What else can we do? We don't want to steal, but sometimes we have to.'

Another man, a Romanian this time, said to me: 'A man who has a full stomach reasons in a different way from one with an empty stomach. If you or your children were starving you would steal too.' I had to agree with him. In *The Brothers Karamazov*, I remembered, Dostoevsky had written of the Russian peasants, 'First give men bread, then ask them to be virtuous.'

Of course some Gypsies stole more, some less and some did not steal at all. It was the same with the Romanians and the Saxons. It was wrong to make generalizations. Of the biggest thieves in this particular village, one was a Romanian, one a Saxon and one a Gypsy. There was in Halma an equitable distribution of light-fingeredness, regardless of race or creed. There was no justifiable basis for discrimination.

A Gypsy named Conta was one of the more inventive thieves. For some reason Nicolae had given Conta the job of 'looking after' fifty of our sheep. He was supposed to tend them during the day while they pastured on the hill, and then return them to the fold for milking. One evening, however, he did not return to the fold. He had simply walked away with all his charges, through the forest and over the hill. I had to admire his nerve but was astonished by his stupidity. Where on earth, I thought, did he hope to hide an entire flock of sheep?

Nicolae leapt on to his horse the next morning and set off through the forest towards the village of Bîrnău. Someone had seen a flock heading in that direction. As Nicolae approached the village he saw the sheep on the outskirts several hundred yards away. He put the horse into a gallop across the open field. Conta looked up, saw him approaching and ran, disappearing into the forest 'so fast he left a trail of dust behind him', as Nicolae described it. Once he was among the trees Nicolae on his horse could no longer keep up with him. Two of the sheep had already been sold to unsuspecting villagers; the rest were unharmed. Conta returned (sheepishly) a month later to the village. He met Nicolae in the street, and went down on his knees to beg forgiveness.

'I couldn't bring myself to give him the beating he deserved,' Nicolae told me. Conta agreed he owed us two sheep, but of course we never saw them or any money. Perhaps Conta was not so stupid after all.

Conta and his family were possibly the most notoriously light-fingered of the Gypsies of Halma, and their thefts were the stuff of many a village story. One of the most entertaining of these was of the cow they had stolen some years before, strapping gumboots on to all four of its hooves so as to disguise the trail in the mud – a ploy remarkably similar to that used by Hermes when he stole the cattle of Apollo. Old Moş Petru, the owner of the cow, had come sleepily into his stable that morning, sat down on the milking stool, brought over the bucket and put his hand out to feel for the udders to wash them. He felt about in air – there was no cow in the stable, and he had not even noticed. Everyone would fall about when they heard this story for the umpteenth time. Of course, as always, the Conta family were caught (just as Hermes had been). By mistake they had tied the two left-foot gumboots on the two front hooves. As a result, instead of the trail being disguised it was all too easy to follow.

THE HAPPIEST PART of the winter for the Gypsies were the twelve days of Christmas. This was the season of music and dancing which was, of course, what they really enjoyed. It was also the season of carol singing, of the *Capra* and of the gathering of food, drink and a little money. Motley collections of Gypsy children, adults and musicians would go around the village on Christmas Eve singing carols for which they received a few lei, or a slice of cake, or a glass of *rachiu*. Some of the more stingy villagers would close their gates and not allow the carol singers in. But for most it was a time of good fellowship, to drink with others, to enjoy oneself, and an opportunity to give a few presents to the poorest of the village.

Then on New Year's Eve the same groups tramped from house to house but this time performing the story of the *Capra* – the goat. The *Capra*, like a medieval hobby horse, with horns and clacking wooden jaws, rigged up with string to open and shut like a bite, came dancing along the street, accompanied by the musicians, terrorizing the dogs as it came. To jaunty music the *Capra* pranced into houses and danced its frenzied and demoniacal dances, snapping, *clack, clack, clack*, in the spectators' faces. Children ran for cover. Then the assembled mummers would act out a short satirical play with a goatherd, a Gypsy, a doctor and the goat (during which the Gypsies good-humouredly parodied themselves), and when it was concluded cakes and *rachiu*, and more lei, were handed round to all. Using this money the company would throw a wild New Year's party. There was no bourgeois thrift amongst the Gypsies. Money was spent as soon as earned.

That year Eugen, Marishka's brother, dressed up as the *Capra*. Marishka shouted at him as they were setting off around the village:

'Eugen! Come back! Where is the blanket off our bed?'

'I borrowed it to play the goat. Don't worry, I'll bring it back tomorrow,' he shouted as he disappeared out of the courtyard.

We received the blanket back several days later with a large hole cut out of the middle, through which Eugen had stuck his head to wear it as a cloak.

ON 6 JANUARY there were solemn religious rituals to be observed. The priest and his attendants processed through the village blessing the houses on the feast of the Epiphany. We tidied the house and, as is the custom, put a glass of *rachiu* or wine for each man, a cake and a small contribution to the church funds, on the kitchen table.

'They are coming,' said Marishka, craning out of the window. We checked that all was ready and stood waiting by the door.

We waited patiently, but the expected tramp of feet on the wooden steps did not come. Marishka went to the window only to see the small procession, clutching cross, holy water and the aspergill made of box and dried basil, walking along the snow-covered track towards the centre of the village. Other Gypsies had come outside wondering why the priest and his entourage had not entered their houses either. They had deliberately missed all of us out. Marishka was livid.

'It is because we are Gypsies,' she said. 'They have put a fence in the cemetery to separate our graves from theirs, and now they don't even stop to bless our houses. And you mended the roof of the church!' It was all too much for her: the disappointment, the shame and the injustice. She rushed out of the door and I saw her striding towards the ecclesiastical party with a murderous look on her face.

When Marishka reached the procession gathered in the square she protested that they had missed us out and must return.

'I'm afraid we can't come back,' said the priest. 'It is not permitted to go backwards or anti-clockwise when blessing the houses.'

'So William has repaired your church roof and you don't even come to bless his house.'

'It was an oversight. We did not know you were there. But we simply can't come back now.'

'Oh really? We will see about that,' said Marishka. 'If you don't come back this instant, I am going to start shouting *everything* I know about you for *everyone* to hear. You have ten seconds to decide what you are going to do.'

For ten seconds a flustered priest was seen gesticulating, endeavouring to persuade his attendants that church principles could perhaps be overlooked under certain circumstances, and thus steps could theoretically be retraced. Unsmilingly, they returned to the house. With his aspergill the priest sprinkled the walls with holy water while declaiming prayers of benediction, drank the *rachiu*, pocketed the money and quickly departed. Once again Marishka had succeeded in infuriating the Romanians.

'I don't know why you wanted him to bless the house when you know what a rogue he is?' I said after the stilted ceremony had been completed.

'Who else will do it?' she said. 'He's the priest.'

'Don't have it blessed at all,' I suggested.

'No, the house must be blessed, even if it's by him,' she said, 'it is the custom, and in any case, people will try to cast evil spells upon us, you can be sure of that, and this will help to protect us.'

I suspected that the scene might have been provoked more by her injured Gypsy pride than anything else, but felt that, on balance, with spells whizzing around all over the place, there was no harm in taking precautions.

THE WINTER WAS long and much time was spent huddled inside in the warmth of the house. But on mornings when the sun was shining and there had been a fresh fall of snow, tired of being cooped up indoors, we would take to the hills on the horses. Riding on snow was more slippery than on grass, but at least if we fell the landing was less painful.

The boy who milked the cow would let the horses out soon after the sun came up and we would hear the muffled clunk of their hooves on the snow-covered cobbles as they trotted out to the village fountain for water. This muffled clunk was our gentle alarm clock. Having eaten our fill of scrambled eggs, Eugen and I would saddle up the horses and with Marishka, and anyone who cared to come with us, we set off at a gallop across the virgin white hills, lumps of snow thrown up by the hurtling hooves of the horses in front bouncing off our faces. The Gypsies liked to go at full tilt, not just for the thrill, but also to show off their horsemanship to any-body who, with luck, might be watching. There were terrifying descents back to the village, hooves slipping and sliding on patches of ice, and Marishka, Eugen and I would arrive back in the square exhausted and exhilarated, our fur hats flecked with snow.

Then in the evenings we would crunch our way along white paths, toboggans rushing past us accompanied by the delighted screams of children, to warm ourselves by the stove in the *crîşma*. The road, normally a rough and bumpy track, was now smoothed by the passing of a hundred horse-drawn sleighs and toboggans. The runners of the sleighs had made the snow so smooth and glassy that at night their tracks reflected the glow of the few twinkling street lights.

Around the stove the talk would move from the mundane to the supernatural. One New Year's Eve I told the assembled company about the necromantic customs in the Maramureş on the evening of the last day of the year, and on St Andrew's Day, when the girls tried with various devices to look into the future to see whom they might marry. A girl in the Maramureş had explained to me how they ate salted dough balls in the evening so as to dream of their future husbands.

'Just like when we give salt to the cows before they go off to see the bull,' her brother had mischievously suggested.

'Oh shut up, you stupid idiot,' she had shouted at him as she chased him out of the room with a broom.

Here, said Marishka, a girl steals a strand of basil from the priest's aspergill when he is sprinkling the house with holy water on 6 January. If she puts this sprig under her pillow that night, she will dream of the man she will marry.

This talk prompted Marishka's uncle Gheorghe, the metal-worker, to tell us about the bizarre behaviour of the sorceresses in his native village on the eve of St George's Day. That evening, he told us, was the evening when all the *vrăjitori* (witches) of the vil-lage, both women and men, would go about collecting the basic ingredients needed for their spells the following year. In his village St George's Eve had some special potency, just as St Agnes's Eve had a special potency in Keats's England. The witches, he told us, as he lit another cigarette with a match struck on the seat of his trousers, would first collect water from nine wells. Then they would strip naked, and in the middle of the night, literally the 'witching hour', creep up to the graveyard on the hill where they would carefully put the earth from nine different graves into bags. Gheorghe's grandfather had told Gheorghe and his friends that they should hide in the shadows near the graveyard and wait for the witches to appear. When they saw them coming they should leap out of their hiding places and beat them with their carting whips and send them scurrying home. Gheorghe waited for three St George's Eves run-ning until he saw his first witch. He and his friends jumped out in front of her and chased her, cracking their whips and falling over themselves with laughter, all the way back to the village. In this way, he explained, they had prevented her from spreading her evil over the village in the coming year. She had not been able to gather the essential raw materials necessary for her incantations.

Gheorghe then told us about the witch from his village who would seek out entwined snakes, and separate them using a special hazel switch. With this same switch, waving it in the appropriate way, she was able in a swish to separate courting couples or hus-bands and wives. Gheorghe's stories reminded me of the Macbeth-like magic of the Maramureş, and the uses of wolves' windpipes and bats' wings. Romania seemed, wherever you went, to be like a great bubbling cauldron of magic, you could not get away from it: spells and the work of witches were always simmering just below the surface.

After an evening's chatting in the *crîşma*, warmed by beer, wine or *rachiu*, or all three, we would return home, the snow glittering on the roofs in the moonlight, load the stove with wood and jump into our blissfully warm bed. All sorts of icons and sanctified charms from monasteries hung on the walls around us, and Marishka had even placed them under the pillow to protect us from all the evil eyes which she was sure would be watching us.

20

The Calm Before the Storm

Transylvania had been a familiar name as long as I could remember. It was the very essence and symbol of remote, leafy, half-mythical strangeness; and, on the spot, it seemed remoter still, and more fraught with charms.
Patrick Leigh Fermor, *Between the Woods and the Water*

S PRING CAME AGAIN in a spectacular burst of blossom. The pear trees at the front of the house whose branches had recently been weighed down with snow were now adorned with a new white covering of blossom. In April the stream swelled with meltwaters from the hill and the fields were yellow with dandelions and cowslips. On May evenings Maybugs whirred about out of control and in June the toads began a chorus of croaking in the middle of the village long into the night.

The sheepfolds were taken higher up the hill and, once the heated negotiations had been concluded as to who should rent which parcel of land for grazing from the town hall, the pens and shepherds' huts were set up for the summer. Nene Niculaie, in shaggy cloak and with shepherd's round velvet hat upon his head, could be seen leaning on his carved shoulder-high staff, accompanied by his huge dogs, standing upon the banks beneath the forest.

As the weather warmed up meals were taken on the veranda in the shade of the wide-leaved vines which curled up the wooden columns and tangled themselves along the eaves of the house. Horses and carts, piled high with hay, clattered along the road outside, sending the chickens, ducks and geese squawking in all directions and the dogs barking in excitement. Sometimes it was Nicolae or Eugen whom I had asked to bring a cartload of hay for the horses. They would drive the cart through our gate, the load brushing against the posts on either side, and into the huge oak-beamed barn, which was twice the size of the house. Here the flower-filled hay was heaved into the loft with pitchforks, and the cart, when empty, was driven out the other side of the barn and through the orchard, weaving its way in between the ancient, twisted apple trees, and away back to the fields up near the forest to fetch another load.

DURING THOSE DAYS one of the ducks went missing, and although we never found her, we did find her nest. In it were eight eggs and we persuaded a broody hen to take them on. Before long the eggs hatched and the hen became the proud mother to eight ducklings, and looked furiously at anyone who dared to come too close. All went well for a few days until, to the hen's great alarm, all her 'chicks' jumped into the stream and started swimming and splashing about happily in the summer sunshine. The hen was thrown into confusion. For days she walked up and down the bank, clucking and fretting and calling to her chicks to see sense and return to dry land.

WHILE I BUSIED myself mending walls and roofs of the village's eighteenth-century houses Marishka looked after domestic matters. Although she now made an incomparable scrambled egg, she did not concern herself unduly with food preparation, and meals were often few and far between. For cleanliness, however, she was a demon. The house was washed and scrubbed every day, and there was always a ready supply of freshly laundered clothes and sheets.

She also looked after the garden, although there was a lack of urgency about her arrangements. Planting usually happened late, and I had to drop heavy hints about the appropriate time to hoe and weed. But we usually produced enough vegetables to last us at least through the summer and autumn.

Food, it seemed, was something which she trusted would always appear from somewhere, somehow, either from family or friends, or bought from neighbours at the last minute when hunger was clamouring. In any case, she herself would happily go without food all day. As a result eating became a haphazard affair for me as well, provided I had a good breakfast. What Marishka could not miss was the gathering in the village square prior to the cows coming home, or the evening's ensuing entertainments in the *crîşma* invariably involving music and dancing.

She also enjoyed expeditions; it was perhaps an inherited trait. She liked being on the move, going to town, or just happily walking in the hills, or driving the cart up to the forest, where we lit a fire, cooked food, and drifted off to sleep on rugs in the warmth of summer evenings. Marishka was an expert at comfort. She had the suppleness of a cat. She could curl up on a chair on the veranda, or stretch out on a rug and doze with feline ease, her head resting on her brown arms in a pose of perfect relaxation. Looking at her as she rested her head on my lap, I could not understand why people could so dislike the Gypsies.

'Well,' I said one afternoon as we dozed on the hill, 'for the moment people seem to be leaving us alone.'

'Yes,' she murmured, 'we have been lucky so far. But they are not happy about the sheep.'

'I have noticed,' I said.

Certainly there was a lot of talk. Villagers whispered to me that the shepherds were tricking us. They told me the sheep were not being looked after properly. Nicolae was not a shepherd, they said, and did not know what he was doing. I would lose money. The sheep were grazing on other people's land and I must be careful or I would have trouble with the police. These comments were intended to persuade me to sell the sheep. But I did not want to sell them, especially if pressurized to do so by the envious whisperings of those who disliked Gypsies. Besides I enjoyed going up to the sheepfold in the evening to watch Nene Niculaie making cheese, his leather face lit up as he bent over the boiling milk, flames licking and curling around the base of the blackened cauldron. And in the spring it was a delight to see the lambs jumping and playing, shaking their ears and racing each other back and forth across the meadows.

When it was not too hot, Marishka and I would take the horses further afield, perhaps to visit the blacksmith in Bîrnău to reshoe the horses, or to look for horses or dogs for sale, or grain for the animals. Some of my happiest moments were spent galloping over the hills and across the meadows, with Marishka or her brothers, tears running horizontally across our cheeks as the wind streamed into our eyes. They had only two speeds, walk or gallop. Trotting bareback was too uncomfortable, and cantering was too tedious. So we would hare over the hills, as if we did not have all the time in the world to reach wherever we were heading, and only slowed down in order to rest the horses.

When I went with Marishka to neighbouring villages we would stop on the way in glittering oak glades, picnicking on bread, cheese, wine and wild raspberries or strawberries. We took the saddles and bridles off the horses to let them graze freely, and lounged in the shade of the oaks. There was never anyone around, and there never seemed to be any hurry. We sipped and dozed away the summer days. We did not know that this happy time would soon be brought to an end by the envy and spite of others.

ONCE ON AN expedition to find sheep we discovered some new cousins for Marishka. We were in a village several valleys away from Halma and were having a drink in a *crîşma*. A Gypsy girl sitting at a table asked us from which village we had come and we told her.

'My grandfather was said to be from there,' she said.

'Oh really, what was he called?' we asked innocently. She then gave Valentin's name. On one of his musical jaunts, it seemed, her mother had been conceived, and now, lo and behold, Marishka had happened upon several new cousins whom she had never known existed. The girl summoned her siblings and for an evening there was much mutual congratulation and drinking of *rachiu*; then we headed back over the hills and never saw them again.

As an excuse for a jaunt, we would also travel over the hills to visit the tremendous fortified churches, which, just as in Halma, stood magnificent in the middle of all the neighbouring villages, their bastions, portcullises, pointed towers and ring-walls 'bristling with purpose like bits of armour', as Patrick Leigh Fermor described them. Marishka often waited for me outside. She knew the Saxons did not like the Gypsies to enter their churches and she thought it best not to provoke them. Nor was she especially interested in Saxon churches.

One September day Marishka and I went to visit the church of the neighbouring village of Floreni. I had not been there for some time and wanted to see whether the church roof might need patching. We decided to take a picnic and rugs and so went by cart. I put into the basket a bottle of wine, glasses, plates, boiled eggs, Nene Niculaie's cheese, gherkins, apples and pears from the garden, a bar of chocolate. It was a warm and sunny day and we trotted out of the village, the little dark Gypsy children in their ragged clothes chasing us, jumping on to the back of the cart and shrieking with joy.

We climbed the hill, one of the village storks soaring above our heads, and passed through the forest at its narrowest part. Here the track descended over the same fields that Marishka and her family had walked up when they had fled from Sighişoara nearly twenty years ago. We pulled up the horses beneath a beech tree for shade and ate our picnic overlooking the valley. In all directions the forest spread out as far as the eye could see. The horses, as always, moved slowly off to find the best grass, while we ate our picnic, drank the wine and snoozed in the warm afternoon air. Birds sang in the tree above us, I even heard the strange whistling sound of a golden oriole coming from the thick greenery of a distant clump. Marishka rested her head on my knees and I told her about Floreni.

In Floreni all the Saxons had now left. I had known the last two who had lived there, an old lady called Anna and her son Kurt. When I first visited them in 1991 they still stored the village hams in one of the bastions, the *Speck Turm* – the 'Bacon Tower', as it was called – just as they had for centuries, so that there was always food available inside the walls in case of attack.

In 1990 there had been nearly two hundred and fifty Saxons in Floreni but by 1994, everyone, even the parson, had gone. Only Anna and Kurt remained. They could not bear to leave their home and their church to its fate.

By themselves Anna and Kurt soldiered on, doing their best to look after the church. Anna swept and dusted, and weeded the flower beds. Kurt carried out whatever repairs he could. Even though there were no other Saxons in Floreni Kurt would ring the bells morning, midday and evening as they had always been rung. Every other day he would climb the steep oak steps to wind the old clock, slowly ratcheting up forty feet the heavy weights which powered the clicking and clacking mechanism for a couple of days. When the clock stopped working they paid out of their own pocket to have it mended. There was no one else left to contribute.

Gradually, however, life became unbearably lonely for them. They had Romanian and Gypsy friends, but even after living side by side with them for many years they felt different, and could not understand the way the Gypsies lived. In December 1989 Kurt had gone to fight alongside other Romanians in the streets of Bucharest during the Revolution that deposed the dictator Ceauşescu. Little did he know that his valiant efforts and the ensuing execution of Ceauşescu and his wife would spell the end for the Saxons in Floreni.

Finally Anna and Kurt decided to leave as well. One April morning which should have been so full of hope, with ploughing and seeding for the year ahead, Anna and Kurt packed their bags. Anna, with tears running down her cheeks, rang the bell for the last time. Kurt climbed the ladder to the oak-boarded platform where the clock ticked in the reassuring way it had done for centuries, and wound it up for the last time. Then, taking only what they could carry, they departed from Floreni for ever, leaving the village without Saxons for the first time in over eight hundred years. Since then the bells have not rung and two days after their departure the clock quietly stopped.

Marishka had fallen asleep. She woke up towards the end of the story.

'So there are no Saxons left in Floreni,' she said drowsily. 'I wonder what will happen to the place?'

As we descended into the village we passed houses which were already in ruins. In the centre there was a new *crîşma*, named the 'Bar Tropicana', with a couple of simple palm trees painted on the wall by Gypsies. In front of the bar stood the solid defensive walls of the church, an indecipherable Communist slogan still just visible, painted in red along its length, and there, as always, on top of one of the corner towers was the customary storks' nest.

Marishka and I entered through the gates, passing under the two encircling defensive walls. As there were no Saxons left Marishka did not feel so out of place. The paths and flower beds which Anna had kept so neat were now overgrown. Weeds were even growing out of the walls halfway up the tower.

We stepped through the stone Gothic doorway into the church itself. There was a feeling of damp and dereliction in the air and layers of dust had built up on the pews.

'How sad it is here,' said Marishka. There had not been a service in the church for nearly a decade. The grand old gilded baroque organ still functioned, but a Saxon organist's fingers had not wandered over its keys for years. Now, if you pumped the time-polished foot pumps, dust blew out of tarnished pipes.

Everything, however, was still in its place in the church. On the pews were the Gothic-script hymn books; a velvet and gold cloth lay on the altar; even the black and white painted numbers, also of Gothic form, announcing the hymns of the day, were still hanging on the wall. But there were no people.

On the organ stand I found a book of music. I blew off the dust. Turning the pages, among any number of Lutheran hymns which had once trumpeted out beneath this vaulted nave, I found a piece entitled: '*Für den Geburtstag des Kaisers* – For the Emperor's Birthday'. 'God save, God protect, our King-Emperor and our land' were the first lines. I looked for the date of the book: 1875. It was to be played on Franz Josef's birthday. A few notes showed it was the tune from Haydn's Emperor Quartet, later used as the famous German patriotic song, the *Deutschlandlied*. One could imagine on 18 August each year the church echoing to the strains of this rousing hymn, and on that day congregations all over the Empire and the Hungarian Kingdom joining in one voice to wish their King-Emperor a long life. He did have a long life, and a long reign. He was eighty-six when he died, having reigned for sixty-eight years. But when he died, in 1916, his empire was almost finished. After just a few years, this village and all the others for hundreds of miles around would become part of Romania. Mihai of the Maramureş had been born into the Austro-Hungarian Empire, but by the time he was a year old Breb too had become Romanian.

The end of the Empire had been a blow for the Saxons. Without their caring Emperor, life became ever more difficult and uncertain. Romania gave them no special treatment, and felt no medieval obligations towards them. German influence in Central Europe was diminished. There was a brief resurgence with the rise of the Third Reich, but this only brought down greater troubles upon the Saxons' heads. Many fled from Transylvania in 1944, in front of the advancing Russian armies, fearing reprisals against ethnic Germans. Of those who remained behind most, like Frau Knall, were deported to Russia for five years where many died of disease and starvation. Then came forty years of Communism followed by the great exodus after 1990. It had not been a good century. The Saxons had, to a great extent, been victims of remote political decisions and had been caught up in wars which had nothing to do with them. They were a peaceful, peasant people, whose lives were torn apart by a tumultuous twentieth century. Now in Floreni there were no Saxons left at all.

Riding away out of the village, the hooves of the horses clopping on the cobbles, you passed the blue, buff and green-washed eighteenth-century Saxon houses, many now abandoned and falling into ruin. Huge cracks were appearing in their walls, and tiles slipping from their steep terracotta roofs. I found it hard to believe that such beautiful places were being allowed to crumble away.

On the edge of the village Gypsy families still lived in brightly coloured houses. The children ran to the front gates and waved, while discussing among themselves the merits of our horses. Music emanated from the windows and courtyards, and the young lounged on simple verandas in the evening sun, some dancing, others waving or whistling as we passed by. They had an entirely different outlook on life. The Saxons would have been working in the fields. The Gypsies were busily taking life easy. You could not necessarily say that one way of life was better than another. They were just very different.

All around you could see what the Saxons had left behind – not just the crumbling village houses and the castle-church whose ter-racotta roof and pointed spire were lit up orange by the evening sun, but also the huge oak and beech forests cloaking the hills, the neatly cobbled streets, and the pear trees planted all along the roads in which now, in the autumn, Gypsy children clambered like mon-keys and gorged themselves on the fruit.

Coming down into Halma, columns of smoke rose from chim-neys into the blue evening mist, the occasional dog barked, and on a slope on the other side of the village we could see the cows and horses returning from their daily pasture, and even catch the hollow clang or tinkle of their bells. The sounds carried easily in the still-ness of the evening. On the slopes beneath the trees we could just make out a flock of sheep recently let out to pasture following the evening's milking. It was an idyllic and peaceful scene, and Marishka rested her head on my shoulder as the horses slowly made their way down from the hill.

We rolled into the square and the horses headed for the drinking trough. The Gypsies, even though it was nearly dark, were finish-ing repairs I had asked them to carry out on a nearby roof. The portly and ancient figure of Frau Knall, in her aprons, could be seen sitting on her bench, her hands on the rounded handle of her walk-ing stick, watching and smiling benignly.

The sun was settling behind the spire of the Saxon church, and a pale moon was coming up over the hills to the east. The mother stork circled above the square and landed in her nest on the top of the tower, while in the bar one of Marishka's uncles was playing on the accordion he had inherited from his father. Above and beyond the village, however, the dark forest looked down. 'The poetic gentleness of the flowery slopes was all too deceptive in obscuring the wildness of the deep forests.'

21

A Time of Troubles

The thief who is not caught is an honest man.

Romanian saying

ANOTHER WINTER FROZE the land solid, and covered it for
months in a mantle of white. *Fe'Martie* followed, as uncomfortable, miserable and muddy as ever, but little by little the sun rose
higher in the sky each day and the end was in sight.

During the winter Nicolae came to me and suggested we buy
some bullocks and heifers to graze with the sheep. If we already had
the shepherd, he said, they could graze and grow fat up on the hill
at no extra expense to us, and we could then sell them in the
autumn. It seemed to make sense, so in the spring we went to the
markets, found seven well-grown calves and brought them home.
Before the sheepfold was set up they grazed harmlessly on the margins of the village.

One evening, however, one of the bullocks failed to return
home. Nicolae searched high and low but it was nowhere to be
found. There were, however, whispers: someone had spotted Goga
leading the bullock off the hill and into the bottom end of his
orchard, just as daylight was fading.

Nicolae with some friends went to Goga to ask him if he had the
bullock.

'I'm not a thieving Gypsy like all of you!' he shouted, picking up
an axe. 'Get out of here.'

The next day, however, in front of many witnesses, including the
under-policeman Lucian, the bullock was found in Goga's cowshed

and Nicolae lodged an official complaint with the police. For a while nothing happened. Then, after several weeks, there was a reaction, although it was not quite the one we were expecting.

It was a warm May evening and we threw a party on the grass up on the edge of the forest. We lit a large bonfire, the flames licking up into the sky, and everyone danced and enjoyed themselves in their usual spontaneous and unaffected way. Marishka and I lay there on the rugs under the silver stars, watching the light and shadow from the fire flickering in among the oak trees. It was a beautiful evening. We left at two o'clock and wandered back across the fields chatting and laughing together. We dropped into bed exhausted and fell into a deep sleep.

A few hours later, sometime between five and six o'clock, there was a loud hammering and crashing on the door of the room where we were sleeping. Marishka shook me violently.

'Wake up, wake up! They are taking Nicolae,' she screamed. 'You must save him.'

I was only half aware of what was going on. My sleep-filled mind was trying to grasp what was happening. Someone was screaming outside the door. It sounded like the wailing or keening which women in Romania make when a person has died.

'Get up!' shouted Marishka desperately, shaking me. 'You must be quick. Please! Wake up!'

I struggled to my feet, dragged on a pair of trousers and a jersey and ran outside. Natalia was there with tears running down her cheeks, wailing and moaning.

'Hurry. Hurry. They will kill him!' she was saying as though in a trance, swaying from side to side.

Marishka and I had been sleeping at Attila's house that evening. Nicolae and his wife and two small children had been in the blue house. Within a minute we were there. The road in front of the house was full of police, and the courtyard was swarming with men dressed in black, with black balaclavas and carrying machine guns, sprays, handcuffs and truncheons. There were between twenty and thirty police altogether, along with various ominous-looking prison vans.

In the middle of the track stood a fat policeman who seemed to be controlling operations. I went up to him and started to shout. I demanded to know what was going on.

'There have been complaints,' said the fat policeman.

'What complaints?' I said.

'Complaints,' he replied, and left it at that.

I then saw Nicolae being led out by several burly masked men dressed from top to toe in black.

Marishka started screaming. I told the fat policeman that if they laid a finger on Nicolae I would go straight to Bucharest.

There were many policemen all watching me. In the background I could see Barbu. He and the others were laughing at my futile anger.

Nicolae had by now disappeared, but the back of one of the vans swung open. I saw him sitting there.

'Now you see how Barbu treats us,' he shouted.

'Shut that door!' barked the fat policeman crossly, at last showing some emotion.

The door was slammed in Nicolae's face.

The van then drove away. At the same time the fat policeman came over and asked to see my papers. '*Documente!*' he said gruffly.

My passport was in my pocket and I showed it to him.

Marishka was next to me.

'They will kill him,' she sobbed. 'You must do something. They will beat him in the van. We must follow them!'

All around me women were wailing as though someone had already died.

The policeman slowly perused my passport. It seemed he was keeping me there as long as possible. At last he gave it back.

A Gypsy woman standing nearby said to me, 'You must go to the police station quickly. They will kill him. Go. Go!' The urgency in her voice frightened me.

AT THE TOP of the steps at the police station there were two black-clad and masked Jandarmes. I walked towards the door but they blocked my way.

'I want to see Barbu,' I said.

'You cannot. He is busy.'

I tried to push between them but they shoved me back.

'Let me go!' I shouted. 'I want to make sure they are treating my friend properly.' This was the police station where Andrei had been taken, and had died the following morning.

I again tried to push through, but again they threw me back. So I started shouting anything I could think of through the door. In this way Barbu would at least know that I was there.

Inside two black-masked Jandarmes stood next to Nicolae smacking truncheons into their gloved hands. Barbu was facing Nicolae over a desk. He placed a piece of paper in front of him.

'Sign here!' he said, thumping his finger on to the paper.

'Why should I?' asked Nicolae. 'What is it anyway?'

'You know what these people can do,' said Barbu, indicating the sinister mask-wearers. 'Just sign it.'

An officer came in. 'The Englishman is outside shouting and screaming,' he said.

'Don't let him in whatever happens!' said Barbu.

'Sign here!' he yelled and slammed his fist on the table.

Nicolae signed although, as he told me afterwards, he had no idea what he was signing.

Some hours later Nicolae emerged from the police station. Marishka rushed up and hugged him.

'Are you all right?' I asked.

'I'm fine. They didn't touch me. They just made me sign this,' he said, handing me a piece of paper.

I took it and read it as Marishka covered him with kisses.

'O frățiorul meu! Oh my little brother!' she was saying over and over, tears pouring down her cheeks.

The scrawl was difficult to read. It was clearly some sort of statement. I deciphered it word by word. Nicolae had, according to the note, irresponsibly allowed the bullock to wander into Goga's garden, where it had trampled his newly planted vegetables. The bullock had then entered Goga's cowshed, it said, where it had remained unnoticed until it was found.

The note was enough to exonerate Goga. And sure enough, soon after, an official letter arrived from the local procurator to tell us that there was no evidence to suggest Goga had stolen the bullock, and the case was closed.

At the same time another letter arrived. It was a fine for Nicolae for not properly controlling his animals.

MARISHKA TOLD ME that I had saved her brother. 'They would have killed him if you had not been here,' she said. 'They have wanted to get their revenge for a long time. Everyone knows it was Nicolae who hit the policeman when they tried to arrest my father.'

Even Natalia was generous when I saw her. 'I am glad that you did not leave after all,' she said.

A few evenings later in the *crîşma* a Gypsy, unrelated to Marishka, came up to me, kissed my hand, in the way of the peasants and Gypsies, and hugged me.

'You are like a father to us,' he said. It was a touching compliment.

I was popular with the Gypsies following the raid – they had seen that I was prepared to stand up for them – but not with the Romanians. I was harassed more than ever in the village for having dared to accuse one of them of stealing, and for having foiled their plans to deal with Nicolae.

Then one morning a motorcade swept into the village square. The passengers climbed out and walked down the road to our house. Many of them were wearing suits, the others were policemen. When they reached our house they hammered on the gate and asked us to come outside. It was, it turned out, a delegation from the Prefectura, accompanied by the local police, among them Barbu, and the Commandant from the town, Barbu's immediate superior.

They wanted to know if there was conflict between the Gypsies and the Romanians.

The officials and assembled police waited for my reply.

'No, there is not conflict. To me there appears to be injustice.

The law here seems to protect only friends of Barbu,' I said, pointing to him standing opposite me.

'You must have faith in the police,' said one of the officials.

'How can I after what happened to Marishka's uncle?' I asked.
'He was taken to the police station where he was questioned for
hours. The next morning he died, aged thirty-four.'

'He was beaten,' said Marishka.

'That is not true!' shouted Barbu, furious. He tried to continue
speaking, but the Commandant intervened.

'Silence!' he shouted. Barbu obeyed.

'And then they raid our house in the early hours of the morning
for no reason that I can understand,' I said.

'Why did you raid their house?' asked an official from the
Prefectura.

'There had been complaints,' said Barbu.

'What complaints?' asked the official.

'They were having noisy parties,' said Barbu.

'Is it necessary to raid the house with masked gunmen if we are
having noisy parties?' I asked.

'Who made the complaints?' asked the official.

'Several people here,' said Barbu.

'Let us talk to them,' the official replied.

Barbu walked down the street but he could find no one willing
to speak.

Gratifyingly the delegation seemed to be losing patience with
Barbu and decided to leave. Before departing, however, one of
them gave me his telephone number and whispered in my ear.

'We'll sort out this policeman. Come and see me.'

They then disappeared as fast as they had come, and left us
standing in a cloud of dust.

FOLLOWING THE OFFICIAL'S invitation I telephoned and arranged
a meeting.

'You have to find witnesses who know what happened to
Marishka's uncle and who are prepared to testify. At the same time

you will need to talk to Andrei's widow to request that the case be reopened,' he said.

I returned to the village and told Marishka. She, with her usual courage, tried to find witnesses but no one was prepared to speak out. Everyone was too frightened.

'It is always like this,' said the official when I told him. 'It is a hang-over from Communist times. Dammit! If they want their situation to improve they should testify. How else can we make progress?'

'They are afraid,' I said.

'Yes, it's hard. I sympathize with them,' he said. 'They have to live in the villages from day to day.'

There was no more Marishka could do. On the face of it our situation was now precarious. Marishka and I had publicly brought up the subject of Andrei's death. We lived every day expecting some form of retaliation. At night I would suddenly awake imagining I heard the vehicles of the masked police outside coming to take us away. I was worried. Barbu, if it was he who had beaten Andrei, as the Gypsies believed, might like a rat in a corner be capable of anything.

ONE MORNING I was walking down the road when a certain Mr Ursan, a friend of Barbu, came driving by in his car. On the track was Marishka's old grandmother walking slowly with a stick towards the village square. The car was moving fast on the rutted track and throwing up a trail of dust behind it. It appeared to be heading straight for her and did not slow down. It whooshed by and the old lady was enveloped in a cloud of dust. When the air had cleared she was lying face down on the road. She was lifted up, brushed down and taken to the doctor who declared that she had a cracked rib. Marishka's family complained to the police.

A week later a summons was handed to me by Mrs Goga, the village postmistress. I was to answer the charge of 'Slander' against the policeman's friend Mr Ursan at the town courts.

'Slander?' I said. 'I never said anything slanderous about Ursan. What on earth is going on?'

'I don't know anything about it. I only deliver the letters,' said Mrs Goga smugly.

I rang a lawyer who told me that 'Slander' was a criminal case. If I was found guilty I would have a criminal record and might even be forced to leave the country. So, despite the absurdity of the matter, I was forced to take it seriously and appear at the first hearing. Ursan, however, was not there. The case had to be adjourned. I requested the judge not to fix the next hearing before 20 September, explaining that I was going to England and that my return ticket was booked and paid for the 19th.

In due course the summons for the next hearing arrived. I was called to appear on 18 September. To be there in time I had to buy a new ticket. Ursan was once again nowhere to be seen. The case, due to his repeated absences, was closed and I never did discover what slander I was accused of uttering. It seemed the whole process had been arranged simply to distract attention and to cause me trouble.

Needless to say Barbu did not follow up what had happened to Marishka's grandmother. The old lady simply sat on her usual bench by the side of the road wincing with pain as her rib slowly mended.

ONE DAY THE sympathetic official from the Prefectura was passing near Halma and paid us a surprise visit. This time he was alone.

'You should know what people are saying about you,' he told me. 'They don't like you. There was a meeting at the county hall where they discussed you. In front of the Prefect a high-ranking policeman stood up and declared that you were organizing a *răscoală* – an uprising – amongst the Gypsies, that you were deliberately stirring things up. It was for this reason that we all came here a few weeks ago. To find out what was going on.'

'A *Gypsy uprising*?' I said. 'I am astonished they should think I am so dangerous, but it is absurd. I am doing the very opposite.

Whenever there is trouble between Gypsies and Romanians I try to stop it.'

'He was clearly misinformed,' said the official. 'Let us hope everyone calms down soon. I just came to warn you. There are people who would like to be rid of you from here and from Romania. They will want to cause trouble. They are saying all sorts of stupid things at the moment, just bravado probably, but you should be careful.'

Our friend climbed into his car and, with a wave, disappeared.

THE FIRST MENTION of Halma in historical records was in the fourteenth century when a certain Hungarian count complained to the Voievode of Transylvania of the Saxons in Halma and the sur-rounding villages allowing their animals to stray on to his land. It was not long before present events began to follow historical prece-dent. After the police raid, our animals were suddenly found to be straying on to other people's land with alarming regularity, and indignant villagers kept appearing at my door in the early hours of the morning. Wearily, I went to Nicolae to ask what was going on.

'It is not true what they are saying. They want to create bad blood between us so that you will sell the sheep,' he said. 'Just tell them to talk to me.'

When they saw that shouting at me was useless they tried a new tactic. They brought our animals down into the village to enclose them, claiming they had been grazing illegally. Nicolae tried to stop them and was attacked by a certain Mr Lupescu wielding a pitchfork. Lupescu, however, was no match for Nicolae who pulled the pitchfork out of Lupescu's hands and walked away with it as evidence that he had been attacked. Lupescu immediately rushed off to report the incident to the police. Nicolae should have com-plained as well, but from experience he realized there was no point. It would only make things worse.

A week later a letter arrived for Nicolae ordering him to pay a fine of 15,000,000 lei for not controlling his animals and for having attacked Mr Lupescu. Fifteen million lei was equivalent to five months' wages. It was a huge fine, and there had been no investigation into what had happened. Lupescu had simply made his complaint to the police, supported by his friends as witnesses.

I did not have 15,000,000 lei so I rang Mrs Dima, the human rights lawyer who had advised me during the earlier case with Ursan. She told me that we must contest the fine within fifteen days. So we wrote a statement, filled in forms, had them stamped and legalized, and handed them in to the court.

When some weeks later the case was heard, there was an impressive row. Halfway through Mrs Dima's defence the judge attempted to silence her.

'I have a right to defend my clients,' Mrs Dima shouted back.

'Silence!' yelled the judge. 'We have heard enough.'

'But I have not presented my witnesses. If I am not permitted to speak', Mrs Dima shouted, 'I insist it be noted in court records that I have not been allowed to finish my defence and I will make an official complaint to the Chief Justice in Bucharest.'

The judge backed down.

Mrs Dima's courage and the quality of her arguments won the day. The judge was left with no option but to find Nicolae not guilty.

'I have never seen anything like it in any court in Romania,' said Mrs Dima as she came out. 'It was disgraceful.'

'The judge is their friend,' said Nicolae. 'She is the neighbour of Lupescu's sister.'

When I returned home I told Marishka of our victory.

'Serves them right, stupid idiots,' she said.

'We have to show Barbu and the others that we will stand up to them. Otherwise things will only get worse,' I said pompously, echoing what she had once said to me.

'But you are always telling me *not* to argue with the bullies,' said Marishka.

'Yes, but this is different,' I told her.

'Yes,' she said, 'because it is easier.'

'Well then, that is a good reason for it, isn't it?' I argued.

'No, because when someone attacks you with a knife you can't put them off until the next court case.'

THE GYPSIES OF Halma were constantly surprising me. At about the time of the second court case one of them came to ask me if I would help them repair the village hall.

'We have no proper place to hold dances, wedding feasts or baptisms,' he said.

If I would supply the materials he would persuade the Gypsies to work for free, he said. I was confused. I had thought the Gypsies did not care about the hall, and had found it more useful as a supply of free firewood.

'But it was Gypsies who pulled it to pieces in the first place, wasn't it?' I said. 'If we repair it, won't it just be pulled apart again?'

'No,' he said. 'You have been misinformed. It was the mayor ten years ago who destroyed it. He gave away the windows, the curtains, the mirrors, the chairs and even the huge cast-iron stoves.'

'Who did he give them away to?' I asked.

'To his friends, except the chairs which went to the mayor's offices. The stoves are heating Ursan's big cattle sheds.'

'Might we recover some of these things?' I asked.

'Perhaps. We can try, but I don't think there is much left. The windows were given to Goga's brother-in-law and have disappeared. Ursan will not be amused at being asked to give the stoves back.'

Nonetheless, I agreed to help. There was now a new mayor and to my surprise he agreed to supply the several hundred tiles needed to mend the roof. I ordered new windows and doors to be made, the holes in the roof were patched, and the interior plaster was repaired.

Before long the work was finished, and soon the villagers began to use the place for dances, and for baptism celebrations. Sadly I was unable to persuade anyone to return the things which the previous mayor had given away, and Ursan, so I was told, said he would rather smash the stoves with a sledgehammer than let us have them. In the end the stove problem was solved by one of the resourceful Gypsies who made a new one out of scrap metal.

At many a celebration I watched the villagers laughing and dancing and the Gypsy musicians playing. Sad to say, the friends of the policeman steered well clear of the village hall and avoided the parties, but a few Romanians and Saxons did turn up from time to time. Either way, everyone theoretically now had this new space in which to enjoy themselves, all because of the initiative of the Gypsies. We were all very proud of what we had done. Herr and Frau Knall were astonished by the Gypsies' work, and happy to see the hall, which had originally been built by the Saxons, put back in action. They were beginning to change their minds about us.

FLORIN WAS MARISHKA's first cousin and everyone agreed he was an excellent fellow. Hard working and dependable, you would often see him heading off to the fields with his scythe over his shoulder or harnessing his horses to go and collect hay or wood. When we saw him he was always cheerful and friendly. He was also enthusiastic about repairing the village hall. The circumstances of his early death – he was only twenty-two – added a sinister new dimension to our troubles.

Romania, and especially the Gypsy side of it, was obsessed with magic, witchcraft and superstition. Almost every move a person made was given a supernatural cause. Marishka and her family believed in all forms of magic. Every unfortunate event was ascribed to a spell having been cast against you, or the priest having performed a malicious Mass. Every dream or twitch of an eye was said to have some special necromantic meaning.

It was the Black Masses, the *Slujbe Negre* as they were called, which upset Marishka more than anything else. It was because God was involved. If a Black Mass was aimed in your direction it suggested that even God was against you.

I had heard the words *Slujbă Neagră* – 'Black Mass' – for the first time while hoeing in the fields in the Maramureş. My curiosity aroused, I interrupted my chatting companions to ask what exactly a *Slujbă Neagră* was.

'Well, if you have a problem with someone,' they explained – 'perhaps a person has stolen from you but the police cannot do anything, or perhaps he has offended you in some way – you can pay the priest to carry out a Black Mass to put a curse upon him.'

'And then what happens?' I asked in amazement.

'Well, he dies, or suffers some terrible misfortune.'

'And if in fact he didn't steal anything?'

'Then nothing will happen,' they said.

One day when Mihai and I were walking through the church-yard, he had shown me two identical wooden crosses side by side.

'These are the graves of two friends who stole a ram,' he said. 'The owner paid the priest for a Black Mass, and both friends died soon after, almost at the same time, one struck by lightning, the other killed in a mining accident.'

'But why didn't the man who had lost the ram just go to the police?' I asked.

'Because he wasn't sure who the thieves were. When these two boys both died so soon afterwards, everyone knew it must have been them.'

Any number of similar stories were brought out to demonstrate that wicked people would always have their comeuppance.

'You really mean it is the priest who performs these Black Masses?' I asked.

'Of course,' they replied, as though it was the most normal thing in the world. Everyone was quite open about *Slujbe Negre*, even though it seemed obvious to me, in my simple Anglican way, that Black Masses were things which priests, far from practising for financial gain, should unequivocally condemn.

That year Marishka's cousin Florin had been given the grass of the Halma cemetery in exchange for ringing the church bells. Florin had dutifully rung the bells all year round and was now looking forward to filling his barn with the promised hay. The priest, however, was drinking more than ever, and many an evening he could be seen walking home taking a route which was by no means the straightest. In need of money for more drink, he sold the grass which he had promised to Florin to someone else. This man promptly scythed it and carted it away. When Florin discovered, he was hurt and furious. He went immediately to the *crîşma* – it was the first place to go when looking for the priest.

'You have sold my grass!' he shouted. 'You've been selling the icons from the church and now you have sold my grass!'

The priest was furious at such a public accusation. He retreated to the door of the *crîşma*, and as he left he lifted his finger. 'You will regret what you have just said,' he spluttered.

Over the next few days there were murmurings that the priest was saying Black Masses against Florin, and people shuddered.

That summer was a particularly hot one, and on an August holy day a group of friends from the village decided to go on an excursion to the communal swimming baths in the town. Florin was with them, and they set off in jovial mood.

At the pool someone jokingly suggested to Florin that he might be afraid to jump in. Florin could not swim but, not wanting to be laughed at, and not realizing how deep it was, he walked up to the edge and jumped into the murky waters of the municipal pool. After five minutes everyone was asking where Florin had gone. Nobody knew. They peered into the waters, but being so cloudy they could not see if he was there or not. Another five minutes passed and there was a shout. He had been found lying motionless on the bottom. They hauled him out and tried to revive him, but it was too late.

From the pool Florin was taken to the morgue. There he was dressed in his best shirt and suit, and shaved by a friend from the village.

'I didn't need water to shave him', he told me afterwards, 'as my tears were falling on his face.' Florin was brought back to the village in a coffin on the back of a lorry.

At the wake he lay in a pine coffin surrounded by his weeping family. I went to pay my respects. 'Look,' his mother said to me, 'you see he is crying too', and sure enough drops of water were flowing down his pale cheeks. He had died just three weeks after the argument with the priest. When things like this happened it was not surprising that people were even more afraid of God than of the police.

MARISHKA WAS DEVASTATED by Florin's death and by the manner of it. It seemed that everybody was against us, even God. Everything was going wrong. Not only was it dispiriting, it was exhausting as well, having to fight one court case after another, and to make so many journeys to the courthouse in the town. Our peaceful and carefree life had become a tormented round of documents, stamped and double-stamped, meetings with lawyers, and always more paperwork. It was time to make more positive steps to improve our situation. Things could not go on like this. I decided to pay a visit to the Commandant, the head of the police force in the local town.

I announced myself to the stern-looking policeman who guarded the entrance of the police station. Before long I was ushered into the Commandant's office. I went in with trepidation. I was walking into the lion's den. The Commandant was, I knew, the man whose job it had been to catch Nicolae when he had been on the run. This was the man who had torn the photograph of Nicolae in two with his teeth, and had said, 'When we find him, I will eat him!'

I shook the Commandant by the hand. He asked me what he could do for me.

'I came to talk to you about the problems in Halma,' I said. 'Certain people, it seems, are trying to present me as being anti-Romanian. They are even suggesting that I am deliberately stirring up the Gypsies to rebel against the Romanians. I hope you realize that this is nonsense. I have come to you because I want to calm everyone down, as all I want is to be able to live in peace. I hope you do not mind.'

'Of course not,' he said.

'I want to show you that I am not anti-Romanian.'

I took out an article I had written for the colour supplement of the *Daily Telegraph* in June 2001. In it were photographs showing scenes typical of Maramureş life, of Mihai and Maria, and of me scything the Maramureş meadows.

'This is one of the best-selling newspapers in Great Britain,' I told him. 'And here is an article about Romania and Romanians which is more complimentary than any I have ever seen, and it was written by me. Most foreign journalists write about the poverty, the orphanages and the miners coming to Bucharest to terrorize intellectuals. I am one of the few who write articles full of praise for Romania, and yet I am hounded out of the village where I am living by the local policeman. I know it has nothing to do with you, but you do understand – it is absurd. I cannot live like this any more.'

'I am sorry,' he said. 'But how can I help you?'

'I don't know,' I replied. 'I just wanted you to know so that at least someone here knows that I love Romania and that I am not trying to cause trouble.'

'I understand,' he said.

'Do you see now that the idea of my leading a Gypsy rebellion could not possibly be true?'

'Yes, I think so,' he said. He kept his cards close to his chest, but I sensed that he was sympathetic. Perhaps I had managed to sway him a little, and he now suspected that Barbu might have misinformed him.

Before leaving I told him of how the Gypsies were repairing the Halma village hall.

'You are really not paying them anything?' he asked.

'No,' I said.

He nodded as if impressed, or perhaps he was incredulous?

When I departed he shook my hand and gave me a piece of paper.

'This is my telephone number. Ring me if you need help,' he said.

★

I WAS SITTING quietly one evening on the wooden bridge in the square talking to Gypsies who had been helping me mend the roof of one of the village houses, when Ion Goga came out of the *crîşma* accompanied by his city cousin Traian. Both had had plenty to drink and came over to taunt me.

'Hey! You!' Ion shouted. 'You had better keep control of your sheep or there will be trouble.'

'Nicolae looks after the sheep. Talk to him about it,' I answered, using my standard reply.

'No. We are talking to *you*, because they are *your* sheep. *You* don't control them properly,' he said.

I was sitting down and by now he was leaning over me. I stood up.

'Before you start telling other people how to behave', I said, 'perhaps you should put your own house in order first. What, for example, happened to my bullock which disappeared and was found in your stables?'

'You will regret saying that,' he slurred. 'We will get you, Englishman, we will sort you out.'

'Your threats do not frighten me,' I said. I was sure Ion would not dare attack me for fear of what Nicolae would do to them in return.

The Gypsies nearby were worried, however. They took me by the arm.

'William. I think we should leave.'

We left. Ion and Traian did not attack, but walked away down the street. At that moment Marishka appeared from the *crîşma*. Someone had run to tell her of the trouble brewing in the square.

'What is going on?' she asked.

'*Nothing!*' I said firmly.

'Rubbish! I have been told how they spoke to you.'

'It doesn't matter. I don't care. Please forget it,' I said.

My words had no effect. She was already advancing down the road towards Ion and Traian. I followed her. By the time Marishka reached them Traian had doubled back and was heading towards me.

'I am going to sort you out now,' he said.

Marishka stopped him. 'If you lay a finger on him Nicolae will kill you,' she said.

'Who is Nicolae? What do I care about him?' answered Traian – being from the city he did not know the local personalities.

Ion knew who Nicolae was. He ran up to his cousin, took him by the arm and pulled him away.

'Let's go home,' he said. Traian reluctantly agreed, but as they went he turned his head and shouted that, in good time, he would 'sort me out'.

Five minutes later Nicolae appeared.

'What is happening?' he asked.

'Nothing,' I said again.

Marishka, however, told him and the two of them set off in the direction of Ion's house.

'Wait here!' they said as they strode off up the hill.

'Don't do anything stupid!' I shouted.

'Don't worry,' said Nicolae, 'I'm just going to ask Ion what he wants.'

After a few minutes I decided to follow them. If there was trouble I might be able to stop it. When I turned the corner at the top of the hill I could see people gathered on the track ahead, and could hear shouting. It was night-time but there was light from the moon. I walked up to the crowd and found myself in the middle of a brawl. There in the semi-darkness I caught sight of Nicolae facing Ion Goga. Ion had a stick and was lashing out. Nicolae was advancing and retreating, waiting for his moment.

'Nicolae!' I shouted. 'Stop fighting!' He heard me and stepped backwards.

All around me, I could hear stones landing on the road, although I could not see from which direction they were coming. Then, *bang*, one large stone hit me on the leg. Nicu was standing near me. He saw what had happened.

'Are you all right?' he asked.

'I'm fine,' I said.

Nicu shouted to Nicolae. 'They have hit William with a stone.'

I did not see what happened next as I was hobbling away down the track and reached the house in pain. Five minutes later Marishka and others, including the Lad, appeared.

'Are you all right?' asked Marishka.

'My leg hurts a bit but I'm all right,' I said.

'We showed those shits!' said the Lad. 'We have taken revenge for you. They'll think twice about speaking to you like that in the future.'

The Lad enjoyed a good scrap (as I had observed on several occasions) and more than anything else he hated the Goga family. All such feelings overcame any old grudges he might have borne against me. I noticed he had blood on his knuckles. I dreaded to think what had happened. I soon discovered. The Lad and others had seen Traian with a knife in one hand and throwing stones in my direction with the other. The Lad picked up a blunt instrument and they flew into the fray. They knocked Traian down, jumped on him and punched and hit him until he stopped resisting.

Nicolae and Nicu then arrived at the house.

'You should see Traian. You did a good job,' said Nicu, addressing the Lad. 'His face is so covered in blood you can't recognize him.'

'That is what he deserved,' said another Gypsy named Pipaşi.

'There is going to be trouble now,' said Nicolae. 'They shouted at us that they were going to call the Jandarmes. They said they'd be here at first light.'

My heart sank. I could not bear the idea of another dawn raid by masked gunmen, but going on past experience a raid was more than likely. When Gypsies fought with Romanians they would come in force, masked and armed with a panoply of weapons. Marishka too was anxious. She knew Barbu still entertained the idea of teaching Nicolae a lesson.

I, however, had a new friend. Maybe he could help. The Commandant had given me his telephone number. Now was the moment to dial it. It was late, nearly ten o'clock, but there was reason enough to call.

At the only telephone in the village, where you first had to contact the switchboard in the neighbouring village by winding a handle, I was given a line to the town.

'*Domnul Commandant*,' I said, 'I am sorry to ring so late but there has been a fight in Halma and I have been injured.'

'Are you all right?' he asked.

'Yes, I'm fine.'

'Then you must go and make a complaint,' he said. 'Has the fight calmed down now?'

'Yes,' I said, 'but the Gogas say they will call the Jandarmes to come and deal with us in the morning. That is why I am ringing. Is this true? Will the Jandarmes come?'

'No,' he said, 'they will not come.'

'Are you sure?' I asked. 'Perhaps Barbu will call them.'

'No, I give you my word they will not come,' he said. 'You can sleep soundly.'

From the telephone I went to the police station in the neighbouring village where I gave a statement to Lucian, the duty officer. I showed him the now livid and spreading bruise on my leg.

'You must go to a special "Legal" doctor to get an official opinion on the injury,' he said. 'You are lucky I am here. Barbu would not tell you this.'

I thanked him.

'You'll have trouble,' said Lucian. 'Ion Goga is Barbu's godson.'

True to the Commandant's word no Jandarmes appeared, either the next morning or on the following days. True to Lucian's word a summons arrived two weeks later ordering me to appear in court charged with the customary 'Slander'. The Lad and Pipaşi were charged with causing bodily harm. We were comforted that both Ion and Traian had also received summonses following my accusations against them.

The day after the fight I had found a 'Legal' doctor in the city of Târgu Mures. He measured the bruise with his ruler, hummed and hawed and wrote out a description of the injury: 'A haematoma . . . 12 centimetres long . . . hospital 5 days.' His note was stamped and signed, and he handed me a document which would be accepted as evidence of my injury by any court. It only remained for me to prove who had inflicted the wound. There were many Gypsies who had witnessed what had happened, but how many would dare to testify?

On the appointed day we all turned up at the court. All three cases were to be heard on the same day. Once again, if I lost my case I would receive a criminal record. Both the Lad and Pipaşi faced going back to prison. Pipaşi too had been there once before.

As a result I brought along a lawyer – a new one this time, as the indomitable Mrs Dima was unable to attend. He was called Bogdan. In preparation for the case Bogdan and I had read the witness statements, which were written in Barbu's hand. In them I was described as walking through the lines like a general during a battle organizing my Gypsy forces. I smiled at this embellishment which seemed designed to give credence to the idea that I was leading a Gypsy uprising.

Before the cases were heard Ion and Traian asked to speak to Bogdan. They agreed to drop their charges against me if I dropped my charges against them. But I knew that if I agreed to this the Gypsies would be left high and dry, and off to prison they would go.

'I will drop my charges only if they drop their case against the Lad and Pipaşi as well,' I said to Bogdan. The Lad, Pipaşi and others had rallied to my defence with their fists. It seemed only fair that I should now try to defend them. Without my help they did not have a chance. They could plead self-defence but it would not be accepted as they, and a whole crowd of Gypsies, had been outside Ion's front door.

'Never,' said Ion and Traian to Bogdan. 'We will *never* drop charges against the Gypsies!'

'The case will have to continue then,' I said to Bogdan, when he came over to report.

When we found ourselves in front of the judge Ion and Traian asked for time to find legal representation and the hearing was adjourned. A month later we again reconvened in the courthouse. I was worried. The last thing I wanted was to have to fight the case against me, and perhaps to lose and find myself with a criminal record. But I had to appear relaxed so as to convince my opponents that I would only back down if they dropped charges against the Gypsies.

After a period in which we eyed each other up, they approached Bogdan and asked if I had reconsidered. He told them I had not. Bogdan then asked them if perhaps *they* had reconsidered.

'*Certainly not!*' they replied.

An anxious half-hour followed.

They then called Bogdan over.

'We have had a discussion and we agree to withdraw our charges against the Gypsies,' they said with pained expressions on their faces.

And later, in front of the judge, this is what they did. I, in return, dropped my charges against them.

I was immensely relieved. Once again we had been prepared. I had been to the doctor and had proof of my injury. I had talked to Gypsies who had agreed to testify. Ion and Traian knew we had fought and won the previous case. Usually in the courts they would have been sure of victory. Now we had sown seeds of doubt and they had given in. It seemed to be a turning point. The fact that they had caved in meant that they were worried. It was an indication that we might now be able to live in peace.

The poorest Gypsies in the village had sampled a morsel of justice. They were astonished. As we walked out the Lad shook me by the hand.

'Thank you,' he said, 'I didn't think we had a chance. We are Gypsies after all. And if we had lost we would have gone back to prison.'

'I know,' I said as he walked away, 'I was just returning the favour.'

I then shook hands with Ion Goga.

'I hope that we can now live in peace,' I said.

He shook my hand and nodded in agreement.

★

AT LAST THE tide seemed to be turning. On 15 May, exactly a year to the day of the police raid, Mr Goga died aged fifty-four. He had been in hospital and his operation went wrong. They could not save him. He was brought back to the village in an open coffin on the back of a lorry. Attila was in the village square when the lorry arrived. Goga had been a big man. The coffin was heavy and all those nearby were asked to help unload it into the house. Attila looked at Goga in horror. 'He had turned black,' he told us.

22

The Cherry Trees of Breb

Lyubov: *All, all white! Oh my orchard! After the dark gloomy autumn*
and the cold winter, you are young again and full of happiness, the
heavenly angels have never left you . . .
Gaev: *Yes. And the orchard will be sold to pay our debts; it seems*
strange.

Anton Chekhov, *The Cherry Orchard*

I DROVE OVER the forested passes of the northern Carpathians and
down into the green and quiet valleys of the Maramureş. Only
this time there was a difference. This time Marishka was with me.
I had asked her if she would like to come to visit Mihai and Maria.
I had thought it was time for a rest and a change of scene.

'But Mihai is Romanian and he will not want a Gypsy staying
in his house,' said Marishka.

'Mihai and the people from the Maramureş are different,' I told
her. 'He will welcome you.' In the end she agreed to come.

As we descended into the village the cool air smelt of grass and
we saw the men with their distinctive tasselled straw hats, and the
women in headscarves and skirts, all purposefully working in the
fields, methodically scything line by line, raking and building ricks.
Many too were still wearing *opinci*, the old home-made moccasin-
like shoes. It was a surprise for Marishka, just as it had been for me
when I first arrived, to see people dressed in this way. As we drove
into the village many friends waved and shouted welcome. It was
like coming home.

Secretly I too was worried how Mihai and Maria might react to having a Gypsy staying in their house, but I had wanted Marishka to meet them. I need not have worried. Mihai and Maria greeted her warmly and Mihai behaved as the perfect gentleman that he was throughout our visit.

'How wonderful that you have come to visit us,' he said. 'I do hope you will stay as long as possible. Stay for ever.'

We gave them a hunk of fresh sheep's cheese made by Nene Niculaie. 'This is the best cheese I've ever tasted,' said Mihai to Marishka. 'I'd so like to come and see your sheepfold but perhaps I am too old now. I used to be a shepherd a long time ago, you know.'

He chatted to Marishka and showed her the house.

'The Gypsies who made the bricks for the house,' he told her, 'they lived in a tent in the garden. And they were the cleanest and tidiest people I have ever seen. Everything in their tent was perfectly ordered.'

I was happy to see that Mihai, who I respected so much and who was like a father to me in Romania, approved of Marishka. 'You don't need to untie yourself from her,' he said to me that evening, 'she is a fine girl.'

At supper Mihai talked of what had happened to us in Halma.

'One idiotic policeman has to spoil all the goodwill,' he said. He was upset that a Romanian could have behaved so badly towards us. It hurt him. He was, he said, ashamed for his country.

'It does not matter, Mihai,' I said. 'It was not a pleasant experience, but everywhere in the world there are stupid people. This one man cannot destroy the goodwill so easily.'

Mihai was happy to hear this. We drank *horincă*, laughed over dinner, and Marishka and I slept the deep sleep one sleeps in such peaceful places.

MARISHKA WAS WELCOMED with open arms wherever we went. The villagers of Breb were as gentle as ever. We walked about the village watching people quietly at their work. They put down their tools and sat on the ground to talk, to ask me how I was getting on in the outside world and to ask Marishka where she came from. The courtesy and kindness of the Brebeni was the very essence of the Romanian peasant, the sort that I had read about in many books. All my old friends, even though they knew Marishka was a Gypsy, treated her as they would treat one of their own, without showing any hint of uneasiness. When living in Breb I had noticed that the Gypsies were treated with respect. The family of the blacksmith was always included in village celebrations, and Maria used to take bowls of soup to the fat Gypsy woman who lived at the bottom of the garden; then when the Gypsy had married, everyone in the village had donated food for the wedding feast. The Gypsies were different, nobody pretended otherwise, but they were a part of the community. They provided services to the Romanians – working metal, playing music, making baskets – and they were accepted and treated with respect.

The families of Breb and the Maramureş had remained much the same as they had been for centuries. A girl or a boy might marry into the next-door village but rarely any further, and even this was a big step. 'I would not want to marry between villages,' I heard girls saying when I first came to Breb. Perhaps this was why Breb was so different from Halma. Halma had been affected not only by the movement of peoples in Communist times, but also by the departure of the Saxons. As is common throughout the world it is often newcomers who cause the problems. Sure enough, in Halma Goga, Lupescu and Ursan were all from other parts of Transylvania, Barbu was from Moldavia.

WE WERE VERY happy in Breb, but for me there was a certain wistfulness. I could not help noticing that life in the Maramureş was changing. I did not want to notice it, and tried to ignore it, but it was all too evident.

The changes had been accelerated when the old stone and dirt track into the village had been tarred. Previously the journey from the main road to Mihai's house by car had taken a quarter of an hour. You could travel no faster than walking pace. Now it took just a few minutes.

The tarmac had arrived several years before, while I was still living in Breb. I remember well how over several weeks the black asphalt had slowly slithered its way into the village. The roar of the lorries bringing the tar and gravel seemed to me like the sound of the axes in *The Cherry Orchard*. For the villagers, however, the new road had been a cause of celebration. People had started describing things as being 'as smooth as asphalt'.

I had prophesied doom, and people looked at me surprised.

'Children will not be able to play in the streets any more,' I said.

'Oh well, they will have to play somewhere else then,' they replied.

'But you will start to worry where they are, and you will not be able to live as peacefully as you have lived up till now.'

Nobody had taken much notice. The road was a sign of progress. Other villages had asphalt roads. Now they had one too. Besides, there were speed limits.

Soon afterwards, however, the eight-year-old grandson of the story-teller, to whom I had given the Austrian scythe, was killed by a speeding car, and people lost some of their enthusiasm. More tears had been shed at that funeral than at any I had ever been to. It was too late for the boy, however, and too late for the village. The road was already there.

Western advertising and the new-style television programmes glorifying the modern world, programmes often sponsored by international companies, had been infecting villagers' minds for several years already. Now the new road allowed this modern world to enter the village, and in it blundered, trampling pitilessly upon the gentle, traditional way of life.

The most obvious change was in the clothes people wore. For the first time in the history of the village, girls started to wear trousers instead of gathered skirts and petticoats. The fashion had started in the villages nearer to the town and worked its way to the remoter places.

Not long after the arrival of the new road I bumped into the daughter of a neighbour on my way to the fields. She was wearing a pair of jeans. It was the first time I had ever seen her in trousers rather than a skirt. I was sad. Even here the traditional clothes now seemed to be on the way out. I asked the girl why she had suddenly taken to wearing trousers. She looked embarrassed and said that all her skirts were being washed.

'That is not true, is it?' I said.

'No,' she replied. 'You must understand, William, that it is difficult for us. I can't easily afford modern clothes, and in any case I prefer to wear skirts as they are more comfortable and more beautiful, but if you do not wear the latest fashions people laugh at you and say that you are poor. Before it was easier for us because we made our own clothes. Each year there would be a new stitching or knitting pattern which became that year's fashion. Now we have to buy things. Whether or not you are well dressed has become purely a matter of money.' After she had told me this I felt ashamed that I had asked her.

With the new road came also the new kiosks set up by people from the town selling modern factory products. All the products were packaged in plastic. Such packaging had never been seen before in the village and the villagers did not know what to do with it. Gradually the beautiful stream began to fill up with litter and its waters became contaminated by the new detergents. Walking back from the fields one day I was accompanied by the ten-year-old son of a neighbour. With pride the boy told me the names of all the trees and flowers which we passed. But then we reached the stream in the middle of the village near the church and saw the piles of plastic bags and bottles along its edge.

'A few years ago', he told me, 'when I put my bucket in the stream to fetch water for the house there was a fish in it when I pulled it out. But now there are hardly any fish left. The boys who go fishing have told me.'

Modern travelling salesmen also ventured down the new smooth road. They were very different from the colourful, happy-go-lucky Gypsies who used to arrive in their carts to sell useful enamel saucepans in part exchange for walnuts or old bottles for recycling. The new salesmen arrived by car and offered for sale a perplexing array of goods to the bemused peasants. I remember Mihai endeavouring to understand a hairbrush with vibrating bristles for massaging the scalp, as one of the new breed of sales-men in the inevitable ill-fitting suit demonstrated it to him with great seriousness. 'With this hairbrush we are offering a free bar of soap,' said the salesman. 'This is a very special offer, a once only opportunity.' This hairbrush, and the special offer, seemed to sym-bolize the pathos and absurdity of the whole sad but inevitable process of change.

AFTER A WALK in the village one morning, Marishka and I returned to the kitchen and found Mihai, spectacles on the end of his nose, with a needle poised on the end of a thread, stitching away. He put aside the harness he had been working on and sat down with us to a glass of *horincă*. He was in reflective mood.

'Have you noticed?' he said. 'You can no longer see the cherry blossom. Everyone has been chopping their cherry trees down. Foreigners came and offered money for them. It used to be so beau-tiful at this time of year, the white blossom all over the hills. People would not have chopped down all the cherry trees in the old days.' He shook his head.

'It is not good,' he said.

Up until then people had lived in harmony with their surround-ings. They had lived on the food from their crops and their animals, and from what the natural world around them provided. The cher-ries of course had provided fruit. People never threw anything away and felled trees only for firewood and as building materials for themselves.

But now the new slick television advertisments had been mes-merizing villagers with images of all sorts of tempting items which they had never needed or wanted before. The advertisements went on, over and over again, ramming the same idea down people's throats, that they could not possibly live without washing-up liquid or Coca-Cola, or some sort of automatic vegetable slicer. In the end, bludgeoned into submission, people gradually began to buy, and once a few had bought others were obliged to do the same or be considered poor or backward.

The traditional, harmless way of life of the Maramureş communities had endured for thousands of years, surviving even the forty years of Communism. The modern television, with its insidious advertising, was a threat against which they were defenceless. Money was desperately needed to purchase the new products. As a result the cherry trees had to come down to be sold to the foreigners. Then it was the walnut trees, and then the oaks and the beeches.

'I don't know what is happening to us,' said Mihai. 'People have taken leave of their senses.'

He returned to stitching the harness he was making. He did not want to think about such things any more. Mihai and Maria's way of life had not changed and would not change.

ONE DAY MIHAI and Maria went up to hoe a field of maize. Marishka and I went with them. Maria packed lunch into a round-bottomed basket, which she covered over with a white cloth, heaved it on to her back and set off for the fields. She refused to let me carry the basket, even though she was seventy-seven. *Domni* – gentlemen – should under no circumstances be asked to do such things. Of course *domni* should under no circumstances have allowed *her* to carry the basket but she was adamant. She did however make a concession and allowed me to carry the small wooden-handled enamel churn containing the soup.

We walked along paths which led through courtyards and back gardens, paths symbolic of the way people's lives in the Maramureş are woven together, and across wooden bridges over mountain brooks, through orchards of plum trees, to the maize-sown strip up above the village.

On that day fields all over the Breb lands were being hoed. Teams of people in lines, their hoes going up and down in front of them like the hammers of a piano, could be seen all over the hills. Still, although times were changing, you could see people in their smocks dotted about the hillside, specks of white, like the blossom of a pear tree fallen on a path.

We joined a happy party of female friends and relations of Mihai and Maria. Hoeing was considered to be women's work. They were hoeing the weeds from around the maize shoots, working from one side of the strip to another, and resting on the grass on the edge of each section. It was a strip I had once ploughed when I had been living there. The women talked almost non-stop, though always remaining attentive to the work. In among the maize there were also little cabbages emerging, and the first tiny green evidence of beans and marrows, and none of these must be uprooted by mistake.

Marishka and I were only ever allowed to hoe for a few minutes. It would of course not do for gentlemen and guests to dirty their hands. Hoeing is tough work and, even for the short stints I was allowed to join in, it was not long before my back was aching. The women of Breb, however, were well used to it. I would stand up and put my hand on the small of my back.

'Is your back hurting?' they would ask.

'Just a little,' I replied, not wanting to be told to stop.

'Don't worry,' said one, 'it will straighten out in bed.'

At lunch we laid down our tools, and, as Maria unpacked the food, we went down to wash the earth off our hands in the stream and returned with a pitcher full of cool clear water. We all sat on the ground and were given bowls of bean soup. They gave to Marishka first and then to me. We then ate slices of salted pork in our fingers, and for pudding doughnuts filled with bilberry jam. Throughout the meal we took swigs of *horincă* from the bottle and then, dreamy from work, food and drink, lay down to sleep in the shade of trees by the edge of the strip.

After half an hour's snooze we were back at work. The women, and even the younger girls, were as tough as hoe handles. They worked all day long in the hot sun bent double, with just a few breaks, and with barely a word of complaint. They chatted happily, and the hours passed. Many talked of their husbands or sons going abroad to find work, and how sad and difficult it was to be left alone to look after everything without them.

'But this is democracy, isn't it?' one said, wistfully. 'This is how things work in the modern world.'

When Marishka joined the team for a short while a girl offered to sing her a song of the Maramureş. Her clear voice flowed over the hill, accompanied by birds and the sound of our hoes cutting into the earth. For a moment others in nearby fields leant on the shafts of their tools to listen.

'The forest feels sad for its lost green leaves,' she sang, 'But I feel even sadder for my lost childhood.'

In the evening we came down from the hill through the orchards with hoes and baskets on our shoulders. I was tired and in reflective mood. How long would it be, I wondered, before these strips were abandoned? How long would it be before most of the people of Breb were lured away to work abroad or in factories in the towns, and the village houses became the holiday homes of whey-faced city dwellers? Then some of those city dwellers might pass by the fields where we had just been working and would say to each other, 'Look! You see those raised strips? They are the remains of the old medieval field system.'

23

A Last Letter

*The peasants are the great sanctuary of sanity . . . when they disappear,
there is no hope for the race.*

Virginia Woolf, *The Common Reader*

MARIA DIED IN 2002. She was seventy-eight. Mihai went into
deep mourning. I had not been able to go to the funeral. I
came instead for the *Parastas*, a religious service performed six
weeks after Maria's death, at the time when the soul of the dead
person is said to leave the earth. Marishka came with me.

Mihai, now wearing a beard of *doliu*, signifying his bereavement,
welcomed us with open arms, but was tearful as he talked of the
funeral, of the musicians he had brought to play and of all the
hundreds of people who had come.

'I am very sorry that I was not here,' I said.

'It does not matter. The great thing is that you are here now,' he
said.

MIHAI WAS NOW eighty-five and knew he too was soon to die.
He wanted to be properly prepared. Over the years he had been
building their tomb. Maria had now been placed in one part of it.
Mihai's space next to her still remained empty. Both Maria's and
his names, and the dates of their births, had been already carved on
the tombstone. The dates of their deaths, like Stephen the Great's,
were left to be filled in after they died.

Mihai took us to see the grave.

'I come and sit here often by the grave,' he said.

'Just getting used to the view,' he would tell people when they walked by.

'It is nice to see the meadows up there on the hill where we used to work, isn't it, Willy?' he added.

Back in the house, as we were having lunch, Mihai said:

'I'll soon be moving house, you know. In any case, people here do not know how to live properly any more.' I was taken aback. He had lived in this house all his life.

'I've built myself a new home,' he said. 'Do you want to see it?'

'Yes,' I said, confused.

He led us through into the back room.

'There it is,' he said, pointing, with a smile on his face. 'What do you think of it?'

There, supported by two chairs at either end, was his coffin.

'LOOK AFTER WILLY,' said Mihai to Marishka when we left, 'and tell him to come and visit me sometimes.'

He waved goodbye until we were out of sight. I waved and looked back, not sure if I would ever see him again.

We headed back on the beautiful road which leads over the mountains to the south. As always we passed the charcoal burner's conical piles of ash, plumes of smoke pouring from the breathing holes, and then the lime kilns with their glowing furnace fires beneath them.

A little further on, beyond the town of Dej, we came across a group of Gypsies camped on the side of the road in a lawny dell. They were semi-nomadic Gypsies, like all the travelling Gypsies of Romania today. When in Communist times all the *Corturari*, the 'tent' Gypsies, were given a place to live, the entirely nomadic Gypsy became a thing of the past.

These Gypsies were of the metal-working *Căldărari* tribe. They were on their summer migration, making money selling cauldrons and copper stills. Like all the other semi-nomads they travel in the warm months and return each autumn to ramshackle settlements where, for the duration of the winter, they huddle together in their brightly coloured, mud-plastered cottages, with ogee arches over the verandas and decorative flourishes reminiscent of India, just managing to keep warm enough to survive the freezing temperatures outside for the seemingly endless icy months. Then in the spring they hammer boards over the doors and windows to secure their houses and set off, the horses pulling the wagons tossing their heads and breaking into a trot, longing once more to be on the open road.

The capacious tents of these *Cǎldǎrari*, made of canvas and nylon sheeting, and held up by three long poles which protruded from the top, stood in a line, their openings facing the sun. Smoke issued from the camp fires. Marishka was suspicious of the travelling Gypsies, and indeed the *Lǎutari* considered themselves to be a cut above the *Cǎldǎrari*, but she knew there were often fortune-tellers and magicians among them. She begged me to stop.

'We still have a long journey ahead of us, Marishka,' I said, hoping to be able to avoid entangling ourselves in expensive sorcery.

'Oh please! . . .' she said.

So we walked in among them. The men were busily engaged in beating the copper seams of a bulbous still, but they chatted to us as they worked. They told us of the difficulties of travelling on the roads today. Even to be semi-nomadic these days was not easy in the changing world.

'The big new lorries, which go so fast, try to run us down or drive us into the ditches,' they said. 'They pass by as fast and as close to us as possible and when they are next to the cart they blare their horns to frighten the horses.' This story was familiar to me. I knew that many people and horses had been killed in this way. Often I had seen the fear on the faces of Gypsy children in the back of their wagons as they saw the huge roaring lorries approaching. Sometimes the lorries hit them and there was a carnage which one shrinks from describing.

As we talked, from among the tents there emerged an old woman dressed in voluminous coloured skirts and with long plaits on the end of which dangled gold coins. She was a fortune-teller. Just as we had predicted, every Gypsy encampment had at least one.

She hobbled over and offered to 'untie' us from any evil spells which may have been used against us. Marishka did not need much persuading.

'It will work against the priest,' she said to me.

'How can you take any notice of that alcoholic charlatan?' I said crossly.

'But you remember what happened to Florin?'

'Of course I do, but that is absurd. That was a coincidence,' I said.

But the old woman and Marishka were both so insistent that eventually I agreed to let her work her magic.

She sat us down next to the fire upon which steamed and bubbled a pot of brown watery stuff in which unidentifiable things were floating about. I was praying we would not be asked to drink a ladleful of it as part of the ceremony. It turned out to be the Gypsies' lunch.

She took Marishka's hand and crossed the money we had given her over her palm.

'*Să creapa pământul, / Să intra urâtul* – May the earth open up and swallow the evil,' she chanted. 'He who made this evil, may it turn itself upon him.' She spat symbolically on the money.

As the spells proceeded I watched her. In her braided hair I noticed she was also wearing shells, just like the family I had met on the road when I had first come to Breb.

The sorcery concluded, we thanked the woman for her assistance and wished her *bacht*. Then, as we were leaving, it came into my mind to ask her where the shells in her hair had come from.

'I picked them up on the beaches of the Black Sea,' she said, 'when we were walking back from the concentration camps in Transnistria.'

MARISHKA AND I had been together for three years now. Things had not always been easy. We had lurched from one crisis to another, in the usual Gypsy fashion. It had been tiring, but now life was a little easier and the crises fewer. Goga was no longer around and Lupescu had recently died as well. Then the priest disappeared. No one could tell me what had happened to him, he had just upped and gone, and the priest from the neighbouring village took over the Halma services. At the same time the village postmistress was replaced. It seemed as though there had been a clean-out of all the rotten apples.

Then the best thing of all happened. Barbu was pensioned off from the police service, aged forty-five. The Gypsies of Halma danced a jig or two when they heard this wonderful news.

I was overjoyed. Marishka was more circumspect.

'Others will come who are just as bad,' she said.

'Oh come on,' I said. 'You know what Barbu was like. You must be pleased.'

'Well yes, I suppose I am,' she admitted.

A bloom of peace suffused our lives. We no longer lived with the assumption that someone was always plotting against us in the background. Marishka, at my urging, was becoming better at preparing for winter. She bottled peppers and cucumbers in vinegar, and the crop of potatoes, beetroot and spinach was respectable this year. But although things were improving for us, the world in Halma, like the world of Breb, was changing.

FROM VALLEY TO valley the news spread. In the *crîşma* people listened open-mouthed to stories of the untold riches you could earn working in Western Europe. At the same time life in the Romanian countryside became ever more difficult. The old collective farms had shut down. There was little work, and the cost of living was always rising. Going abroad was hazardous, and a shock for the average Romanian. Western Europeans were found to be unfriendly and inhospitable. If you were thirsty and went to the nearest house to ask for a glass of water you would have the door shut in your face. Can you imagine it? But despite the dangers and disappointments some Romanians found jobs working in factories or on building sites earning reasonable salaries and the news filtered through.

It was not long before people from Halma were leaving in the hope of finding work. Up until then complicated visas had been necessary to travel to Western Europe, but now there were fewer restrictions. In any case if there were problems you could always bribe your way through. The borders, it seemed, were almost entirely porous. The Hungarians accepted bribes as readily as anyone. Indeed many people were making themselves rich out of this emigration. As the hopeful Romanian workers crossed Hungary the Hungarian police lay in wait for them and held them up until yet more money was extracted.

The journey to Western Europe was not easy, but regardless the young and able of Halma took whatever opportunities came their way and the village gradually began to empty. In the bar when workers returned I used to hear about their experiences. Some came back boasting. One returned from a small town near Reggio di Calabria in Italy to relate how she had had coffee every morning with Leonardo DiCaprio. Others came back with flashy-looking cars, although fairly soon pieces started to fall off them. We who had stayed at home had a good laugh at their expense.

Others returned from the big wide world and told the truth. 'We worked for a month in Calabria pruning olive trees,' one told me, 'and at the end of it the man said we had not done it to his liking and paid us only ten euros a day instead of the fifty he had promised. There was nothing we could do. They all have guns in Calabria. While we were there we heard of Romanians who had disappeared. No one knew what had happened to them. We heard once of a Romanian who had been killed because a Calabrian took a fancy to his wife. The Romanian became angry and the Calabrian just shot him and threw his body in the sea.'

The boy who used to chop our wood and bring us water was called Romi. He was a Gypsy. He was a polite and hard-working boy, but one day he announced that he had found a job in Germany working on a farm where he would be earning seventy euros per day. He and a friend, Dumitru, the eldest son of Marishka's uncle Andrei, set off full of hope. We heard nothing from them for three months. Then suddenly one day they returned. Romi told us what had happened. It was from him that I learnt of the modern-day Fagins of Italy, and how the more innocent Gypsies fell into their nets. He did not try to pretend that they had had a good time.

Instead of Germany, after a long journey in a van, they found themselves in the city of Salerno in southern Italy. There they were brought by their 'Boss' to the empty shell of an unfinished apartment block. Inside there were hundreds of Romanian beggars sleeping on rags and mattresses which had been salvaged from rubbish dumps. There were rats everywhere. Romi and Dumitru could scarcely believe their eyes. This was to be their new home.

The next morning they were pushed out on to the streets to beg. Romi was in tears. But in his tearful state he earned good money, especially outside the churches. He pocketed over a hundred euros on the first day and in the evening he tried to conceal some of it from the 'Boss'. He was told to strip. They found the money and beat him. They beat Dumitru as well because he had earned only ten euros.

After that on most days Romi made good money, but all of it he was forced to hand over to the 'Boss'. Dumitru, however, was not an effective beggar boy and was beaten every evening. The 'Boss' punched him in the stomach and slapped him in the face and warned him that if he could not earn more they would cut off one of his legs. He was even taken to one of the big bridges which pass over the river in Salerno. The 'Boss' and his friends wrestled him over the parapet of the bridge, and held him dangling by his feet.

'If you don't earn more money this is where you are going,' they said, indicating the water below. Of course Dumitru could not swim.

That evening Dumitru was crying and terrified. Romi promised him that the next day he would give him some of his money before they returned home. This was what he did and life marginally improved. But there were still scares.

One day a visitor arrived. It turned out he had come to buy Romi and Dumitru. He offered two thousand euros. The 'Boss' said he wanted three thousand. Romi heard their conversation. The man said they looked too healthy. He would have to break their legs or arms so they could beg more effectively; this was inconvenient and so he could offer only two thousand. To Romi and Dumitru's immense relief a deal was not reached. Another boy there had a twisted foot. He told them what a narrow escape they had had. It was this man who had broken his leg and bent it round before selling him on to Romi and Dumitru's boss.

Somehow Romi and Dumitru endured this miserable life for three months until, out of the blue, they were taken back to Romania. Romi's family knew with whom the boys had gone to Italy, and the 'Boss' decided it was best to return them home to avoid trouble. When they reached Romania they were let out of the van and given £10, just enough to reach Halma. They arrived home with two pounds' worth of lei in their pockets, having worked for three months.

MARISHKA AND I remained in Halma. Marishka was not interested in going abroad. Even when I tried to teach her English she had resisted.

'But what if my friends or family want to speak to you?' I asked.

'They could learn Romanian,' she suggested.

So we stayed at home and with the peace gained through winning the court cases, we now had time to think about other things. This was not, however, necessarily a good thing. We had been so busy protecting ourselves against Barbu and others we rarely thought about our own situation – whether, for example, we were suited to live together permanently.

Marishka now had time to consider whether I was faithful to her. She concluded that I was not. People in the village were still trying to separate us, only they were now using different, more subtle means. They would take Marishka aside and whisper into her ear. I remembered Byron's lines from *Don Juan*:

> They whispered he had a lover, some said two;
> But for domestic quarrels one will do.

Often they would whisper to me as well. 'Marishka has cast spells to entrap you,' they would say. 'You do not know what you are doing. You must go and have the spell reversed without delay.' They would also tell me that she too had a lover.

Marishka was much more affected by their intrigues than I and domestic quarrels ensued. I rarely took any notice of the whisperings; and the less notice I took the angrier and more suspicious Marishka grew. She wanted me to be jealous. If I was not jealous it was sure evidence that I was falling out of love with her, and this served only to increase her distrust and in turn her jealousy. The more jealous she grew, the more exasperated I became.

'Don't you see, Marishka?' I urged. 'They are trying to cause trouble. It's the same as before, only they are using different methods. They want to make us suspicious of each other.'

Then one day Marishka discovered the bag of charms given to me by Ileana, the white witch of the Maramureş. After Ileana had given them to me I had put them in a box and forgotten about them. This box I had then brought from the Maramureş to Halma unaware that the charms were in it.

Marishka had visited a woman who read the future in cards. This woman told her that I had concealed magical charms somewhere in the house. When I was out Marishka searched for them. Eventually, turning everything upside down, she found them in the box from the Maramureş. She recognized them immediately as intended for magical purposes. There was the bag of earth, the bundle of elder twigs, the wood with nails driven through it, the chips off the loom tied up with thread and the bent nail piercing a dried onion. Immediately her head began to ache and she felt faint. The charms, she said, had such evil power that they were making her feel ill.

Marishka took the charms to a priest. He told her that all the objects were from dead people: pieces of wood chipped off a coffin, nails from a coffin and earth from a grave. The priest would not touch them. He picked them up with a sort of metal hook.

'You must take these things to fast flowing water', he told her, 'and throw them in, and as you throw them in you must recite these lines', he gave her a piece of paper, 'to return the evil to the witch. But be careful, you must not touch these objects. They are very dangerous. They could even kill you.' He gave her the hook as a present.

When I next saw Marishka she was fuming.

'You have been trying to work magic against me!'

'Of course I haven't. The things in the bag were given to me by a white witch in the Maramureş. She said they would protect me against evil. She gave them to me. I did not ask for them. I don't even believe in them.'

'If you did not believe in them why did you keep them?'

'Because they were amusing curiosities.'

'You have no idea how dangerous such things are,' she said. 'Thank goodness I found them and disposed of them.'

I tried to calm the jealousy and the superstition but I did not succeed. We had been through much side by side, but this was more difficult to put up with than anything else as we were not united by it, but separated. Little by little our relationship deteriorated. The occasional missile flew across a room. Items of crockery were smashed. Our life together became ever more difficult. Finally on one sad day I decided it was best to leave. I think Marishka had seen it coming.

'I WILL MISS you,' said Marishka as we parted in the village square.

'And I you,' I said.

'I don't believe you,' she replied. Tears were welling in her eyes and dropping down her cheeks. She turned her head to hide them and walked away across the dusty village square.

'How can you leave after all that we have been through?' she said.

Later the same day, when I opened my suitcase I found she had stuffed a note inside. I unfolded it.

To you from Marishka, who loves you very much and who will never forget you. Goodbye. I don't know if we will ever meet again. You are a stubborn ass and a rascal. I would have liked for us to be together for all our lives, and that nobody or nothing on the face of the earth could have separated us. But you did not want it. I will cry much, but what can I do, this was my fate, not to have luck in life. I will suffer, but in the end I will have to forget you. Goodbye, I kiss you a thousand times, I will miss you and I will think of you always, please believe me.

PS. When you return to this village I want you to take back everything you ever gave me, even my clothes. I would not be angry, as I only want you to believe that I loved you.

I had left with a heavy heart, and having read this note it weighed even heavier. But I kept asking myself, being from such different backgrounds, how we could possibly live happily together for the rest of our lives? What happened next provided at least the hint of a clue.

FIVE MONTHS AFTER I left I heard that Marishka was pregnant. A couple of months later she gave birth to a son. He was, as Romanians delightfully put it, *un copil din flori* – a child of the flowers, that is to say a child born out of wedlock and likely therefore to have been conceived in the fields or in a newly made haystack. Since, however, most of the many children in the village were *copii din flori* this did not mark him out as any different.

Marishka called him Constantin. I had not seen her since we separated and it did not seriously enter my head that I might have been the father. Marishka, however, insisted that Constantin was my son. So one day I paid a visit to Halma. When I walked through the door of Marishka's house, she was holding Constantin in her arms feeding him. She first chewed the food in her mouth and then turned her head and passed it from her mouth into his waiting mouth, like a bird to its chick. It was a touching sight watching him instinctively turning his head to receive the food from his mother.

He was a sweet child but when I first saw him I did not notice any obvious resemblance. It was only later that I came to realize that what Marishka said was true. By then there was a noticeable resemblance. I became very attached to Constantin, and he to me, and I came to spend more and more time in Halma. Marishka was happy for me to be there, and she saw the pleasure it gave to Constantin. I too was glad to see that his Gypsy family doted upon him and all joined in looking after him. If he was not with Marishka he was with his grandmother, or with Attila, or Natalia, Nicolae or Eugen, or involved in rough and tumbles with some of his many cousins, his happy face appearing from the mêlée.

He was smothered with love and affection. His grandmother would make him stinging-nettle soup in the spring, and a range of herbal and other remedies when he was not feeling well, as well as mashed potato with garlic to keep worms away, a rag around his neck soaked in sheep's butter against bronchitis, milk brought fresh from the udders of the ubiquitous goats, and whispered, inaudible incantations to fend off any lurking evil eyes. All the women of the village wherever he went would go weak at the knees.

'Oh *puiul mamii!* – Oh mother's chick! How sweet he is,' they would say, and then invariably go through the motions of symbolically spitting. 'Pew, pew, pew!' they went, and said, like a spell, 'I spit in the face of the evil eye that he may not be bewitched.'

Attila, though more used to drinking, singing and fighting in the bar, was happy to spend hours playing with Constantin. Nicolae and Eugen also joined in his upbringing, taking him for rides in their carts, teaching him how to hold the reins and the appropriate commands to shout – '*Gyeh neah!*' to move off and '*Ilu!*' to stop or in our two-horse open sleigh, trundling over the snow, the bells jingling, much to Constantin's inexpressible delight. In the summer they took him up to the sheepfold where he played with the lambs and the kids, and the puppies of the sheepdogs, for hours without tiring.

Natalia was still in Halma. She had a daughter and the little girl's name was Elena. But suddenly Natalia had gone to live in Spain, part of the great migration westwards from Romania, and had left Elena behind. Elena became Constantin's greatest friend. He thought she was wonderful. Whenever she came to the house he would rush into her arms with a beaming smile on his face and they would play, rolling about and laughing together for hours. Then Elena would put a cassette into the tape recorder, she would clap her hands and Constantin would dance his eccentric version of the Gypsy dances.

But one spring Natalia came to pick up Elena and take her to Spain. On the last evening before she left Marishka and Constantin bathed her in a tub in the middle of the kitchen floor so that she was scrubbed and clean for the long journey. Then the next morning, with tears in her big eyes, Elena departed on a bus. Constantin over the following days kept asking where she had gone, and in Spain Elena cried herself to sleep.

Constantin had to become accustomed to life without Elena. In the village I would watch him playing with the other children and used to wonder what his life was going to be like being brought up in such a place, and living among the Gypsies. Certainly I was glad that he would be a part of this old country world, however eccentric it might be. One thing was certain, his early life scampering about the dusty tracks and running freely over the hills or through the echoing woods of Halma was going to be similar to the sort of upbringing I had had when I was young, and unlike anything he would be likely to have in the altered England of today, so changed by the modern world. In Halma the children were released in the morning and would roam all day long, until in the misty summer evening the cows gently descended into the village square. Constantin would learn early about all the habits of the animals and birds. He would come face to face with indignant broody hens and hissing geese, he would see how the lambs would butt each other in play, he would watch the swallows in their weaving flights above the square and see how they brought up two broods of chicks each summer before departing to warmer climes, and would watch the young storks in early flying lessons, all flying in a line behind their mother, and coming in to land one by one on the nest on top of the tower by the Saxon church.

I wondered of course what sort of education he would have. I imagined Marishka would like him first and foremost to be a fighter, not to be afraid and to stand up to the bullies. I wanted that too, but hoped that however much of a fighter he might be, he would at the same time help those who were weaker than himself, in the same way as his uncle Nicolae.

I also wondered how his life might be as half-Gypsy and half-Englishman in Romania. How would people treat him? Would Romanians and Saxons whisper behind his back that he was a Gypsy? I was happy to watch him playing with all the other smiling Gypsy children, and it did not bother me in the least that he was not dressed in uniform and going to a school in England, but I hoped he would not be looked down upon or treated unfairly because of his Gypsy blood.

It was a good sign that Frau Knall did not seem to be averse to talking to Constantin. On the contrary, she was enormously fond of him, and had long forgiven me for consorting with the Gypsies. Her face lit up when we walked through the door. She would speak to him in German to try to turn him into a linguist. Although since Marishka spoke Romanian to him, I spoke English, and Attila Hungarian, I was worried that he might become confused.

On one of our visits we found Frau Knall with another old Saxon lady. They were the two oldest Saxons in the village. While Constantin was playing with the cat I asked them more about their days as prisoners in Russia after the war.

'There was a song we used to sing while marching to work,' said Frau Knall. 'I still remember the words.'

Slowly, she started singing, and her friend joined in. Together in their old but clear voices they made their way through the song of sixty years before. Outside the window there was snow and ice, a horse and sleigh passed by the window, and as they sang the years slipped away. One could almost imagine them in the icy winters of Siberia, marching back and forth from work every day for four years, ten months and eighteen days, without one single day of rest. Even Constantin was in awe and watched them silently as they sang.

Morning and evening we march, Lines of Saxon workers to the mines. Who will ever thank us? We work by day and by night, Hunger dries out our bones, And the work destroys us. We had done nothing wrong, And now we have to be prisoners. On a simple grave there grow no roses, On a simple grave there grows not a single flower. Our only pride is the coal from the Dombas, And the hot tears which our mother cries.

When we were leaving that day Frau Knall said:

'I am glad to see you are spending more time in Halma again.'

'There is Constantin to think about now,' I said.

'Yes,' said Frau Knall. 'As the Romanians say, "When you have joined the *Hora*, you have to dance until the end".'

IN THE SUMMER of 2007 Marishka and I took Constantin on a trip to visit Mihai. I had very much wanted Mihai to meet him and I particularly wanted to have a photograph of them together. Mihai was overjoyed to see us and welcomed us with his usual warm smile. Constantin too was overjoyed to be in Breb, as there were even more chickens, kids and lambs than in Halma, which he had more fun than ever chasing. The Maramureş women in their head-scarves and skirts could not resist kissing him, and smothering him with affection, and constantly spitting symbolically in the face of the evil eye.

It was a happy time.

'Well, Willy,' said Mihai as we watched Constantin running about the yard. 'You have a fine son. You can be proud of him.' He said the same to Marishka. We thanked him. We knew how poignant it was for him to see the children of others happily playing. He and Maria had had no children, but of course what a wonderful father he would have made!

Walking around the village he was happy to see Constantin running about over the meadows jumping about on the grass like a foal. But as we walked back up the hill to the house Mihai had to pause for breath.

'Now I know what it is like to be an old tired horse with a heavy load, but just having to keep going on,' he said.

Mihai had become much older. But I was relieved that he and Constantin had met, and I had one or two photographs as proof. Mihai would die soon, it was hard to say how much longer he would live as he was so tough, but their meeting gave Constantin's and my Romanian life a continuity. As Mihai grew weaker, Constantin grew stronger and was slowly moving into the space from which Mihai was gradually taking his leave.

On the evening before we were due to go Mihai and I talked. Constantin and Marishka had drifted off to sleep and we were having a glass of *horincă* quietly in the kitchen.

'You will come to my funeral, won't you, Willy?' he said. 'I would feel much better if I knew for sure.'

'Of course I will come, Mihai,' I said. 'I promise I will come. But please don't die too soon.'

When we departed the next day Mihai shook Constantin's little hand; tears as always filled his eyes and his voice was choked. 'Willy, dear boy,' he said, 'I don't think we will ever see each other again.' This time, with tears welling also in my eyes, I felt more than ever that this might be true.

As we drove away he walked slowly around the corner, although bent with age, so as to see us for a few more seconds and waved until we were entirely out of sight.

ON 8 JANUARY 2008 I returned to England. Over Christmas I had been with Constantin in Halma. We had had a merry time with the carol singers and the dancing *Capra*, and with the snow and the sleighs. But while I had been in Romania, although I had wanted to, I had not managed to travel north to the Maramureş to see Mihai. It was not so easy in the winter. The next day, half an hour after I had arrived home in England, I received a message to tell me that Mihai had died. The journey home had taken two days, but immediately I repacked my bags, climbed back on to a train heading for London, and early the following morning boarded an aeroplane taking me back to Romania.

Everything was white all around as, from Bucharest, I headed northwards. The iron wheels of the train sliced through the snow. It made its way across the plains, through eddying mists and fogs, and then over the Carpathian mountains where pine trees climbed steep slopes up to jagged cliffs and peaks which towered above the train on either side. In Transylvania we trundled through forests and along remote valleys, stopping at village stations where the lights of houses and Gypsy cottages on the outskirts winked out, and smoke rose from tottering chimneys perched on their now white roofs. Looming high above them were the tall spires and towers of Saxon churches. Then once more we were plunged back into the darkness and the swirling snow.

I told my companions in the train that I was on the way to a funeral in the Maramureş.

'You've still a long journey ahead of you,' they said.

They handed me their bottle of *ţuică* so that we could drink a toast to Mihai – 'May God let him rest in peace!' we all repeated together.

Leaving the town of Sighişoara the next morning I travelled by car through northern Transylvania, over the snow-covered mountains, and came down into the old Maramureş, just as I had done for the first time many years before. The nearer I approached to Breb the slower I went. I knew Mihai was dead. I knew this would be the first time he would not be there to greet me with his invariably smiling face and his warming words of welcome. No longer would I be able to ask his wise advice, and laugh about the follies of the outside world from the safe haven of his simple kitchen. The car went ever slower. I did not want to see Mihai dead, as only then would I truly know that my faithful friend was no longer there.

I walked into the house and into the back room accompanied by two of Mihai's old neighbours. They had arrived to pay their respects at the same time. Both were wearing *opinci*. One was Gheorghe a Curatorului, the story-teller to whom I had given the Austrian scythe, the other was Maria, wife of Costin. Both I had known for many years. Both embraced me fondly with warm smiles on their faces and I felt as though they were almost like family. Mihai had gone but these delightful old people were still there.

Mihai's nephew took off the lid from the coffin and there lay Mihai, at peace, his hands folded on his chest. He was wearing a fur hat, a *cuşmă* as they call it in the Maramureş, a new wide-sleeved smock of spotless white, and a brown *pănură* waistcoat. Next to him was his walking stick, a loaf of bread with twenty-four coins stuck into it to pay the gatekeepers at the twenty-four gates he would have to pass, and a half-litre of *horincă*, something which he had never been without on any journey.

'Oh look how beautifully they have arranged him. Haven't they dressed him up finely?' said Maria alui Costin. 'Look, such a nice clean shirt, and brand new waistcoat.' She straightened out a fold in the material.

'And he has his *horincă* with him,' said the story-teller. 'I remember when old Gheorghe of the Meadow was digging a grave a few years ago, his spade hit upon an ancient bottle of *horincă*. By the evening everyone wondered where on earth he could be. Eventually they found him in the bottom of the grave, fast asleep, with the empty bottle next to him.' We all laughed.

'Well, Mihai, *Dumnezeul să-ţi ohidnească* – May God let you rest in peace,' said the story-teller and Maria alui Costin as they left.

'How wonderful that you have come, Willy, and from so far,' they said. 'Mihai was always talking about you. It is good that you have come.'

Outside I met Mihai's niece Maria. She had looked after Mihai since Maria had died. 'Mihai asked so many times whether I thought you would come,' she said. 'I told him that of course you would, and I am so glad that I was right.'

I asked her how he had died. It had all happened suddenly. There was no possibility that I could have reached him. A vein in his leg had burst and he lost a lot of blood. Weak from the loss of blood he had died the following evening sitting in his chair. So many tough old people, who have worked hard in their lives, die sitting up, as though they were just taking a rest.

We toasted Mihai and drank *horincă* late into the evening.

When I was on my way to bed Maria stopped me for a moment.

'I wanted to tell you. Your mother sent Mihai a Christmas card,' she said. 'It arrived during the second or third day of January. With the card was a picture of your son Constantin. Mihai was so happy to see it. He showed the photograph to everyone who came here, almost as though Constantin was his own grandson.'

THE COURTYARD WAS arranged with benches and tables. In the middle was a table where the coffin would be placed. All morning women had been preparing food in the kitchen, chopping meat and potatoes to make the goulash. Then guests began to arrive. The first were those who had walked over the hills from neighbouring villages, many of them in full traditional dress, and their feet wrapped in *opinci*, which in the cold weather were of course the warmest and most comfortable of footwear.

Soon hundreds of people were assembled. A short service was held in the back room. Holding a candle, I stood with a few of Mihai's closest friends and relations around the coffin as the priest intoned and waved incense.

Mihai had lived on this plot all his life. He had been born here. Now after ninety years he was to be taken away. The coffin was lifted to be carried outside into the courtyard and the keening began. The songs were not like those at Ion and Vasile's funeral. Mihai had been old. In this case they were quiet sad songs sung by old women. They seemed to me to be songs of mourning not just for Mihai, but for the whole of the old Maramureş way of life which Mihai's passing brought ever nearer to its end.

The courtyard was now full of people, and the crowds overflowed into the vegetable garden and into the neighbour's yard. I was glad so many had come. The coffin was placed on the table in the middle of the yard that I knew so well. Here Mihai had taught me to beat out the blade of the scythe, here we had cut wood, here Grigor had pottered and the hens pecked, and here we had laid out all the wooden forks and rakes ready to take out to the fields for haymaking.

I stood by the coffin holding my candle. I was agonized that I had not been with Mihai when he died. But if, as Romanians believe, the soul of a dead person lingers on the earth for six weeks after their death, then at least he will have seen that I had kept my promise.

The funeral service continued. The priests made their solemn speeches. My mind drifted to memories. On the lid of the coffin was a jar filled with wheat in which stood a candle. I remembered wistfully how at a funeral many years before I had asked Mihai the significance of the wheat in the jar. When I first arrived in Breb I was always looking for symbolic meanings. 'It is to stop the candle from falling over,' said Mihai.

Among the crowd looking on were familiar faces of friends with whom I had worked in the fields. I knew almost all of them. It was reassuring to be again among such a dignified and gentle people.

Then the priest's voice changed tone. Mihai, he said, had written his own *Iertăciuni*. These were his last letters addressed to his family and friends. He had written them over the previous year, but I had not known about them. The first was to the niece who had looked after him for the last five years. The second was addressed to me. In front of all the hundreds of people the priest read the letter out loud:

I say my last goodbye to our beloved William.

Now has come that day when we must be separated for ever, and with tears in my eyes I write these words, dear William, because for so many years we were all so happy together. We lived many years side by side. You helped us always with work in the fields, you took us to the doctor, to the hospital, and with all and any other things just as though you had been our son. You spoke only in a kindly way to us, and always concerned yourself with us and our welfare. We had no children, but we were glad because we now had someone who cared about us.

Please do not forget us, and please do not abandon our house, and our village. Please come sometimes to our grave and throw upon it a strand of grass, because you were our son and we loved you. May God give you all the good things in the world, and to Constantin, Marishka and your friends and your mother, as well as your brothers and their families. And if we ever, somehow, did you wrong, I beg you now to forgive us.

As Mihai was carried out of the courtyard for the last time three shepherds, standing on a small knoll, blew on their shepherd's horns a last mournful blast which echoed all over the village and across the hills.

Note

M UCH HAS CHANGED in Romania in recent years. Crucially, members of the old Communist police, many of whom remained in their jobs after the 1989 Revolution, have been weeded out from the modern Romanian police force. Since then life has improved for the Gypsies in Halma and for many people all over the country. In other respects too the Romanian government is making laudable efforts to improve the situation of the Gypsies, notably through education.

Comments about individuals should by no means be interpreted as judgements about groups or institutions.

As regards names of people and places, for Breb I have left all names as they are. For Halma they have all been changed. Indeed Halma itself is an invented name. I changed names in order to protect people and their privacy. For the same reason, the occasional time sequence and a few minor details have been altered or toned down. Conversations are not verbatim, but as I remember them.

THROUGHOUT THE BOOK, with few exceptions, I have used Romanian spellings for names and places, and have included both the Communist 'î' and the pre- and post-Communist 'â', depending on which is most suitable for English readers.

In pronouncing Romanian words readers should be aware that:

1. 'ţ' is pronounced 'ts'
2. 'ş' is pronounced 'sh', so *crîşma* is pronounced 'crishma' (more or less)

3. 'i' at the end of a word is almost imperceptible (so *Floreni* is pronounced 'Florayne')

I have used the modern Romanian spelling of 'Romania'. I
apologize to those, especially Rudolf Fischer, who feel that
'Romania' is not the correct, and certainly not the phonetically
correct, usage in English, and that properly I should have written
Rumania, or at the very least Roumania.

ON PAGE 225 I refer to a book I had been reading. This fascinating
book was written by Marianna Koromila, and is entitled *In the Trail
of Odysseus*.

Acknowledgements

OVER THE YEARS innumerable Romanians have, without hesitation, and without knowing me, offered a bowl of soup or a bed for the night, either in the warm comfort of their cottages, or under the stars in their 'Hazel Hotels' – the shepherds' shelters on the hills, better known as *colibe*, which are constructed of bent hazel wands. There were so many welcoming people that there is no room to thank them all here, even if I knew all their names, which I do not. I can only offer to them as a whole my heartfelt thanks: *Să trăiţi la mulţi ani cu bine!* – May you live happily for many years!

There are many others who helped me during the time I was living in Romania. Rudolf and Dagmar Fischer have been unstintingly generous and, in their book-lined sitting room in Budapest, placing a glass of Hungarian red wine in my hand, they have shared with me their deep knowledge about every aspect, however esoteric, of Romania and Romanian life. Patrick Leigh Fermor, who understood from the first moment why an Englishman should choose to live in Romania, has given an abundance of much-appreciated encouragement. His unflagging enthusiasm is infectious and hearing him recite the *Mioriţa* recently has prompted me, at last, to learn it properly myself. Manfredi Manera's adventurous spirit has impelled me on many exotic journeys to places I might never have thought of travelling to, including parts of Romania, and Gail Kligman and Liviu Vânău made the original suggestion that I might find Breb an interesting place to visit on my walk. Those wishing to know more about life and ritual in the Maramureş should read Gail Kligman's excellent book, *The Wedding of the Dead*. A great many thanks to all of them.

My brother, Barnaby, has given invaluable editorial advice – I would recommend his services to anyone. There were others too who were kind enough to read drafts of the book and offer suggestions: among them, Bogdan Burghelea, Philip Chapman, Jasper Guinness, Louise Lamont, Sue Macartney-Snape and Aura Neag. To all, my thanks.

I also owe much gratitude to Caroline Dawnay for her enthusiasm and wise guidance, to Roland Philipps and Helen Hawksfield at John Murray for their astute advice and good humour, and to Howard Davies for his scrupulous copy-editing.

There are many others whom I would like to thank for diverse kindnesses related in one way or another to this book. There is Patrick Paul, for his generosity and encouragement, which makes so much difference to struggling scribblers and conservators; Isadora and Emma Caulfield, for giving me the spur to write early chapters; then in alphabetical order, Dr John Akeroyd, Mark Almond, Antony Beevor, Brian Blacker, Rohan Blacker, Hugh and Caroline Boileau, Rory and Miranda Carnegie, my aunt Diana Cavendish, Ioan and Lucica Ciombului, Dr Mihai Dăncuş, Sara Dootz, Charlotte Duthie, Philip Eade, Will Ellsworth-Jones, Natasha Fairweather, Caroline and Walter Fernolend, Esther Gisin, Zac Goldsmith, Istvan Haller, Jan Hülseman, Bernard Houliat, who has written wonderful books about the country people and Gypsies of Romania, Ileana lui Ghiula, Christoph Klein – the Saxon Bishop of Transylvania, the late Gabriel Lambescu whose work in keeping the old buildings of 'Halma' and many other Saxon villages standing is beyond reckoning, the London Library, the Mihai Eminescu Trust, Beatrice Monti and her late husband Gregor Von Rezzori whose blue eyes, as we talked of Romania, became misty with nostalgia, David Packard, my cousin Willy Peel, Rob Penn, Giannozzo Pucci, my uncle Hugh Rathcavan, Ross Somervell, David Summers (who was a dear and faithful friend to Mihai and Maria), Jonathan Sunley, the Tiran family of Breb, the Mihnea family, the late Vasile lui Irimei, Laura Vesa, Maria lui Voda, Rupert Wolfe-Murray, the Anglo-Romanian Trust for Traditional Architecture, and the many people in positions of authority in

Romania, including policemen, who have over the years gone out of their way to help me.

I also give warm thanks to all those in Breb who generously, and with smiles on their faces, helped me in so many different ways. It was a great honour to live in your village.

Finally special thanks to my mother, and late father, who gave my brothers and me the freedom to roam the hills and woods of Sussex and of Ireland when we were young, and so to learn about the countryside and appreciate its beauty, and who did not try too hard to stop us following our mildly idiosyncratic paths through life.